The Duel of the Giants

The Duel of the Giants

CHINA AND RUSSIA IN ASIA

by **DREW MIDDLETON**

CHARLES SCRIBNER'S SONS • NEW YORK

Library of Congress Cataloging in Publication Data

Middleton, Drew, 1913–
The duel of the giants.

   1. China—Foreign relations—Russia. 2. Russia—
Foreign relations—China. 3. China—Defenses.
I. Title.
DS740.5.R8M48   327.51′047   78-9305
ISBN 0-684-15785-3

1 3 5 7 9 11 13 15 17 19 V/C 20 18 16 14 12 10 8 6 4 2

PRINTED IN THE UNITED STATES OF AMERICA

CONTENTS

PREFACE

THE northeast corner of Asia is one of the world's flash points. The interests of the three greatest modern states—Russia, China, and the United States—converge there. The existence in the same area of Japan and the rival North and South Korean republics complicates the military and political situation.

This book is primarily the result of a three-week visit to the People's Republic of China. What I saw and heard in the People's Republic strengthened my conviction that the confrontation between China and Russia, though vitally important to these two countries, is also of great significance to the United States. This book, then, is one man's assessment of the military, political, and economic situation in East Asia.

My Chinese hosts insisted, and I am very glad they did, that I must also see some of the industry and agriculture of their country on which, in the event of war, China's ultimate survival would rest. Since I was unable to visit Siberia, I have done my best to provide some idea of that area's economic potential.

Charles E. Bohlen, that gifted diplomat, said once that there were two phrases that were palpably false: "Alcohol doesn't affect me" and "I understand the Russians." I make no claim to understand the Chinese or the Russians, but I believe it is fair to say that I was shown more of the Chinese military establishment than any other foreign journalist. Thus, if I do not "understand" the Chinese, I do have a fairly comprehensive view of their defense position.

What the Russian military is doing and has done in Siberia is not a mystery in these days of satellite observation; Russian intentions are. It is evident, however, that the Soviet military position in Siberia, like that in Europe, is far in excess of what would be needed for defense.

My thanks are due to hundreds of Chinese who with unwearying courtesy assisted me during my stay in China. I also am grateful to the diplomats of the Department of State in Washington and in Peking who answered my innumerable questions; to members of the American and Allied intelligence communities; and to my editor, Norman Kotker of Scribners, for his unflagging support.

Finally, of course, I must thank my colleagues on the *New York Times:* the executive editor, A. M. Rosenthal; the managing editor, Seymour Topping, whose splendid book on China was an invaluable corrective to my more ingenuous impressions; and James L. Greenfield, foreign news editor at the time of my China visit.

Since beginning the writing of this book, I have read a great deal of literature on China and Russia. I must single out O. Edmund Clubb's monumental *China and Russia: The Great Game* (New York: Columbia, 1971), to my mind the best work yet done on the historical record behind today's confrontation.

Drew Middleton
Westport, New York

The Duel of the Giants

1

From Mao to Hua:
The Search for Stability

THE train slowed down going north from An Shan to Mukden. A column of truck-towed antitank guns was halted on a road running parallel to the tracks in a driving rain and a harsh wind, a wind that the Chinese say "comes from the bears in the north," meaning the Russians. Two officers were scanning a map while an NCO stood at attention. How many times in how many countries had I watched that scene whose opening line in any language is, "Where the hell are we?"

One officer said something to the NCO, who saluted and returned to his truck. The officer, making a gesture old as war, raised his right hand and swung his arm toward the north. The column of weather-beaten trucks and obsolete guns moved along the road that led north.

"Why, of course," said a young officer on the train. "They go north. That is where the Russians are. That is where the danger is."

We had been walking through the air-raid shelters, which the Chinese call tunnels, under Dairen for forty minutes when one of the guides tugged at my sleeve and pointed to something stowed against the wall. It was a steel plate about a foot and a half square studded with steel spikes. I asked what it was for.

"To catch the Russians when they come," the guide replied with a happy smile.

The elders of a village southeast of Peking led me proudly

through a network of tunnels under their village. I scrambled up a rude ladder and, through slits in the rock, looked out at the village pigpen.

"From here we shot the Japanese and the Nationalists," an old man said. "From here we will shoot the Russians when they come. All enemies try to steal our pigs."

The three incidents occurred during a tour of China that covered more than two thousand miles in the autumn of 1976. They illuminate perhaps the most pervasive element in the Chinese national attitude: the conviction that the Soviet Union is China's enemy; that the Russians will attack China; and that, with or without modern weapons, with their bare bodies if need be, the men and women of China must resist and ultimately defeat that attack.

An understanding of the depth and pervasiveness of these sentiments is vital to an understanding of contemporary China. The Sino-Soviet antagonism is the cardinal fact of political-military life in China today. Sooner or later, any conversation with a steelworker, an official, a farmer, a shopkeeper, or a soldier will lead to mention of the danger from the north. A factory manager, giving his views on the extent of the danger, may be interrupted by a worker who wants the American to know, through the interpreter, just how dangerous he thinks the situation is.

In Manchuria's Liaoning Province I thought that the sentiment might be stronger because there the Russians are nearer and the province is rich in industrial resources and installations. The Soviets have been there. They know its wealth.

But in Nanking, a thousand miles and more from the nearest frontier with the Soviet Union, the feeling was equally strong. A brisk young woman showed us over the great bridge across the Yangtze that is one of China's prides. Asked if it could be destroyed in the event of a Soviet advance, she became very grim.

"Yes, of course. But we will defend it. The Russians will never have it. This is *our* bridge!"

And in Shanghai, in Mukden, in Peking men and women repeated what became the central theme of my visit: we must be prepared to defend our country against the Russians.

The death of Chairman Mao Tse-tung apparently had not affected the national view of the danger. Officials at the defense and foreign ministries and senior officers of the People's Liberation Army (PLA) all emphasized the gravity of the country's military situation, and the officers described the manner in which China would meet and overcome the Soviets.

I was first inclined to attribute these remarks to a practice common in all authoritarian states. The government raises the specter of foreign encirclement or invasion to divert the populace's minds from internal difficulties, to incite it to new prodigies of production, to make it more obedient to the ruling group.

I had seen this in the Soviet Union in 1946 and 1947. Stalin and his subordinates had presented the Russians, terribly mauled and lethargic after four years of war, with a dire picture of the military ambitions of the United States, which then enjoyed a monopoly of nuclear weapons. Making Russia strong enough to defeat this imaginary American threat, the people were told, demanded greater efforts on the part of every industrial worker and farmer and complete obedience to the policies of Stalin.

The atmosphere in China was decidedly different. Across the barriers of ideology, race, and language the Chinese conveyed the conviction that their fear of the Russians was genuine. Older workers in factories, on railroads, and in Shanghai's thriving shipyards recalled how the Russians had taunted them when the Soviet Union withdrew all technical assistance in 1960.

"They told us we'd never complete the factory," said a worker in an electrical machinery works in Mukden. "They took the blueprints with them and told us we could grow cabbages on the land where we planned the factory. Well, we built the factory. They'll never get it back."

Chinese antagonism toward the Russians, the gradual increase in the quantity and quality of the Soviet forces along the long frontier between Asia's two giants, and the PLA's overall inferiority in the quality of its weapons are elements in one of the world's most dangerous military confrontations. The ramifications of that confrontation are infinite. It affects all of northeastern Asia. What is its influence on North and South Korea? What is its meaning for Japan, Asia's strongest industrial power? And, farther afield, how does it affect China's relations with the United States? Finally, how permanent is it? What are the chances for a rapprochement between the two largest Communist nations? Any Sino-Soviet relationship that duplicated the one that flourished before 1960 would have a shattering impact upon the present global balance of power.

The feud with the Soviet Union has developed at a particularly awkward time for the Chinese. It creates requirements for modern military technology at a moment when China's planners must choose their priorities carefully. From what the visitor is shown, it is fairly safe to assume that the central question is how much should be invested in any one of a half-dozen critical areas of national development. Should the maximum investment go to heavy industry, to agriculture, to transport and communications, to consumer goods and services, or to the armed forces?

Tension with the Soviet Union and the consequent efforts to prepare a defense against a Russian invasion are obstacles to success in China's struggle to modernize the country by the year 2000, a goal set by Chou En-lai when he was premier. Accomplishment of this truly herculean feat appears possible only if China enjoys years of stability or, to use a favorite Chinese word, tranquility. Modernization, of course, would include the armed forces, but an extensive program there would divert resources from other fields.

No great nation, not excepting Russia and Germany, has had a national experience in this century as chaotic as China's. The fall of the Manchu Empire, the foundation of the First Republic, and the political rivalries and military combats of assorted warlords were only preludes to more massive disturbances, some of foreign origin and others homegrown. The Japanese invasion was followed by World War II. The war was hardly over when Chiang Kai-shek's Nationalists and the Communists plunged China into civil war. The Communist victory was followed by extensive purges which, as they always do, liquidated or drove into exile some of the ablest people in the country. Then came Chairman Mao's Great Leap Forward, which had an essentially destabilizing and counterproductive impact on the national economy. This was followed by the Great Proletarian Cultural Revolution, which came close to ruining education and which created turbulence in the industrial labor force. Finally, there was the struggle for power between Hua Kuo-feng and Mme. Chiang-ching (Mao's widow) and the other members of the Gang of Four.

There can be no stronger testimony to the endurance, the flexibility, and the basic self-confidence of the Chinese people than their emergence from three-quarters of a century of political and military strife still purposeful, still believing in their destiny as a nation.

Are the Chinese united? Like all authoritarian countries, China gives the impression of unity. The visitor is constantly told ''we'' are all happy about the succession of Hua to Mao's role, about the disgrace of the Gang of Four. Tomorrow, of course, the visitor may be told that ''we'' are equally happy over the choice of a new leader. Moreover, in a country as large, as highly populated, and as diverse as China, there is always the probability of sectional disputes and rivalries between personalities bent on seizing power.

Indeed, to a considerable extent the rivalry between the triumphant Hua Kuo-feng and the Gang of Four and its followers was a simple struggle for power, although it was presented to the people as an ideological conflict in which the verities of the Communist faith were at stake. Here were two groups thirsting for power. As in the Soviet Union after Lenin's death, each claimed to be the rightful heir to the dead leader, in China's case the sainted Mao Tse-tung.

To a visitor in China in late 1976 it seemed an uneven conflict. Hua Kuo-feng held the high cards, the support of the People's Liberation Army and the bureaucracy. Neither group evidently supported him 100 percent. But Hua had enough support
to hold the position he had taken and launch an extensive propaganda campaign against Madame Chiang-ching and her associates and supporters. No village, no city street corner, no
railroad station, no airfield was without its wall newspaper and
wall posters denouncing the Gang of Four.

One of my strongest impressions about authoritarian propaganda—from the left or right—is that sooner or later it encounters the law of diminishing returns. In Moscow it is quite
evident that the fulminations and exhortations of *Pravda* and *Iz-
vestia* have little real impact upon the unfortunates whose daily
news comes only from those newspapers. The same is true of
radio and television.

An experience in Shanghai reflected a possible difference between the two peoples. Below my room in the Peace Hotel,
built by the British as the Cathay, was a small square dominated
by an enormous screen the size of a football scoreboard. The
board was covered with wall posters and cartoons vividly re-
counting the wrongdoings of Mme. Chiang-ching and her collaborators in detail and, at the end, consigning the group to hell.
When I first looked out at lunch time there were over three
hundred people gazing at the screen. The audience was about
the same size after dinner. By 11:00 P.M. it had dwindled to
about two hundred men and women. I slipped out and stood in
the back row. The silence was broken only by trucks rumbling
up and down the bund. The Chinese around me had every appearance of anxious attention as they studied the charges. Some,
which had been translated for me earlier in the day, were so extravagant that it was difficult to believe they would be accepted
by any rational person. But the Chinese read them in silence.
They are a humorous people, apt to burst into laughter at
absurdities, but there was no laughter, no smiles that night on

the bund. Of course, the propaganda campaign had only just begun.

Life is far too complicated to allow us to ascribe to any event a single cause. But my strong impression was that the acceptance of Hua and the new regime was because the new leaders promised what all from the best educated to the peasants perceive as China's major need—a lengthy period of stability. They have had their fill of power rivalries, of grandiose schemes for remaking the country. An open rivalry between Hua and Mme. Chiang-ching might push China back to the unsettled times of the warlords' feuds.

My estimate is that Mme. Chiang-ching has many supporters in China today. But I believe most will keep quiet and offer tacit support for Hua because that is the course that offers some guarantee of national tranquility.

This intense desire for a period of stability in which China can be modernized is closely related to the universal detestation of the Soviet Union and its leaders. The Chinese see Soviet aggressive intentions as a destabilizing influence on the whole of East Asia.

My visit to China took place in the weeks immediately after the death of Chairman Mao, the transfer of power to Hua, and the opening of the campaign against the Gang of Four, including the arrest of all four. In the year since then I have consulted with those in Washington, London, and Paris who keep a watchful eye on the People's Republic of China; I have compared reports, official and unofficial, of what was happening with my own impressions as recorded in my notebooks; and I have read an extraordinary amount of material about the developments in China since the succession.

The most important and significant aspect of the Chinese puzzle in the months since Mao died is that there have been no violent changes in the society. The arrest of the Gang of Four, the replacement of officials in the administration and the economy believed to be loyal to the gang, and the reappearance of Teng

Hsiao-ping as one of the country's most powerful leaders were all important. But no great crises developed in the year after Mao's death. The great people were shaken by the passing of a revered leader; another took his place; adjustments, which may well be considered minor in a nation of nearly a billion people, were made; and the great republic rumbled slowly into an unknown future.

What did happen was a discernible shift in emphasis, in priorities. As Harry Harding of Stanford University points out in a pamphlet distributed by the China Council of the Asia Society, Hua assumed the leadership of a country that for two decades had been torn by two conflicting views of the correct road to economic and social fulfillment of the Communist party's goals.

On the one hand there were the moderates, symbolized and led by Chou En-lai, who argued that economic modernization must be given priority. The stability of political life, their argument ran, is a requirement if economic progress is to be made. Consequently, in Harding's words, the society must accept a "degree of social and economic inequality for the sake of economic efficiency" and accept the belief that progress toward a communist society demands a long period of economic growth.

The radical viewpoint was that the revolution must continue, a concept that found its most powerful advocate in the works of Chairman Mao. The radicals argued that there must be a constant class struggle, involving, in some cases, political disorder, to prevent the emergence of "revisionism" in China. *Revisionism* is one of the names that the Chinese apply to what they perceive to be the Russian retreat from the fundamentals of Communism in the direction of a middle-class, "social imperialist" state.

Conversations with Chinese officials led me to the conclusion that the many radicals had not at the outset desired the political disorder that marked the Great Proletarian Cultural Revolution.

"The whole program, good though it was in theory, got out

of hand,'' an official in Nanking said. ''They couldn't control it. And some of the disorders cost us many years.''

This fundamental conflict naturally ranged far beyond essential economic priorities. The radicals in their quest for a new revolution supported worker participation in economic management, frowned on pure science, wanted all scientific work directed to the solution of industrial problems, and encouraged trade unions and student groups to rebel against the party leadership if it was deemed incorrect. The moderates stuck to their guns. All this, they contended, would slow national economic modernization and reduce industrial efficiency, because neither was possible without political tranquility.

The internal conflict pitted those who, taking their cue from the all-wise chairman, believed in continual revolution and those who, correctly assessing China's weariness with continued turbulence, opted for concentration on the reduction of political turmoil and the conquest of economic problems.

Most authorities, including Fox Butterfield of the *New York Times,* have concluded that since Mao's death there has been an appreciable shift to the right, that is, toward the position taken by the moderates in the preceding ten years. My impression was that the bureaucrats, the technical experts, and the young officers who desired military modernization were moving toward control of the system and that the concept of permanent revolution was unwelcome among people face to face with the staggering problem of dragging China into the twenty-first century as a modern, viable society.

Unity, stability, and the promotion of production are the rallying cries in post-Mao China. What is left of Mao's revolution is directed against his widow and her friends and supporters. Ironically, the Gang of Four's own slogans have been turned against them; they are now ''the enemies of the class struggle.'' But, bitter and pervasive though propaganda of this sort may be, it is matched by a torrent of propaganda appeals stressing the importance of maintaining a centralized and unified leadership, reflecting, perhaps, apprehensions over a residual internal opposition.

Although the consensus of foreign opinion is that modernization of China's economic structure is clearly vital, it is prudent to recognize that in certain areas the economy did very well in the critical year 1976, which saw the deaths of Mao and Chou En-lai, the struggle for power within the upper echelons of the party, and the severe earthquakes in Tangshan. Despite these events, China registered a record $1.2 billion trade surplus for 1976.

Political turmoil had a great effect on Chinese imports but little on exports, which remained at $7.2 billion, the same figure as in 1975. However, imports fell from $7.4 billion in 1975 to $6 billion in 1976, a drop attributed to the leadership's failure to agree on the new five-year plan and to a continuing debate over trade policy.

Yet even though the majority of import cuts affected trade with Western countries, the share of non-Communist countries in China's trade in 1977 was 82 percent, only two points below the 1975 figure.

With the new government firmly installed, 1977 was devoted to an active foreign-trade policy, with Chairman Hua and his colleagues stressing the importance of foreign trade to internal economic development. Throughout the first ten months of the year the emphasis in public speeches and propaganda was on the link between overseas trade and an expanding economy. At the foreign-trade conference in Peking in July, workers in the foreign-trade sector were urged to do "a still better job in importing advanced technology and equipment" and "to grasp well the work of exporting."

Foreign suggestions for improvement in the quality and packaging of exports were heard and implemented. Government departments are doing their utmost to improve the efficiency of the ports through which imports and exports move.

Although the overall picture in this sector of the national economy is better than might be expected, the country clearly still suffers from the turbulence created by the Cultural Revolution, a turbulence that affected every aspect of society. For example, at the height of the revolution, high school graduates were sent arbitrarily into the countryside or into industrial plants to "strengthen their understanding" of the peasant and industrial working classes. In Nanking, I asked a teacher if it was possible during the revolution to keep in touch with bright students who otherwise might have been headed for the university. She had tried, she said, and failed. How many potential nuclear physicists, industrial managers, and aircraft designers are out there in the back of beyond hoeing cabbages or running lathes in village factories?

The new government's emphasis on the importance of production, which, ironically, is considered a means of furthering the revolution, has been accompanied by the jettisoning of many of the Cultural Revolution's most cherished programs. These include the concept of "open science," which involved workers and peasants in research work in scientific institutions and the activities of "worker-peasant propaganda teams" in universities and high schools, where they were supposed to exercise "mass control" over the "bourgeois specialists" of the faculty.

But the Cultural Revolution's effects on the economy are still there. The "political" work stoppages of the revolutionary era demoralized work forces. Factory managers, usually entitled vice-chiefs of the revolutionary committee, suffered outside interference during the revolution, in addition to the daily battle with a maddeningly slow bureaucracy and mounds of paperwork. By the time I had a chance to visit industrial plants, the work stoppages had ended, but as the reader will see, I found most factories overmanned and, by Western or Japanese standards, inefficient.

The swing toward the moderates may also salvage some of the students hustled out of the schools and onto the farms and factories during the last years of the revolution. Reports from Hong Kong say that in 1977 more and more students were being allowed to move directly from high school into the universities with intellectual ability rather than ideological fervor increasingly becoming the criterion of entry. The new leadership also has dropped the idea that scientific research should be restricted to problems tied to current industrial production.

Educational reform, meaning the revival of old policies, has been given a high priority by the new leadership, which understands the relationship between economic progress and an educated work force. Politics have not left university halls; students devote at least half a day each week to political studies. They must also perform some unpaid physical labor at a commune or factory, although an effort is made to relate this work to studies. University enrollments rose slowly in 1977, but generally they are well below the figures for the years prior to the Cultural Revolution.

None of these changes, mild and halting though they may seem, has been accomplished, or indeed could have been accomplished, without some drastic changes of personnel at the apex of the government pyramid. The Gang of Four is the only remnant of the old regime whose arrest and disgrace has been publicly celebrated. But there has been a general replacement of officials loyal to the gang and its concept of the Great Proletarian Cultural Revolution by men and women more in sympathy with the new policies and with greater expertise in implementing them.

The emphasis on experienced expertise in economic planning and management was reflected by the composition of the new Politburo elected in August 1977. Li Hsien-nien, one of China's best-known economic planners, was made a vice-chairman of the party. Yu Chui-li, head of the State Planning Council, was elected to membership in the Politburo. The new group also includes two officials experienced in administering scientific programs, Fang Yi and Nieh Jung-chen, and two others with a wide background in foreign economic relations.

Before these appointments were made, an alternate member of the Politburo had been demoted, six cabinet ministers dismissed, and about one-third of the members of the Central

Committee replaced. A similar process has been going on in most of the provinces.

The combination of new men and new—or, rather, resurrected—ideas gives the impression of a party and government tiptoeing delicately away from the precepts of Chairman Mao while mouthing loyalty to those precepts. Some Maoism remains untouched. The ban on free markets and private plots of ground continues. But many of the Cultural Revolution's ideas have been forgotten: programs for improving rural education and public health, encouraging small rural industry, and transfering urban youth to the agricultural communes.

New governments in democracies almost invariably announce at their installation that they intend to take a fresh look at foreign policies, with the implication that this look will lead to changes. No such promises are required from an authoritarian state, nor were any given in China. In fact, China's present foreign policy is very like that pursued by Chairman Mao's government since early in this decade. It still rests on three principles: the Soviet Union, not the United States, is China's chief enemy; China can strengthen her position by warning the Americans, Western Europeans, and Japanese of Soviet expansionist tendencies, in the hope that these warnings will lead to greater military investment on the part of these peoples; and China supports the demands of the Third World for a new international economic order and considers Peking the natural leader of that world, but in the changed political atmosphere of today, Chinese support for liberation movements may be reduced.

Those who believed that the passing of Mao would open a new era of warmer Sino-Soviet relations were proved wrong, at least for the twelve months immediately following the chairman's death. The Russians, however, apparently considered that the moment was right for a new approach, for in December 1976 they sent a special emissary to Peking with proposals—some old, some new—for easing the tension along China's northern border with the Soviet Union.

The Soviet initiative failed. As Harding points out, ''Within a few months . . . the Soviet representative had returned to Moscow amidst Chinese accusations that he had presented Peking with 'poisoned arrows disguised as an olive branch.' "

Since then, Hua Kuo-feng has charged that "the Soviet leading clique has not shown one iota of good faith about improving the state relations" between the two countries. If Moscow "really has any desire to improve" these relations, Hua continued, "this clique should prove it by concrete deeds." And even if there was some improvement in relations, Hua declared, China would continue to criticize the "fascist dictatorship" in Moscow and "wage a tit-for-tat struggle against its [Soviet] hegemonism."

Chinese diplomats overseas were quick to deny that an agreement concluded in October 1977 with the Soviets concerning one frontier area would affect the realities of Sino-Soviet relations. The whole affair, they were at pains to say, had been blown out of proportion by the Western media.

There also was some expectation that the new regime, generally considered more pragmatic and businesslike than that of Chairman Mao, would attempt to improve relations between Peking and Washington. No such improvement has taken place, but Chinese newspaper attacks on the United States are less severe than they have been in the past. The elimination from policy making of Mme. Chiang-ching and her colleagues, always believed to be dubious about the value of relations with America, apparently has made little difference.

The government of Chairman Hua adheres to the three demands on Taiwan first raised by Chairman Mao: the abrogation of the mutual-defense treaty between the United States and the Republic of China, the withdrawal of all American forces from Taiwan, and the severance of diplomatic relations between Washington and the Taipei government. In some respects, the new government has gone beyond the stiff position taken by Chairman Mao: it "will not tolerate" continued American arms sales to Taiwan after the "normalization" of relations, according to Foreign Minister Yu Chan; it will not accept replacement of the present embassy in Taiwan with a liaison office comparable to that maintained by the United States in Peking; and it does not welcome the idea of an American statement calling for peace in the Taiwan straits once relations have been normalized.

Perhaps the most perceptible change in Chinese foreign policy since Mao's death has been the greater interest shown in imports of advanced technology that would assist China's development into a modern economic power. Such imports were a favorite target of the Gang of Four, who saw them as chains binding China to the industrial countries. Today, however, the Chinese say that planned procurement of advanced technology is compatible with Mao's policy of independence and, conscious of China's limited foreign-exchange resources, that foreign technology can be obtained through deferred payments.

Another change has occurred in military policy, especially in the position of the PLA in the organization of the state. The army emerged from the transfer of power as one of the two great organizations (the bureaucracy being the other) upon which the power of the new regime is based. The West does not know, and probably never will know, what occurred in the weeks after Mao's death, but it is my conviction that Hua and his colleagues required the assistance of the army to grasp power. The purge of the Gang of Four, the arrests in Peking and Shanghai of radical leaders, and the strengthening of PLA forces in areas such as Shanghai that had favored the gang were undertakings supported—and, in the last case, instigated—by the army.

One consequence of the PLA's timely assistance has been a stronger role for the military in policy making. Three military men were added to the Politburo after the eleventh party congress. Ten military officers now serve on that body, more than at any time since the late 1960s.

As a result, as we shall see, the military, especially the younger officers, is openly calling for the modernization of the PLA's weapons. Lip service at that level is still given to the concept of drowning an invader in the human sea of Chinese, but repeatedly the point was made to me that China could avoid a long and devastating war only if the people in a people's war received new advanced weapons.

Although my visits with the PLA convinced me of the need for advanced weapons, I remain doubtful about how much can be done. Hua Kuo-feng has pledged to increase both military research and development and the production of modern equipment. But I doubt very much whether more than a handful of military men and industrial planners in China understand the staggering complexity and costs of new conventional weapons or the time necessary to modernize the PLA to the point where it can match the Soviet army in weapons.

The first steps in modernizing the military have already been taken. They do not deal with weapons but with improvements in military training and discipline. But they dodge the key issue of any modernization program undertaken by China: where can the government find the money and the resources for such a program? Military spending is now estimated at 9 to 10 percent of the gross national product, but there are sharp disagreements about the size of the GNP. The United States Arms Control and Disarmament Agency put China's GNP for 1975 at $299 billion; others estimated it at $4 billion more. To complicate the situation still further, China has not published budget figures for seventeen years. One estimate is that China spends about $25 billion annually on defense.

Most Western analysts believe that if that figure is correct, China will be able to improve her conventional-weapons levels as far as the ground army is concerned without spending more. But modernization of the air force and the navy would involve a rapid expansion of defense spending up to 12 percent of the GNP.

What path will modernization take? The answer will have a direct impact on expenditure. If the army is content to invest in modern defensive weapons—surface-to-air and surface-to-surface missiles, new antitank guns, and hand-held missiles—the cost may be manageable for the Chinese economy. But if the military opts for offensive weapons—nuclear- or diesel-powered attack submarines and long-range strike aircraft, for example—then costs will skyrocket.

Despite the obligatory references to Chairman Mao and his teachings, China has embarked on a new course since his death. The new leaders' first goal, one that the people also seek, is stability through national unity. The high-powered ideology of the Mao era, with its high-sounding experiments—the Great Leap Forward, the Great Proletarian Cultural Revolution—has been put in storage even though Chairman Hua has referred to the possibility of new cultural revolutions in the future. The internal turmoil that these experiments promoted and that was so damaging to progress in a developing country has been stilled. There is more pragmatism, more concentration on getting the job done, on efficiency, on an institutionalized government in which the bureaucracy is perhaps the most important administrative element.

Will the new course satisfy the Chinese people, meeting both their rising expectations of a better life and their belief in a China where all workers and all sections of the country are equal? And will the new emphasis on the army and the bureaucracy create, as a similar emphasis did in postwar Russia, that elitist society which Mao and his successor so roundly condemn in the Soviet Union?

These questions cannot be answered today. My view in the days when the first steps were being taken toward a change in course was that the government was conscious of the people's weariness with the alarms and excursions of the Mao years and was responding by leading China into a quieter but more productive period.

Until late in 1977 the assumption in most foreign governments with diplomatic missions in China was that the succession and the subsequent change in China's approach to her problems had been accomplished with very little disturbance and violence, with a few officials demoted here, a few more promoted there. Recently, unconfirmed reports reaching the West have painted an uglier picture. They suggest that thousands of people have been killed, many of them for distributing antigovernment leaflets. Foreign diplomats in Peking documented more than two hundred such cases, estimating that at least one-third of the alleged crimes were political. The *Economist* of London concluded that "the total number must be a good deal higher." An American expert on China accepted the idea of an extensive purge but did not believe it would continue for long. He rejected the suggestion that the current violence could be compared with the purges that took place during the first years of Communist rule, in the early 1950s. We do know that the *People's Daily* has said that inquiries into the activities of Mme. Chiang-ching's supporters will not be conducted in too soft-hearted a manner.

Running counter to the stories about widespread executions is the long, well-established Chinese tradition of reeducation of the political rebel and dissident. A reasonable assumption is that the government has moved quickly and efficiently to crush opposition; first, because it is a new government that can tolerate at this point no public resistance to its rule, and, second, because it has sensed the people's need for a period of calm.

2

Four Centuries of Rivalry and a Decade of Amity

ON March 2, 1969, the long political duel between the People's Republic of China and the Soviet Union erupted in armed conflict. Chinese forces ambushed and severely mauled a Soviet unit on a frozen island called Damanski by the Russians and Chen Pao by the Chinese, in the Ussuri River, which flows between Manchuria and the Soviet Maritime Province. Thirteen days later the Russians retaliated. A heavily armed battalion fell upon a Chinese garrison on the island and defeated it completely. More than a year later, on August 13, 1970, Soviet units occupied a hill two kilometers inside the Chinese frontier in western Sinkiang and defied the Chinese to oust them.

These clashes marked the culmination of a decade of ideological rivalry, heavily weighted with nationalist aspirations, between the world's two largest Communist powers. But in a larger sense their origins can be traced back to that day in the summer of 1579 when Yermak Timofeevich, a Cossack chieftain, led some eight hundred men eastward from the Upper Khama River east of the Ural Mountains into the territory of a Tatar leader, Khan Kuchum. By October 1582 the force had occupied Kuchum's capital, Sibir, and killed the khan's military leader. His capital gave its name to Russia's great new territory, Siberia.

In retrospect, the Russian march eastward seems as inexorable as the American drive to the Pacific in the nineteenth century. The principal difference was that whereas opposition to the American pioneers came from only a minor power, Mexico, and from Indians, the Russians had to face the belligerent Manchu Empire, which by 1659 controlled all Chinese territory within the Great Wall. Beyond the wall the Manchus began to move northward into the territory of the Mongols and into the Amur River region bordering their homeland, Manchuria.

But the Amur region was no longer populated exclusively by the native Tungusi people. While the Manchus were consolidating their hold on China, the Cossacks, supported by a succession of czars, had been expanding into the area. In 1641 a Russian column defeated the Buryat Mongols and eleven years later founded the city of Irkutsk, providing a convenient route to the east around the southern tip of Lake Baikal, a route that was to be of great strategic importance in the future.

Clearly, a confrontation between the two empires was imminent. It came in the spring of 1644 when another freebooter, Vasili Poyarkov, proceeded down the Amur to its mouth, where he was attacked and lost twenty-five men. After spending the winter at the mouth of the Amur, Poyarkov and his men went on to the Sea of Okhotsk.

The pattern on the Russian side developed into one of probes into the Amur region and subsequently of the establishment of trading settlements, at the expense of the tribes in the area. The Cossacks were aware of the richness of the empire that lay to the south. They appear to have been typically Russian in their indifference to the consequences of their operations. The Manchu government had demanded an end to these activities and in 1652 sent two thousand troops to attack the Russian settlement at Archansk on the Amur. The Chinese were repulsed.

Two years later, Onufri Stepanov led a raid down the Amur but was defeated by a much stronger Manchu force. He retreated to a new settlement named Kumarsk, where in company with another Cossack leader, Petr Beketov, he withstood a strong Manchu attack in the winter of 1654/55. But the Cossacks' luck was running out. While on a plundering expedition,

Stepanov was attacked by a superior Manchu force in the summer of 1658. He and most of his men were killed or captured. The Russian penetration into the Amur area was checked, but only temporarily. The Russians continued to expand around Lake Baikal, motivated by hopes of greater trade with China and by hunger for land.

However, the Manchus and their Mongol allies possessed stronger forces. Their aim was to restrict the Russians to the area west of Lake Baikal and the Lena River region. The two parties jockeyed for position and on September 7, 1689, finally reached an accord in the Treaty of Nerchinsk. This was the first treaty between China and a Western power; it was also the first of scores of agreements between China and Russia.

The treaty limited the Russians to an area well west of the Amur region; in fact, the Russians renounced their claims to that area. It provided for commerce between the Chinese and Russian areas and laid down that traders or craftsmen committing crimes of violence in the territory of the other signatory power should be handed over to their own authorities for punishment by the death penalty. As O. Edmund Clubb points out in his definitive *China and Russia: The Great Game,* the principle of extraterritoriality thus was established a century and a half before it was written into treaties between China and the European maritime powers.

The caravan trade between the two countries proceeded spasmodically. Meanwhile, the Russians, growing in military strength, expanded their holdings in Central Asia, in 1717 besieging Khiva, where they were sharply repulsed. Three years later they moved into the area of Semipalatinsk, now the site of one of the Soviet Union's largest missile test sites. For the next two centuries, Russian policy oscillated between an emphasis on trade and more modern and successful versions of the Cossacks' freebooting expeditions.

In 1833 the Asiatic department of the foreign ministry in Saint Petersburg specified that the government's aim in China was political and commercial. The political aim was to preserve and accelerate friendly relations with China; the economic, to expand trade relations for the mutual benefit of the two countries.

Russian activities in the vast new territories in the east were influenced to a considerable degree by the British presence in India. By the last quarter of the nineteenth century, the British and Russian empires were deep into the "Great Game," as Kipling called it, in central Asia. The Russians talked much and did little about an invasion of India. The British on their part sent political missions to woo the khans of the area, with indifferent success. But the British were too late. The Russians had taken Bukhara in 1820 and went on to new conquests until nearly the end of the century.

A type of warfare developed that would have been familiar to the troopers of Custer or Crook. Long marches, sudden forays by superbly mounted light cavalry, ambushes, and the monotonous job of building frontier forts and trading posts were the lot of the Russian troops. Behind the frontier, always vulnerable to sudden raids, the Russian colonies slowly grew. It was not until serfdom was abolished in 1861, however, that any large number of new settlers moved eastward from European Russia. Even then, the population was surprisingly small, considering the size of the eastern possessions. The government estimated it at 2,681,000 in 1851; it was 7,788,000 in 1897, according to Clubb.

This Russian activity did not directly affect the interests of the now-fading Manchu empire. By the end of the nineteenth century, it was more and more concerned over the increasingly aggressive policy adopted by the Far East's most modern power, Japan. The most important step taken by Russia to consolidate its position in northeastern Asia, the authorization in 1891 of the construction of the Trans-Siberian Railway, does not appear to have aroused any apprehension in Peking. The railway, by increasing the speed by which the Russians could reinforce their garrisons, might even have appeared to the Chinese as a help in blunting Japanese territorial ambitions.

The Chinese, if they did indeed see the situation in that light, discounted Russian ambitions. But in 1897 Mikhail N. Muraviev, the foreign minister, was suggesting that Russia seize the Liaotung Peninsula in Manchuria. A year later the Russian government forced Peking to grant it a twenty-five-year lease on the peninsula with the right to construct a railway from Harbin to Dairen.

By the start of World War I, Russia, though beaten by the Japanese in the war of 1904–05, had expanded both territorially and commercially in eastern Siberia. The Chinese, helpless before the aggressiveness of British, French, German, and other European predators, could do little about their neighbors to the north. The Boxer Rebellion had failed to halt the Europeans. China was in acute danger of dismemberment.

The start of World War I half a world away relieved some of the pressure. The British, French, Germans, and Russians gradually became immersed in the greatest conflict that history had yet recorded. Then, in 1917, Russia, the nearest of China's tormentors, was shaken by revolution. After the success of the Communist revolution, the relationship between the two countries entered a new era as turbulent as the early imperialist period.

The Communists began by attempting to place relations with China on a regular basis, an attempt complicated by a series of rapid changes in political leadership in Peking and by British, American, and Japanese intervention on behalf of the White Russian forces in Siberia. Nevertheless, the new commissar for foreign affairs, Georgi V. Chicherin, announced on July 4, 1918, that his government had renounced the rights acquired in China by the czarist government. Clubb reports that he also wrote Sun Yat-sen, the father of the Chinese republic, "setting forth the proposition that Russia and China held common aims in the struggle against imperialism and calling upon the Chinese people to join with the Bolsheviki in that common cause: 'For our success is your success, our destruction is your destruction.' "

This was the first of many appeals launched in the next two decades for collaboration between the two great Asian powers. But Chicherin clearly overestimated China's power and stability and the ability of any Peking government to control outlying areas such as Outer Mongolia.

A crisis developed there in 1920 when the White Russians invaded Mongolia with a force of two thousand men and marched on Urga. They were repulsed by the Chinese garrison, which then turned to the more congenial occupation of looting Russian homes and enterprises in the town. The Whites returned to the attack and, supported by the Mongols, took Urga early in 1921. There followed a chaotic era in which White and Red Russians, Cossack mercenaries, Mongols, Chinese, and Japanese all became involved in the fluctuating fortunes of Mongolia. Warlords contested China's leadership or established virtual fiefs in China's provinces. By 1921 the Soviets had reorganized and, with Mongol help, drove the Whites out of Urga, which had once more fallen to them.

Meanwhile, the governments of China and Russia were moving toward a stable relationship. On Moscow's side the efforts were intensified by the Bolsheviks' conviction that their revolution, now successfully completed, was the forerunner of others and that the peasants of Asia, so long victimized by imperialists, landlords, and militarists, were the raw material for revolution.

This conviction, however, did not deter Moscow from seeking a regularization of relations with the warlords in Peking. Asian revolution was one thing; pulling China away from Japan, which was seen by Moscow as a powerful potential enemy, was another. But not until 1924 was a formal agreement negotiated between the two governments. This treaty provided for the immediate resumption of normal diplomatic and consular relations and annulled all treaties and agreements between China and the czarist government. The Soviets recognized Outer Mongolia as an integral part of the Republic of China and acknowledged China's sovereignty there.

The Russian national, as opposed to ideological, interest in the treaty was expressed by Chicherin, who commented: "The appearance of the Soviet Union on the coast of the Pacific Ocean as a power friendly to China immediately raises the question of the world importance of the basin of the Pacific Ocean. Formerly the cultured world was concentrated around the Mediterranean. Now the political and economic interests of the world reach out more toward the Pacific. It is the ocean of the future."

The meaning should have been clear to both Peking and Tokyo: the Soviet Union intended to maintain Russia's rights in the Far East, probably with greater firmness than had the tottering Romanov dynasty.

Manchuria provided the first test of the strength of the new Sino-Soviet agreement. There was a bitter dispute about the administration and property of the Chinese Eastern Railway, with Moscow sending off ultimatums and Peking taking a high hand with the railway's personnel, especially with its "education" department, which, given the revolutionary fervor of the period, probably had carried out espionage on behalf of the Soviet Union.

The Nationalists were now nearing power in China. Their government was established in Nanking in October 1928. It had relations with the United States and the European maritime powers but none with the Soviet Union. The situation therefore had regressed to that before the 1924 treaty. There was one significant difference: the Nationalists were, like the Russians, vociferously antiimperialist, and the Soviet foothold in Manchuria offered an opportunity for further Nationalist antiimperialist adventures.

There followed a series of unilateral actions by the Nationalists that stirred the Manchurian pot. In January 1929 the Chinese took over the telephone system in Harbin, installed by the Russians of the Chinese Eastern Railway. They then arrested the Soviet consul and consul general in Harbin in May. In July they seized the railway. This was a major stroke. The department heads, all Russians, were dismissed and replaced by Chinese.

Sixty Russian officials were deported to the Soviet Union and another two hundred arrested. The offices of the Soviet Merchant Marine, the Far Eastern Trading Organization, the Naptha Syndicate, and the Textile Syndicate were closed. Soviet trade unions and cooperatives were dissolved.

These arbitrary Chinese acts were backed by a force of approximately sixty thousand troops deployed along the Soviet frontier. China and the Soviet Union were very close to war. But the Russia of that day was not the Russia of twenty years later. Moscow's reaction, when compared with current Soviet behavior, seems remarkably mild. The Chinese actions were strongly protested, but no threats were uttered. Moscow asked for a conference dealing with all questions related to the railway, an early countermanding of all "illegal" actions by the Chinese regarding the railway, the prompt release of all Soviet citizens, and an end to the harassment of others. The Nationalists replied with a tough note that told the Russians to respect Chinese law and sovereignty and to stop distorting the facts.

The situation rapidly worsened. By August both sides reported fire fights along the frontier, while the diplomats wrangled over the future of the Chinese Eastern Railway. Then the Russians bombed the Chinese railway town of Suifenho. The Chinese retaliated by shelling Soviet shipping at the confluence of the Sungari and Amur rivers. The Russians had already established a new force, the Special Far Eastern Army, under General Vasili K. Bluecher and prepared for an offensive.

The first step was an attack by the Soviet Amur River flotilla and by landing parties on the Chinese at Fukien. Chinese forces at Mishan in eastern Manchuria and at Suifenho were defeated, and Chinese units at Manchouli and Chalainor were soundly beaten. The Soviets claimed eight thousand prisoners and said that the Chinese were retreating everywhere along the front. It was time for Peking to abandon the campaign, and on November 26, the warlord Chang Hsueh-liang agreed fully to the terms laid down by Soviet Commissar for Foreign Affairs Maxim Litvinov.

The terms amounted to a complete Russian victory. Soviet administration of the railway was restored. All Russians arrested by the Chinese were released. The Russians discharged from the railway administration were given the right to resume their jobs or to be paid the wages and pensions due them if they did not go back to work. Soviet consular offices in Manchuria were to be reopened, and—perhaps most important from Moscow's standpoint—the White Russian troops were to be disarmed by the Chinese and expelled from the area.

This border "war" had implications for both countries that were far more important than the conflict itself. Moscow concluded that Peking, under any ruler then available, was not militarily strong enough to protect its interests in the border area and that, consequently, the Chinese government could be coerced by force or the threat of force. The events in Manchuria reinforced the Chinese conviction that the new Soviet state was as aggressive as imperial Russia had been. Chiang Kai-shek—who, according to Clubb, had been one of the prime movers of the 1929 adventure—wrote later that Soviet actions were "another proof that Soviet Russia was continuing Czarist Russia's aggressive policy toward China." A third of a century later I found the Chinese describing the Soviet leadership as "the new Czars."

Relations between the two powers were complicated in the years before World War II by the start of Japan's aggression against China and by the rise of the Chinese Communist party. The first prompted the Nationalist government to seek restoration of regular diplomatic relations with the Soviet Union, ruptured by the clash of 1929. The second provided the Russians with an underground ally in China, a revolutionary group that, since its organization in July 1921, had followed Moscow's ideological line with, however, some reservations. By the time the Chinese Communist party called its fourth congress in 1925 it had a membership of fifty-eight thousand. However, it had not yet made heavy inroads into the strength of the dominant Kuomintang.

From Moscow's standpoint the immediate threat was represented by Japan's drive to seize Manchuria from the Chinese and eliminate Russian influences there. This attack, the so-called Mukden incident, on the night of September 18, 1931, must be regarded as the first military milestone on the road to World War II.

The Japanese plunge into Manchuria, which culminated in the establishment of the puppet state of Manchukuo under the "emperor" Pu-yi, rang the alarm bells in the Kremlin. The Russians doubted that the Japanese would stop where they were in Manchuria and saw all of eastern Siberia and Soviet Turkestan as possible targets for Japanese penetration. One obstacle to this supposed Japanese program would be to strengthen Sinkiang and its ruler, Sheng Shih-ts'ai, with money, a loan of five million gold rubles, and Russian technicians and advisors. This was a feeble barrier to the rampant militarism of Japan, which was confirmed by a coup in Tokyo early in 1935 that strengthened the power of the army and navy high command in the imperial government.

Another political weapon, probably inspired by the Soviet government, was a call issued from Moscow by the Chinese Communist party for a united Chinese front against the Japanese invaders. The Chinese Communists had escaped Nationalist encirclement and reached safety after their famous Long March and were emboldened to issue a manifesto, signed by Mao Tse-tung and his colleague, Chu Teh, welcoming any political federation that would fight the Japanese. By May 1936 Chou En-lai and P'an Han-nien, the latter representing the Comintern, met with a representative of the Kuomintang in Shanghai. No agreement was reached; the Kuomintang's political demands were too much for the Communists to swallow. But the affair was not a complete loss to the Communists. As Clubb points out, they had now joined in the national fight against Japan and had strengthened their position with the people. The Communists, however, continued to carry on a desultory civil war against the Kuomintang in widely scattered areas.

On the other hand, the Nationalists, with Chiang Kai-shek as the dominant figure, continued to organize their forces against the Communists and to launch full-scale "bandit-suppression" offensives. Presumably to divert the Nationalists from such attacks and possibly because of genuine concern over Japanese successes, the Communists again, in December 1936, sought a united front. Presenting themselves as the leaders of a Red Army of two hundred thousand (a vastly inflated figure), Mao, Chu Teh, Chou En-lai, and Chang Kuo-tao asked Chiang Kai-shek to end the civil war and join in an anti-Japanese crusade. For the moment the Nationalists paid little attention to the appeal. But events were overtaking both Chiang's stubborn anti-Communism and Mao's suspicions of the Nationalists. The Japanese, attacking at Shanghai, encountered stiff opposition from the Nationalists' Ninth Group Army, a sign that the Nanking regime was finally prepared to fight. The Soviets, who had been helping the Communist forces, now moved toward an arrangement, though not an alliance, to help the Chinese, on both the left and the right, against Japan.

The Soviet government had already provided some financial help for China. The Nationalist government had been granted a large loan in 1937 and in March obtained a more substantial credit of $100 million for the purchase of military supplies. The Nationalist air force was almost nonexistent, so Soviet pilots flew Soviet planes in defense of Chinese towns, shot up Japanese shipping on the Yangtze, and bombed Taipei on Formosa. Russian engineers were sent to build roads and air bases. As Clubb points out, "At a time when Britain and the United States were continuing their profitable trade with the Japanese, the Soviet aid to China was substantial and critical."

The Russians' ability to help anyone, including themselves, was severely inhibited in this period by Stalin's great purges, which began in 1936 and continued with unabated fury through 1937. One of the victims was Karl Radek, at one time director of the Sun Yat-sen University in Moscow and a recognized authority on Soviet Far Eastern affairs. The purges also struck the armed forces but, at the outset, did not affect the Soviet military position in the east; indeed, the Soviet position was strengthened. A new military mission was sent to China, including generals G. K. Zhukov and V. I. Chuikov, both of whom became prominent in World War II, and headed by Gen. A. I. Cherepanov. The mission eventually numbered five hundred officers who acted as advisors at tank and artillery training centers.

Soviet intelligence became increasingly jittery about Japanese plans. Although the ostensible purpose of the campaign appeared to be the conquest of China, there were signs that the Japanese might also be contemplating a military showdown with the Soviets. To Moscow this threat naturally was of greater importance than their program of helping the Nationalists. The Far Eastern command was reorganized into the Special Red Banner Far Eastern Army early in 1937. In June, Soviet and Japanese forces clashed along the Amur River, in which the Russians had occupied two small islands. The Japanese bluffed the Soviet forces out of the islands and drew the conclusion, understandable enough under the conditions, that the purges had seriously weakened command and troop morale in the Soviet army.

The Japanese forces were further heartened by some minor successes along the frontier between the Soviet Union and Manchukuo. By this time the purge had reached the Far Eastern forces, and in a brisk action west of Lake Khasan the Soviets presented a feeble defense. At this point, Moscow removed Bluecher from command of the Special Red Banner Far Eastern Army and put him under arrest. He was replaced by Gen. Grigori Shtern, who was given a large force for that area, including tank battalions and artillery regiments. The military advantage was swinging to the Soviet side, and the Japanese were willing to make peace. On August 11, 1938, a truce was signed that left the Russians in command of the disputed heights along the frontier. The Soviets, with no other active military obligations, were in a good position; the Japanese, according to Clubb, estimated Russian strength at twenty-four divisions, nineteen hundred tanks, and two thousand aircraft.

At the same time, the Soviets continued to strengthen their relations with the Nationalists. The Chiang Kai-shek government signed a new commercial treaty in June 1939 obtaining a new Soviet credit of $150 million. The last summer before World War II had begun, and in Asia, as in Europe, events were moving with bewildering rapidity. The Russians obviously did not believe that the truce along the frontier would last, and they were right. The Japanese were concerned over the manner in which Moscow was strengthening its military position in Outer Mongolia. The Russians believed that the Japanese were preparing an attack in that sector and gave the command of the forces in the Mongolian People's Republic to Zhukov, then emerging as one of the ablest unpurged field commanders in the Red Army.

Zhukov concentrated a force that included five hundred tanks, five hundred aircraft, large numbers of armored cars, thirty-five infantry battalions, and twenty cavalry squadrons into the First Army Group. The Japanese had done some reinforcement as well. They organized their troops into a new Sixth Army and attacked on August 17. Three days later the Russians launched a counterattack that was everywhere successful. The armor tore holes in the Japanese lines. The Japanese were encircled and, by August 30, had been destroyed as a fighting unit. The Russians put Japanese casualties at fifty-five thousand, an exaggerated figure, and their own losses at approximately ten thousand. While this battle of Nomonhan was being fought, the world's eyes were on a different arena. The Soviets and Nazi Germans had signed their nonaggression pact that same month. Hitler, with his eastern flank secured, attacked Poland on September 1, and Europe went to war.

The war on the other side of the world accelerated Japanese operations in the Far East, although after Nomonhan the Japanese left the Soviets alone. The Japanese, at the outset, were as successful in the Philippines, Malaya, and Burma as they had been in China. The united front of Nationalists and Communists in mainland China proved ineffective militarily in all but minor battles, although the Russians had renewed their pledges to support China in a secret agreement signed at Yalta. The agreement said that the Soviet Union had expressed "its readiness to conclude with the National Government of China a pact of friendship and alliance between the U.S.S.R. and China in order to render assistance to China with its armed forces for the purpose of liberating China from the Japanese yoke."

Despite this pledge, relations between the two countries deteriorated. One reason was that the Chinese Communists were gaining strength among the people and new support from Moscow. As their influence increased, the Communist leadership assumed a more aggressive attitude toward the Nationalists, supported in secret by Moscow, which had begun to put pressure on Chiang for a favorable postwar settlement. The settlement was to include, T. V. Soong was told in Moscow, full Russian ownership of the Manchurian trunk rail lines and the coal mines and other enterprises connected with the lines; the restoration of the original Soviet lease, dated 1898, to the Liaotung Peninsula; and recognition by China of the Mongolian People's Republic.

This was a high price—so high, in fact, that President Harry S. Truman protested to Stalin at the Potsdam Conference in 1945. Stalin soothed the president, and the Russians went on with their own plans. The Soviets attacked on the Manchurian front on August 9 and continued their advances until August 23, nine days after the United States, Britain, and China had received Japan's unconditional surrender. On August 14, China and the Soviets had signed a new Treaty of Friendship and Alliance. To this was appended a number of secondary agreements of enormous advantage to the Soviets.

China's sovereignty over Manchuria was confirmed, but the Nationalist government agreed to the joint use of Port Arthur as a naval base and Dairen as a commercial port and gave the Soviets the right to maintain ground, sea, and air forces in the area, which consequently was in effective military control of the Soviet Union. These and other Chinese concessions immeasurably strengthened the Russian position in the Far East. Most historians agree that through a minimum of military effort and intense diplomatic pressure, the Russians had regained the position they had held in Manchuria in czarist days.

Moscow's appetite increased. Chiang Kai-shek was expected by the Russians to accept coexistence with the Communists. The Russians took their time in withdrawing their forces from Manchuria and made the most of their occupation. They dismantled and removed an estimated $900 million in "war booty." They confiscated the gold found in Manchukuo banks and purchased vast amounts of supplies and property with banknotes issued by the Red Army. The occupation force's economic advisors proposed to Chiang that the Russians and Chinese jointly operate 154 mining and industrial enterprises, amounting to 80 percent of Manchuria's heavy industry. Not until May 3, 1946, did the Soviet forces complete their withdrawal from Manchuria, and when they did, they saw to it that the forces of the Chinese Communist party controlled all of the north of the province.

This wholesale looting of China's most important industrial province was accompanied by a new move by Stalin ostensibly intended to bring the Communists and the Nationalists together. Chiang, invited to Moscow, rejected the invitation. The Nationalist high command decided to rely on American military and diplomatic support to maintain the Kuomintang and defeat the Communists. The Moscow suggestion that Communists be included in a broader government was rejected. The final phase of the long, drawn-out civil war now began.

The operations in 1947 demonstrated the new Communist strength. An offensive in May and June resulted in a major Communist victory. Mao called for a national counteroffensive, in reality an uprising, against the Nationalists and the Chiang Kai-shek government. In September the Communist forces won a smashing victory in Manchuria. The Nationalists fared no better in 1948. Their superiority in aircraft, artillery, and tanks could not make up for weaknesses in morale among the ordinary soldiers, the incompetence of many general officers, corruption among the government leaders on a scale surprising even for China, and, finally, the defection of a considerable number of general officers to the Communist side. By early 1949 Chiang had given up his role as head of state, and on October 1 the new Communist regime was established in Peking. To all intents and purposes the civil war was over, with the Chinese Communist party triumphant and the Russian Communists in the role of armorers and paymasters to the new rulers.

Yet even in that moment of victory, the seeds for a future dispute between the two giants were sown. From 1949 until the Sino-Soviet break a decade later, three related situations conspired toward a worsening of relations. One was the Soviet government's rather tardy recognition of the economic resources of eastern Siberia. A second was the new Communist People's Republic's dependence on the Russians for economic aid. A third was the development, in both countries, of national interests—some new, some revived from the past.

German advances along the eastern front in the early years of the war forced the Russians to move industrial plants out of European Russia into the Urals. At the same time, the Soviet government strengthened the economy of Siberia and expanded the region's communications with the western Soviet Union. The Trans-Siberian Railway was double tracked. Airports were built. The Russians, who had first exploited Siberia for its gold and furs, now began the development of its coal and iron deposits and of the oil production on Sakhalin Island. New towns were built to house the European Russians ordered east to man the new industries and expand the collective farms. (A later chapter will underline the enormous importance of Siberia to the contemporary Soviet economy.)

When the Communists assumed control of mainland China, they needed economic help of every kind. Since Mao and his lieutenants had assumed an uncompromising anti-American policy, China had only one place to turn—the Soviet Union. Russia at that time was recovering from the most devastating and costly war in its history, and the amount of economic aid it could provide for the new ally in Asia was limited.

Nevertheless, in March 1949 what the Russians described as a big group of advisors was sent to China to help the new government "sort out the economic chaos." The word *chaos* was not an exaggeration. Western experts at the time reckoned that China needed credits in excess of $3 billion just to begin modernizing the economy. The Russians did not command such resources. They could offer political support, forthcoming in agreements signed on February 14, 1950, which created a Peking–Moscow alliance and which, among other consequences, pulled China away from the United States and other Western powers that might have provided economic aid.

The Chinese paid the first installment on the agreements in blood. In October 1950 the first Chinese troops entered the Korean War in support of the North Koreans. On New Year's Day of 1951 they launched an attack that drove the UN forces, largely American, out of North Korea. Not until June were the UN troops able to stabilize the situation along the thirty-sixth parallel.

Chinese intervention put the People's Republic of China further in Moscow's debt. Soviet arsenals supplied the PLA with tanks, artillery, and MIG fighters, but China was obligated to pay for this aid. In the field of civilian economic modernization an initial Soviet credit of $300 million was soon exhausted. But economic help continued to flow into the new republic. Soviet specialists directed the rebuilding of Manchurian industry and more than a hundred industrial plants were installed in Mukden, according to Russian estimates. The Russians also transferred to Peking, without cost, various properties in Dairen and elsewhere in the northeast. China's trade with the Soviet Union and its satellites in Eastern Europe rose by 45 percent between 1950 and 1952. By the end of 1952 Peking boasted that agricultural and industrial production had risen to the highest pre-1937 levels and that net national production was 20 percent higher than in 1933. The first five-year economic plan was scheduled to begin in 1953.

Soviet material support in the Korean War and in international diplomacy were a matter of record. Now, with China poised to begin modernization, both Moscow and Peking expected that the economic benefits of their alliance would begin to show.

The Chinese had their own ideas of how modernization should be carried out. Although Manchuria was the heart of the country's industry, Peking planned the establishment of new industrial centers.

One reason was strategic. The concentrated industrial installations in Manchuria were, and are, highly vulnerable to attack. Another reason was Peking's belief that new plants should be located near industrial resources. The existing power plants in Manchuria were to be expanded, but the planners also envisaged other power plants built elsewhere in the country. New steel plants were to be built at Tayeh and Paotow to raise steel production by approximately four million tons each year, and production in the northwest was to be expanded.

The Russians, of course, would help with technical advice but not with much money. China still drew on the original $300 million credit and was exporting goods to make payments on the credit. Although the Soviet Union itself was struggling with economic rehabilitation, the Russian economy was in far better shape than China's. As Clubb points out, the relationship of the two countries was that of the countryside (China) to the city (Russia).

By 1954 the Russians were prepared to dole out a few more millions and send more economic aid. At the celebration of Communist China's fifth anniversary in 1954, Nikita S. Khrushchev and his traveling companion, the now almost forgotten statesman Nikolai A. Bulganin, promised to build another fifteen industrial enterprises in China and to extend an additional long-term credit of $130 million. There would be an exchange over the next five years of technical and scientific information and assistance, and the Russians would help in the construction of a new railroad line from Lanchow to Aktogai.

All this assistance naturally increased China's debt to the Soviet Union. There was the original debt of $300 million, the support of Soviet technicians in China, the payments for the ammunition and materiel furnished in the Korean War. China, in theory, was to pay for these out of current production and foreign trade, which concentrated on the Soviet Union.

The demands of China's economic expansion appeared insatiable. Two years later, in 1956, the Soviet Union agreed to build another fifty-five industrial plants and factories in China and supply the equipment and technology for them. The estimated value was $625 million to be paid in Chinese goods. The two governments agreed to develop jointly hydraulic power in the Amur and Argun river basins and to construct a new outlet for the Amur that would enable deep-draft vessels to pass into the river in winter.

Meanwhile, China's debts to the Soviet Union increased. By 1957 the outstanding debt was $2.4 billion, about half of it owed for military equipment delivered during the Korean War. But China needed even more aid in the future if modernization was to be achieved. About ten thousand Soviet advisors had already served in China. More would be needed. The shortage of trained engineers and technicians plagued China then as it does now.

Such economic progress as China had made since 1949 was now interrupted by what was called the Great Leap Forward. Proclaimed in 1958, this was to be a sudden surge of agricultural and industrial production that would accelerate overall economic expansion. Planning was forgotten. Calling on its masses, China would form production armies to win victories in agriculture and industry. Mao's government embarked on an unprecedented propaganda program to claim success for the Great Leap Forward: a doubling of steel production to 11 million tons and of food-grain production to 375 million tons. These "victories," trumpeted to the Communist world, temporarily en-

hanced Mao's reputation as a wonder worker who could overcome China's economic problems through a spasm of national
industry and resolve.

Success for the Great Leap Forward was claimed again in
1959 even when the Russians, who had technical advisors in almost every branch of the Chinese economy, were already re-
porting widespread industrial disruption and delays to Moscow.
The Great Leap Forward was, in fact, a failure. Despite Peking's claims, the output of food grains had fallen, the concept
of the dispersal of heavy industry into backyard blast furnaces
proved impractical, and the labor force emerged from the experience less organized than in the past. China, quite obviously,
still needed assistance from the Soviet Union.

The Russians were still willing. Khrushchev and Chou En-lai
signed an agreement early in 1959 under which the Soviet
Union would provide China with equipment, materials, technical assistance, and training for Chinese personnel to a value of
$1.25 billion. The agreement called for the construction of an
additional 78 large plants in the metallurgical, machine-building, chemical, coal-mining, electric-power, and construction-
materials industries. This brought the total number of plants
built or reconstructed in China by the Soviets since 1950 to 336.
Tens of thousands of Soviet technicians, plus some from Eastern Europe, had played a role in the program.

Curiously enough, it was precisely when the Soviet Union
was extending this massive economic aid, and planning to provide more in the future, that the relations between the two governments and the two Communist parties began to deteriorate.
This was the third of the three elements that led to the break between the two giants. Although their two opposing interpreta-
tions of Marxism played a major role, behind the references to
the sainted Lenin and the invocations of Marx, old, deeply
ingrained national aspirations and interests were important also.
On China's side there was the abiding national dissatisfaction
with what the party leadership called the unequal treaties of the
past—the Treaty of Nerchinsk in 1689, the Treaty of Aigun in

1858, the Tehcheng Protocol, and the Treaty of Ili. These agreements, which the Chinese regarded as unfair because they were imposed on weak imperial governments by aggressive czars, sanctified Russia's expansion into Siberia, including Chinese Turkestan.

The festering resentment over these treaties among the leaders of a highly nationalistic people was exacerbated in the 1950s by the special position in China of the Soviet Union's diplomatic and economic representatives. This irritated a Chinese party leadership which felt, with some reason, that it should no longer be relegated to a secondary role in the politics of the Communist world. Abroad, the Chinese were gaining confidence and winning friends. They had made a brave, if ineffectual, showing against the Americans over the Taiwan issue. They had participated in the Geneva conference of 1954 that ended the first Vietnam war. Their diplomatic missions were making progress in Africa and Asia.

The first signs of an ideological break appeared in the late 1950s with Mao and Khrushchev as the protagonists. Mao believed, then and later, in permanent revolution with its goal the destruction of capitalism. The Soviet leader, far more aware of the realities of world power, plumped for peaceful coexistence and scoffed at Mao's faith in the "omnipotence of revolutionary war," which the Chinese leader said "is good, not bad; it is Marxist."

This dispute over strategy owed much to the situations of the two countries. The Soviet government considered that it faced a triple threat: the possibility of a revived and chauvinistic China in Asia; competition with both the United States and China for influence in the Third World; and the continuing duel with America, whose military and industrial strength was better appreciated in Moscow than in Peking.

Mao and his lieutenants became increasingly distrustful of Khrushchev. They opposed his moves toward reconciliation with Yugoslavia, whose unorthodoxy had long been condemned by the Chinese. They were not consulted about the Russian leader's speech to the twentieth congress of the Soviet Communist party, in which he attacked and largely demolished the Stalin legend. Peking's indirect response was to offer some support to dissident Communists in Poland and Hungary.

The Chinese also indirectly criticized the terms of Soviet aid, particularly the expenses of the Korean War, which the Chinese Communists considered a war fought for world Communism. It was also pointed out, but never in public by Mao or his henchmen, that it would take a decade to repay the loans made by the Soviet Union and that after World War II the United States had excused some of its allies the debts incurred during the war.

Mao at this period began to exaggerate for his own reasons the progress made by Third World countries. In his "the east wind is prevailing over the west wind" speech he suggested that the countries of the Third World had "outdistanced considerably" the powers of the West. From this highly doubtful thesis, Chairman Mao argued that the Communist parties, led by the Soviet and Chinese parties, should take a more aggressive stance toward the imperialists. When the break between China and Russia became final, Moscow revealed that Mao in 1957 had contemplated the death of one-third to one-half of the world's population in a nuclear war, adding that since "imperialism would be destroyed utterly, there would be only socialism left in the world." But by whatever means, Mao sought the destruction of the world's capitalist and industrialized nations and, as Clubb points out, "an early division of the spoils" that would relieve China's poverty.

In retrospect, there seems to be a certain frivolity about Mao's position. In his dealings with the Russians and their East European allies at this period, he seemed to expect them to direct the greater part of their economic energies toward raising the economic conditions of the poor members of the Communist bloc—meaning, of course, China. In a declaration of 1956, in which he advanced his thesis, he also called for a direct confrontation between the Communist bloc and the imperialists, an end to Communist aid to bourgeois governments in the Third

World, and group formulation of international strategy by all members of the bloc rather than by Moscow alone.

Mao's demands ran counter to the thrust of Soviet international thinking at the time. The Russians were much better informed than the Chinese about the strength of the Western imperialists and, consequently, were unwilling to follow an intransigent, revolutionary policy in international affairs. Economic competition supported by diplomatic initiatives, primarily in the Third World, appeared to Moscow a much safer course. Moscow was clearly hostile to any Communist-bloc policies that might bring the bloc to the verge of war and endanger the hard-won gains of the last ten years. It promised Mao prototypes of nuclear weapons but was cool to Chinese appeals for help in modernizing the PLA.

Peking's strategy of indirect political attack was exercised in full. Tito's "revisionism" was bitterly attacked in Peking, but the real target was Khrushchev, whose refusal to accept Mao's proposals for an even colder war with the United States and whose choice of coexistence instead struck the Chinese as "antirevolutionary."

On the surface, formal relations between the two governments appeared tranquil. Khrushchev and Soviet Defense Minister Marshal Rodion Malinovski visited Peking for what was evidently a high-level conference on Communist global strategy in July 1958. Whatever positive results emerged from the meeting were outweighed by China's alarm over a Soviet proposal that the two countries organize a joint naval command for the West Pacific. The Chinese, whose sensitivity to any infringement of their national sovereignty was increasing, saw this proposal as a Moscow plot to control China's strategy in the Pacific. This already included attacks on the Nationalist island of Quemoy, operations that the Russians, now deeply involved in the Middle East, opposed.

Support for the Chinese action against Quemoy was limited to careful comments by *Pravda*. As Clubb points out, it was not until after the Quemoy crisis was over that Khrushchev told

Eisenhower that in the event of a nuclear attack on China, the Russians would retaliate by the same means. No one in Washington had even considered a nuclear attack. The crisis ended in October when the Chinese stopped shelling Quemoy. Mao, undaunted, issued the essay "Imperialists and All Reactionaries Are Paper Tigers," but Khrushchev continued his policy of coexistence with the paper tigers. In the absence of Soviet documentation, it is difficult to trace a connection between this policy and the gradual reduction in Russian military aid to the Chinese.

In 1957 the Russians had promised to help China develop nuclear weapons, and the next year Soviet technicians finished building a nuclear reactor in China. But Khrushchev, already worried by Mao's belligerence, which at that time was directed at the West, decided on June 20, 1958, to cancel the agreement providing for technological aid and information necessary to build nuclear weapons.

The Chinese regarded this action as both an affront to China's position as a great Communist state and as an indication that Khrushchev and the Russian Politburo were pursuing a policy contradictory to China's interests. These sentiments were exacerbated when the Soviet Union took a neutral position toward the frontier quarrel between India and China. When, in late 1959, Khrushchev went to Peking after a conference with President Eisenhower in Washington, he was welcomed with coolness. He did nothing during his visit to heal the wounds he had inflicted on the Chinese. Rather, on his departure, he announced that it was possible to "rule out war for all time as a means of solving international disputes." He also told the Chinese that it would be "wrong" to test capitalism by force.

By the end of 1959, then, it was clear that despite the impressive efforts the Soviet Union had made to assist the development of the Chinese economy, the two governments were pursuing separate and divergent foreign policies. The Chinese, at the very moment when the failure of the Great Leap Forward became obvious, assumed an increasingly belligerent line, whereas the Russians invested their political capital in Third World countries—Egypt, Iraq, Cuba, and India—with considerable success. Although the basis of the quarrel was national interest, the dispute was clothed in ideological terms. The Chinese, in a long article entitled "Long Live Leninism," assailed those who departed from the truths laid down by Lenin, because of changed world conditions. The Russians thought Mao had written the article. The name of the author remains unknown, but certainly the polemic reflected Mao's view that friendly relations between the Soviet Union and the United States must cease and that the Soviet economic penetration of the Third World was a mistake because the benefits could not be shared by China. On the whole, the article also reflected Chinese overconfidence about Russia's tolerance of Peking's criticism.

The Soviets were quick to answer. Otto V. Kuusinen, a member of the Soviet Communist party's presidium, published an analysis that set forth Communist doctrine as interpreted by Moscow. Among other points, it stated that wars are not inevitable and that "the official doctrine of Soviet foreign policy is the Leninist principle of peaceful coexistence of states, regardless of the differences in their social and political systems."

In 1960 the Chinese were given an opportunity to taunt the Russians with the weakness of coexistence, at least with the Americans, when the Russians shot down an American U-2 spy plane twelve hundred miles into Soviet territory. So this is your friend Eisenhower, the Chinese said in effect to Khrushchev, while they applauded the breakdown of the Soviet-U.S. summit conference planned for Paris in May 1960. The Chinese, sensing a reverse for Khrushchev, attacked Soviet policy when the World Conference of Trade Unions met in Moscow and encouraged resistance to Soviet leadership in other Communist parties. None of this had any minatory effect on the Russian leadership. Rather, it appears to have hardened the Soviet attitude toward the Chinese and their policies.

The breach widened rapidly. The Soviets chose a conference of twelve Communist parties in Bucharest as the next battleground. Khrushchev expounded his policies, declaring that "only lunatics and maniacs can now come out with appeals for a new world war." P'eng Chen, China's representative, told the conference that the days of imperialism were numbered and demanded support for revolutionary movements and a tough position vis-à-vis the capitalist world. Khrushchev had the last word. In a private meeting he attacked Mao's internal and foreign programs and compared him to Stalin because Mao fostered a cult of personality.

Although it cannot be said with certainty, the presumption is that by 1960 the Russians, angered by China's attacks on the Soviet Union's political as well as ideological leadership, concluded that the time had come to cut assistance to China and to further Russian interests in other Asian countries such as India and Indonesia. The Soviets were aware of, and irritated by, the Chinese competition for the leadership of the Third World, especially because the Chinese were in a position to participate in this competition precisely because of the economic support given them by the Soviet Union. One example of this competition was in the Mongolian People's Republic, which the Chinese volunteered to help with a loan of 260 million rubles. Earlier they had told Khrushchev that they believed that the Mongolian republic should be returned to China. Such competition could only be won by the Soviets. They had the money, the equipment, and the experts.

The next step was more serious. In July 1960 the Soviet government, in a long note to Peking, declared that Russian experts in China were mistreated, their advice disregarded, and their working conditions intolerable. The Russians also claimed, in a striking example of the pot calling the kettle black, that the Chinese were spying upon the Russian experts by opening their mail and searching their rooms. In consequence, the Soviet government said, it had decided to withdraw all its advisors and technicians in July and August. A Chinese reply did not satisfy Moscow, and by the end of August 1,390 Russian technicians and their families, a total of close to 4,000 people, had departed. Not only had they departed, but they had taken their blueprints with them. Sixteen years later, Chinese still explained to foreigners that this factory or that had been built to their own plans because the Russians had taken the originals.

The Chinese, however, still needed economic assistance from the Soviet Union, and despite the differences between the two leaders, they got it. Early in 1961 the Russians agreed to postpone for five years the payment of China's outstanding debt, about $320 million, and to supply China with half a million tons of sugar on an interest-free credit. Yet while this economic relationship continued, competition in the political field also continued.

Both governments signed treaties of friendship, cooperation, and mutual friendship with North Korea. Each was competing for political and economic influence. A more serious dispute arose over Albania, which for some years had followed the Chinese ideological line of intransigent enmity toward capitalism. At a Russian party congress Khrushchev assailed the Albanians for diverging from the world (i.e., Russian) Communist line and charged them with views comparable to those held in Moscow under Stalin. The charges, of course, were equally applicable to Mao and the Chinese Communist party, who, like the Albanians, believed in the inevitability of war with the capitalist powers. The Russians settled the Albanian issue by withdrawing all technicians from the tiny Balkan state and ending all economic aid. Albania had but one friend in the Communist world, China.

The Sino-Soviet dispute also was affected by international crises involving both countries in the autumn of 1962. China engaged in a brisk and militarily successful action with India on that country's northeast frontier. Despite the military success, the action was politically damaging to China. World opinion saw the Chinese as aggressors and India, shaken out of neutralism, moved closer to Britain and the United States.

Shortly after the Sino-Indian crisis, a more dangerous situation developed between the United States and the Soviets over Cuba. The Soviet Union's initial aggressiveness and final humiliation in the Cuban missile crisis provided Peking with ammunition for the debate over a proper world strategy for Communism. Mao and his lieutenants deplored Soviet "adventurism" and then, in the next paragraph, berated Khrushchev for surrendering to the Americans. The Cubans were told that in a crisis the Chinese would support them to the end, the implication being that the Russians would not.

It was about this time, as Harold C. Hinton has pointed out, that official Peking statements began to mention the fact that czarist Russia had annexed large tracts of territory in eastern Siberia, including the Maritime Province and the Amur watershed, and in central Asia sections of the Soviet Kazakh, Kirghiz, and Tadzhik republics that had been claimed by the Manchu Empire. There were further protests about the inequality of the treaties enforced on the Manchus by the czars. In Moscow, at least, these statements were read as reflecting a Chinese policy aimed at the recovery of these lands. The Russians, then and now, reject any discussion of frontiers, being only too aware that their borders in Europe, as well as Asia, in many areas are the result of forcible seizure.

The Chinese went beyond mentioning the "unequal" treaties of the past. An editorial in the *People's Daily* of March 8, 1963, disclosed that the government had decided years before to examine all old treaties, accepting some and abrogating or renegotiating others "when conditions are ripe." As Clubb points out, the editorial illuminated the Communist leadership's attitude toward international law: "First, it was taken for granted that an 'unequal' treaty, being unjust, was without validity. Second, the Chinese government itself would unilaterally determine which of the treaties it had inherited should be maintained, discarded or renegotiated." Or, as a British expert on China put it, "The Chinese consider their country *above* international law."

As the polemical battle between the two capitals became hotter, trade fell off. Two-way trade between the two countries dropped from $1.65 billion in 1960 to $816.5 million in 1962. The Russians had, by their standards, shown great tolerance toward Mao and his followers. But as Peking continued to extol Maoism as the true faith, tempers in Moscow grew short. The Russians were also aware that the Chinese were making a major effort to divert other Communist parties from ideological allegiance to Moscow, to worship at the true ideological capital in Peking.

By Peking's interpretation, the Russian leadership had become deviationist. In a statement issued on August 15, 1963, the Chinese, with a great show of self-righteousness, announced that "it is our proletarian internationalist duty to point out that they [the Soviet leaders] have now betrayed the interests of the Soviet people and the entire socialist camp." In other words, the Chinese Communist party now regarded Khrushchev and the other Russian leaders as traitors. Mao and his lieutenants directed a series of attacks at the Russians through the middle of 1964 as China moved further from Russia and toward its self-appointed role as the leader of world Communism.

Unfortunately for the Chinese, other Communists did not see them in that light. At a meeting of the Communist-supported World Peace Council in Warsaw, the Chinese suffered two humiliating defeats. A Chinese resolution calling for a militant anti-Western policy line was rejected by an overwhelming vote, and the Chinese delegation's effort to mobilize support for Chinese leadership among African, Latin American, and Asian parties was a failure.

Relations between the two countries took on an acrimony rather like that displayed by the United States and the Soviet Union in the 1950s. Each viewed the other as ideologically deviationist and potentially aggressive. The Chinese increasingly lumped the Russians with the imperialist powers, terming them "social imperialists" who were racist and counterrevolutionary. The Soviet government was accused of betraying Arabs, Algerians, and Cubans. Chinese propaganda appealed directly to the Russian people. An article in *Red Flag* declared, "Now is the time—now it is high time—to repudiate and liquidate Khrushchev's revisionism."

Khrushchev's fall from power in October 1964 did not, however, bring about a change in Soviet policy, although there is reason to believe that Mao considered that the Russian leader had been sacrificed by his associates in an effort to improve Sino-Soviet relations. Chou En-lai expressed hopes that relations between the two countries would now improve. The hopes were soon dashed. Leonid I. Brezhnev, the new first secretary of the Soviet Communist party, speaking on November 5, 1964, made it clear that his leadership would continue the foreign policy of Khrushchev.

The new Soviet leaders, Brezhnev and Premier Alexei N. Kosygin, would have to deal with a China that was gaining strength. The Chinese had exploded their first atomic weapon. Economic progress, without the aid of Soviet technicians, was visible. But these gains were offset by the broadening of the American military effort in Vietnam, including the bombing of North Vietnam. Washington in the past had made it clear that it considered China the source of revolutionary movements in Asia. The bombing therefore had to be considered by Peking as a warning.

This development emboldened the Chinese to make another effort to restore the Sino-Soviet alliance. Foreign Minister Ch'en Yi, speaking at the Soviet embassy, told his audience that coexistence with the American imperialists was out of the question and that "only in concrete action against United States imperialism and its followers can the Chinese-Soviet alliance be tested and tempered and Chinese-Soviet unity be consolidated and developed." The Chinese thus returned to their original proposal that Moscow join Peking in a risky confrontation of the United States. Not only did the Russians refuse, but few parties in the Third World approved the proposed initiative. And when Peking, soured by the Soviet refusal to respond, tried to organize parties in Africa and Asia into a bloc that was both anti-American and anti-Russian, it failed.

Despite these setbacks, the Chinese remained adamant. Ch'en Yi defied the world in September 1965 when he told a news conference, "If the American imperialists have decided to launch a war of aggression against us, we hope that they will come and the sooner the better. Let them come tomorrow! Let the Indian reactionaries, the British imperialists and the Japanese militarists come with them! Let the modern revisionists support them in the North! We will finish nevertheless by triumphing."

There is a note of desperation behind this defiance. The Chinese must have been aware that their anti-Soviet campaign had not produced the expected results. True, they had challenged Russian ideological leadership in the Communist world; had won some converts in the Third World and Eastern Europe; and had, to a minor degree, weakened the Russian hold on the satellite governments in that area. But preaching independence is a hazardous occupation. The Chinese were finding that "fraternal" parties around the world, though increasingly unwilling to accept Moscow's doctrinal leadership, were equally wary of entering the Chinese camp.

China's claims to ideological leadership were further sapped by the launching in 1966 of Mao's Great Proletarian Cultural Revolution. This, it is generally conceded, not only weakened China's international position but turned a society then enjoying a measure of stability upside down.

These developments did not dampen Chinese attacks on Moscow's "revisionist" leadership, which was accused of vilifying China and, even worse, of conspiring with the United States to induce Japan to cooperate in expanding Siberia's economy. The Russians snapped back that they had reason to believe that one of the objectives of the Chinese in Vietnam was "to provoke a military conflict between the U.S.S.R. and the United States so as to be able, as they themselves say, 'to sit on the mountain and observe the fight of the tigers.' ''

The Cultural Revolution was now in full swing and did further damage to Sino-Soviet relations. The Red Guard harassed the Soviet embassy in Peking and was called off only after receipt of a stiff Soviet note. The Red Guard demonstrations against the embassy were renewed in August 1967. The consular offices were looted and burned. Again the Russians responded with a tough note. Chou En-lai, apparently then the one reasonable man at China's summit, warned the Red Guard that it must not attack foreign embassies.

Peking, even in the midst of the new revolution, continued its attacks on Moscow. These took a more militant tone in 1968 when the Russians were charged with 119 violations of Chinese air space by Soviet aircraft in 1967. The intrusions, the Chinese claimed, were ''thoroughly organized and planned by the Soviet government in order to support the kind of atrocious aggression perpetrated against Czechoslovakia.'' The Chinese, understandably, had seized the Soviet offensive against Czechoslovakia as an example of the imperialism of the ''new czars,'' seeing in the condemnation of the action by some other Communist parties a movement away from Russian leadership in the Communist world.

The long history of Chinese–Russian hostility centered in its latest phase on the negotiations over border problems in the north. These talks were utterly devoid of progress. Moscow wanted to restrict the negotiations to local issues such as the ownership of islands in the Amur River. The Chinese, however, sought a comprehensive review of all frontier questions. According to a Russian report—which seems, in light of known Chinese chauvinism, to be accurate—the Chinese claimed 580,000 square miles of Soviet territory. Mao followed this with some belligerent remarks in which he said that the Chinese had not yet asked Russia for an accounting about Vladivostok, Khabarovsk, Kamchatka, and other areas east of Lake Baikal that had become Russian territory in the nineteenth century.

The war of words now gave way to a war of weapons. The guns firing on Damanski Island on March 2, 1969, echoed those of Yermak centuries before.

Four hundred years of bickering, polemics, and occasional outbreaks of fighting between the two giants has been rooted in a basic antipathy between the two peoples. The ideological content of the struggle, so high in the period since 1960, cannot disguise the essential national interests that both parties believe to be at stake. Nor should it mask the xenophobia of both Russians and Chinese. The European Russians, although publicly professing fraternal feelings for the peoples of the Central Asian republics, dislike non-European Russians. There is a strong colonialist aspect to Moscow's rule over these distant republics. Similarly, the Chinese, the inhabitants of the Middle Kingdom, look down on the lesser breeds without the law, a classification that runs from the Tibetans to the Americans. Like the Russians, the Chinese make a great show of their support of their country's minorities. But it is the great Han people who count.

In today's critical situation there is almost no area where the interests of the two countries do not clash. The conflict over frontiers, the disputes over economic aid, the accusations of sharp practice, the competition for diplomatic influence in the Third World, the bickering at the United Nations are all part of a vast pattern of conflict. Unfortunately for the peace of the world, it is not limited to China and Russia, for it affects directly the political and military situation in the North Pacific.

The Chinese, for example, are highly sensitive about the future of Korea. Public policy calls for the unification of the country by a referendum. Privately the Chinese are extremely concerned over the possibility that a united Korea might be dominated economically and politically by the Soviet Union. My visit to China coincided with the last weeks of the 1976 U.S. presidential campaign. Three times, senior officials asked if I thought that Jimmy Carter, if elected, would implement his promise to pull American forces out of Korea. I inferred from their questions and from subsequent comments that they regarded any American withdrawal as destabilizing not only for Korea but for the entire region. With one exception these comments were characteristically indirect. For example, officials would tell me how an American troop withdrawal from West Germany would create a chaotic situation in Western Europe. When I replied that I did not think this was an issue, their replies ran something like this: ''Well, you must admit that any withdrawal anywhere makes a situation less stable.''

My conclusion is that the Chinese believe that an American troop withdrawal, even a carefully phased one that is accompanied by large-scale reequipment of South Korean forces, will encourage the North Koreans, supported by the Soviet Union, to attack. A successful North Korea, they would assume, would have political and military debts to Moscow, and the Russian position in northeastern Asia would be considerably strengthened.

A decade ago, with Mao still in power, the ''Japanese militarists'' were a favorite target for Chinese Communist party rhetoric. The reinforcement of Soviet forces along the Chinese frontier; the prospect of American force reductions in Korea; and, above all, a consciousness among the Chinese of their own military weaknesses have contributed to a more realistic Chinese view of Japan. The Chinese with whom I talked know that the Japanese are not militarists. Indeed, they rather wished that Japan would contribute more to her own defense and that of the northwestern Pacific than the present expenditure, which is under 1 percent of Japan's GNP. They also welcomed in careful, but precise, terms the existence of the security treaty between the United States and Japan, because it requires the maintenance in the area of sophisticated American air, naval, and ground forces, which the Chinese see as a counterbalance to Soviet strength in eastern Asia.

Chinese feelings toward the United States are mixed, the product of memories of perceived wrongs, of exploitation, of the Korean War and the incidents over Quemoy and Matsu. But it was made quite clear that China recognizes the United States as a Pacific power, in some respects the most powerful of all the nations bordering the Pacific. As long as the Chinese see the Soviets as a military danger, they will welcome the American presence. Whether they are prepared to go beyond a mere welcome and seek United States help in the vast modernization program that the PLA so badly needs is a question discussed later in relation to the present status of that army. But the point should be made here, and expanded upon later, that the Chinese military fully understand two prime elements of the military situation: first, the PLA, which embraces China's army, air force, and navy, is woefully dated in its weapons and, consequently, in its tactics; and second, the only country from which, under present conditions, China could obtain the quantity and quality of arms she needs is the United States.

As this review of Sino-Russian hostility and its international effects demonstrates, the present antagonism is not simply the outcome of a doctrinal fight between two Communist demagogues, Khrushchev and Mao, over the location of Communism's true center; rather, it is the culmination of centuries of fear, suspicion, and racial antipathy, exacerbated on both sides by national hunger for land and resources. The quarrel may abate. There may even be a rapprochement between Moscow and Peking, although this would require a revolution in national and ideological outlooks by both parties. But this would lead only to a temporary truce, for the roots of conflict run too deep.

3

The Strategic Triangle: Russia, China, and the United States

YU CHAN, the deputy foreign minister, was an abrasive little man. Unlike some other Chinese officials, he seemed uninterested in the soft answer. When we discussed relations between the United States and the People's Republic of China he asked tough questions and gave tough answers. At that time, three months after the death of Chairman Mao, Americans were looking for an easing of the Chinese attitude toward the United States, particularly since the Chinese spent a great deal of time telling foreigners how frightened they were of the Russians.

What Yu Chan said that cold November afternoon in Peking is interesting in that it did not deviate in any important sense from what Hua Kuo-feng and Teng Hsiao-ping told Secretary of State Cyrus Vance less than a year later. Thus, his remarks can be taken as the basic Chinese position on relations with America. Interestingly enough, I never heard any evidence that China had a diplomatic fallback position. Nor did Vance or other foreigners who have been received by the Chinese leadership. The basic Chinese position is apparently immutable, and Yu's remarks as apposite today as when he uttered them.

Of course, he said, "There ought to be exchanges between our two countries," but as far as bilateral relations are concerned, "the biggest issue is the Taiwan question.

"We said in the past and we are still saying now that there should be three conditions for the normalization of the relationship. The United States must abrogate the mutual-defense treaty with Taiwan, withdraw its armed forces from Taiwan, and cut diplomatic relations with Taiwan. As in what manner we will liberate Taiwan is China's individual affair, and we will not allow others to interfere."

That is where China stood then. That is where she stands now. And that, barring a war with Russia and the consequent need for American supplies, is where she will stand.

Characteristically, Yu, having had his say on Sino-American relations, switched abruptly to the worry that dominates most Chinese officials: the threat posed by the Soviet Union.

"We feel that, apart from the Taiwan question, there are big issues that call for the attention of our two countries: the aggression and expansion of the polar bear."

In discussions of the Soviet–American–Chinese triangle, two interrelated themes always come to the fore. One is China's passionate independence: "We depend on self-reliance."

Yu reminded me that the United States had blockaded and embargoed China and "thought we could not survive. But we did survive and develop. Later on, the Soviet Union learned from the United States and wanted to take us by the neck. But we survived. And we did develop. People must give up the idea that one can take China by the neck.

"We want to trade with you on an equal footing, but we do not desire help," he added. "There should be equality and mutual benefit to bring help to both sides."

So much for independence, mutual benefit from trade, and the customary propaganda folderol. When Yu got down to the nuts and bolts of the triangular situation, he was much more plainspoken—and self-serving.

"Who is the enemy which poses a genuine threat to you?" he asked. "That is the Soviet Union. But you do not concentrate your strength against the Russians. You have dispersed your strength a great deal in the past. You are like a man trying to put ten fingers on ten fleas; the fleas are Vietnam and Taiwan and South Korea. In the end, all the fleas will jump away.''

As I listened, I noticed that Yu, small even for a Chinese, was moving restlessly in his chair. He was, I felt, about to say something unpleasant. He did.

"You Americans cannot appreciate that you should concentrate your forces against the main enemy, and that is why your strategic thinking is dim,'' he said. "You are very fierce in the face of small countries and timid in the face of big countries.'' He glanced at me while I listened to the conversation and continued, "I would like to exchange views in a frank manner: the United States is afraid of the Soviet Union; it not only fears the Russians but helps the Russians.''

Again the sidewise glance. He was, had he only known it, being a good bit less vitriolic than such men as Andrei Vischinsky and other Russians I had interviewed in the past.

Scoffing at Soviet claims that the Russians love peace, Yu said that détente was only a Soviet tactic to disarm the Americans and their allies.

"You Americans are helping the Soviet Union and you say the Soviet Union loves peace and wants détente and wants to be on friendly terms with the United States,'' he continued. "That is to blow the Russian horn. The Soviet Union uses its capital to engage in arms production. But America supplies the Russians with money, you supply food and grain. . . . We cannot understand this. There is an old saying in China: 'To rear a tiger will only entail danger and peril.' Your policy toward the Soviet Union is exactly like that.''

To the deputy foreign minister there are two viewpoints and two kinds of people in the United States. Some, who are aware of the Russian threat, "stand for concessions to appease the Soviet Union,'' but "this is a very dangerous policy,'' since it serves only "to inflate the arrogance of the Soviet Union'' and "accelerate the outbreak of war.''

The other point of view is held by those who "stand for better relations between the United States and its friends so as to deal with Soviet expansionism and aggression.''

Yu paused, looked at his teacup, and asked, ''Can you tell me, will the people who hold the latter point of view gain the upper hand in the United States and will this view have more impact on the administration and on the Congress?''

The deputy foreign minister's comments reflected a certain simplicity of approach to the United States. As far as the Soviet Union is concerned, the Chinese tend to see things in black and white. They may be the subtle, flexible people portrayed by generations of sinophiles, but these traits are not in evidence when they talk of ''the polar bears.'' Consequently, it is understandable that their attitude toward Americans and American policies is didactic; you appease the Russians or you fight them.

The American attitude toward China, the reflection of a diverse, contentious, and singularly unregimented people, seemed beyond the grasp of the Chinese officials I met. They were not stupid men. Indeed, I would bet that their IQs are a good deal higher than those of men in comparable positions in Washington. But they have had twenty-odd years of isolation under a rigid, authoritarian system. For most of that time the United States was an enemy, and enmity, to a Chinese, is not susceptible to gradation. I found it difficult to convince my hosts that U.S. policy toward China today is the result not of official fiat alone but of nearly a century of shifting views on China.

There have been four distinct American approaches to China—''American'' in the sense that they were widely held by the people and thus influenced the making of national policy.

Many can remember the ritual dime or quarter contributed each Sunday to something vaguely known as ''Chinese missions.'' Occasionally the young were herded into an auditorium to watch a jerky, badly focused movie about the work of such missions. To adults and schoolchildren alike, China was a ''good thing.'' American missionaries, doctors, and engineers were bringing civilization to this benighted land of Confucius and Li Po through the altruism of the great, good-hearted, and often fat-headed American public.

U.S. policy was characterized as the Open Door, a stance frequently applauded in editorials and by earnest clergymen seeking more money from church groups. America's policy in the 1920s was only marginally different from the policies of the other great powers infiltrating China: Britain, France, Russia, Japan. But, as Americans have a knack for doing, they wrapped their policy in a mantle of lofty idealism. The U.S. Navy's gunboats, however, patroled the Yangtze, and the Fifteenth Infantry was garrisoned at Tientsin. Businessmen naturally were alert to the promise of a great Chinese market, a promise to this day unfulfilled. Where are those who really believed in 400 million customers? They were succeeded by those who dreamed, a generation ago, of 600 million customers. And, now, a billion?

This curious mixture of philanthropy and good old Yankee enterprise was the main theme of American thinking about China through the period of Japanese military infiltration in China in the 1930s. To many, China became not a country but a cause. The Japanese did their best to increase American sympathies for the Chinese by bombing an elderly gunboat, the U.S.S. *Panay,* roughing up stray missionaries, carrying out the rape of Nanking, and by talking of their "national mission" in China, words to become familiar later in the decade from Berlin.

When the attack on Pearl Harbor blew the United States into World War II and an alliance with China—understood to be Chiang Kai-shek's Nationalist, and dictatorial, government—the American people were prepared psychologically to accept China at Chiang's and their own valuation. China was considered a fourth great power in the anti-Axis alliance, the equal of the United States, the British Empire, and the Soviet Union.

From a military standpoint this was nonsense. Nevertheless, it was accepted publicly by President Franklin D. Roosevelt, by many of his less perceptive advisors, and by those industrial and commercial interests who saw a bright future in postwar China.

America's allies were puzzled. I recall Anthony Eden telling me after the conference at Cairo with Chiang, "FDR does put the Chinese on the same level as the Russians, and there's no arguing him out of it. Odd."

It was indeed odd. Equally curious was the popular inability in the United States to realize that there was not one Chinese ally but two—the China of the Nationalists avidly consuming American weapons and supplies and the China of the ragged soldiers of Chairman Mao's Communists. A few young diplomats like John Paton Davies perceived that the second group exerted a powerful attraction on the Chinese people. Such diplomats were first doubted, then vilified, and finally punished for being correct.

In retrospect, it is clear that neither the Nationalists nor the Communists provided any serious military assistance to the Americans in the Pacific war. In fact, it may be asked with propriety whether the help given by the United States to these two bitterly opposed groups would not have been better assigned to the forces of Nimitz and MacArthur. The Nationalists, however, were adept at producing communiqués that encouraged their supporters in the United States. Like the Soviet communiqués in the first two years of the war, they were long on fiction and short on fact, reminding one of the comment of one of Damon Runyon's characters on *Alice in Wonderland*. It was, he said, "nothing but a pack of lies but very interesting in spots."

The net result of this exaggeration of Nationalist power was widespread shock in America when the facts became apparent. The people and some senior members of the Truman administration were shaken to learn that the government of this fourth great power was waging an expensive and increasingly unsuccessful war against the Communists, a war now known in Peking as the War of Liberation.

American bewilderment was compounded when the Communists won that war. Subsequent events in China produced a drastic change in attitude toward that country, an attitude that still lingers today. The Communist victors, like all rabid revolutionaries, had slight regard for human lives, except, of course, their own. They proceeded to act like any authoritarian group that has fought its way to the top. How many capitalist ''lackeys'' were executed or died in labor camps we do not know and never will; the number was certainly substantial.

These internal events did not, however, shake the American dream of China as much as did the violent anti-American position taken by Chairman Mao's government, then closely allied with that of the Soviet Union.

''As a people you were suffering from unrequited love,'' Lord Trevelyan, for years the chief British representative in Peking, commented. ''Here you'd spent your money and your prayers for the Chinese, welcomed and armed them as allies. And now they were spitting in your face!''

The Chinese did more than spit. They entered the Korean War; fought bravely, if ineptly; and suffered heavy casualties. They talked of invading Taiwan, where Chiang Kai-shek and some of his forces had taken refuge after their defeats on the mainland. They spread the myth that the United States had employed bacteriological warfare in Korea, a myth still accepted as truth by the Chinese. In their ardor, and more certain than they should have been of Soviet support, they contemplated a descent on Taiwan. The probability of the Chinese launching an offensive against Taiwan or taking military action against the United States in the early 1950s seems remote today. But the political atmosphere in the United States was turbulent. The China lobby was fed with information from Chiang Kai-shek and his followers in Taiwan. Chiang's information, like that of all refugees, was highly suspect. This did not prevent the China lobby from swallowing it whole. The result was an appraisal of mainland China's military capabilities and ambitions far different from the facts.

The China lobby assiduously attacked the Truman administration for ''losing'' China. How the United States could lose a country that it had never possessed was never explained. But this reality, like so many others, was submerged in the Red scare of the 1950s. Congressmen who were prepared to believe Sen. Joseph McCarthy were equally prepared to swallow the idea that Harry Truman, Dean Acheson, and Gen. George C. Marshall had handed China over to the Communists.

For twenty years thereafter, attitudes on both sides were marked by fear and suspicion. Cut off from China, Americans accepted the stereotypes of the 1950s. The very few scholars and reporters who were able to penetrate what was then called the Bamboo Curtain returned with tales of an immense national effort to modernize the country, an effort that indicated China had no immediate military ambitions. But such stories were put down as propaganda.

The Chinese Communists did little to help. Mao, as we have seen, took a more aggressive stand than did his allies in Moscow. The United States was the focus for Communist propaganda. Periodically, Peking made warlike gestures toward Taiwan, including the shelling, with no discernible result, of the island of Quemoy. At international conferences, such as that convened at Geneva to sanctify the French defeat in Indochina, the Chinese were truculently anti-American. John Foster Dulles, President Dwight D. Eisenhower's secretary of state, was no less truculently anti-Chinese. He made it clear that he would not sit down and talk with Chairman Mao's representative, an aged former general.

The American intervention in Vietnam increased the hostility. The Chinese, as sensitive as ever about the protection of their frontiers, supported the North Vietnamese and their Viet Cong agents in the south. Periodically, the media informed Americans that the Chinese were about to enter the war militarily. The threat was not taken lightly, largely because accurate information about the PLA was scarce. The tendency was to rate the Chinese at their own valuation, which was high. Only a very few discerned the truth: with the Great Proletarian Cultural Revolution in full swing, China had neither the energy nor the resources to challenge the United States in Vietnam.

Yet Chinese intervention continued to worry Americans until

the last Communist offensive in the spring of 1975. The Chinese did in fact send construction forces to repair bombed railroads and bridges and provided land mines and small arms for the Vietnamese forces. But they were in no position to give massive military aid. At the same time, as the rift with Russia widened, they resented the Soviet Union's assumption of the position of armorer and paymaster for the North Vietnamese state.

The break came in 1972 when President Richard M. Nixon and Secretary of State Henry Kissinger visited China. The new era of cautious groping toward a closer relationship had begun. The reasons why China welcomed first Kissinger and then Nixon are complex. But one factor seems indisputable: the Chinese were increasingly worried over the intentions of the Soviet Union. The Russians had been harassing the Chinese on the Amur River. The Soviets were far better armed in both nuclear and conventional weapons. The hardheaded nationalists ruling China looked around for a possible supporter and balance to Russian power. As realists, they recognized that a link between the two countries would be of value to the United States, which, like China, faced superior Soviet forces.

There were other reasons, naturally. The Chinese needed then, and need now, Western technology to improve the efficiency of their industries and agriculture. They wanted wider markets for their produce. Chairman Mao and Chou En-lai realized, as wise statesmen do, that a great power has no eternal enemies or friends but only interests. It was in China's national interest to repair the breach with the United States. By doing so, the Chinese improved their bargaining position with the Soviets and, possibly, forced the Russians to second thoughts about an attack on Manchuria. The Chinese were aware that Nixon was committed to détente with the Soviet Union, a policy that, as Yu Chan indicated in his conversation, they regarded as unrealistic. They were also aware that once the president and the secretary of state had departed, the Russians might take some drastic action, short of war, in the north. But great as the hazards were, the risks of continued isolation from the United States and confrontation with the Russians apparently seemed greater.

The negotiations between the two delegations were remarkably soothing. The Chinese did not rant and rave about U.S. policy in Southeast Asia. Obviously, they were satisfied that the United States intended to withdraw its forces from Vietnam and that these no longer could be considered a threat to their security. Nor did they say much about the American military presence in South Korea, perhaps because they considered that presence as part of the military balance in northeastern Asia.

The crux of the negotiations between Chou, who was the principal Chinese spokesman instead of the ailing Mao, and Nixon was Taiwan. Both sides were careful of national sensitivities. The Chinese refrained from attacking U.S. policy toward Taiwan. The Americans did not refer to their ties with the government of the Republic of China on the island. These diplomatic courtesies did not eliminate serious differences. Nixon refused to promise anything that could be interpreted then or in the future as an abandonment of Taiwan. The Chinese, for their part, refused to renounce the use of force in recovering what they termed their province.

After the conference, the Chinese put their gloss on the negotiations. The Americans, they said, had promised the normalization of relations between the two countries. What else could that mean, they asked ingenuously, but the severance of American relations with Taiwan, since that, in Peking's view, was the only path to normalization? Nixon and Kissinger, who had purposely confined their comments to vague generalities, thought normalization meant the restoration of full diplomatic relations between the two governments with the People's Republic of China and Taiwan working out their differences by peaceful means.

At the end of the meetings, the two sides issued a joint communiqué, since known as the Shanghai Communiqué. For good or ill, this communiqué has continued to be the basis of Sino-American relations; Chinese diplomats, even after the visit of

Secretary of State Vance in August 1977, still refer to the Shanghai Communiqué when discussing policy. It is a long, carefully written document, notable as much for its omissions as for its declarations. Both the Americans and the Chinese saw it as a frank statement of disagreement and agreement, one that would not endanger the prospects for more-intimate relations between the two countries.

The first section of the communiqué deals with the principles to govern relations between the two countries. It speaks of further efforts toward normalization, which is nowhere defined. Economic, cultural, and scientific exchanges are to be expanded. Relations between the two governments are to be based on the five principles of peaceful coexistence on which the Chinese—at least publicly—put great store. Again, the principles are not individually identified. However, the third principle renounces interference in the internal affairs of another country. The Chinese could, and did, consider this an American promise not to intervene in Taiwan, which they consider part of China and hence an internal affair.

To the Chinese, Taiwan is, in the language of the communiqué, the crucial question obstructing the normalization of relations. Taiwan is a province of China, and no one can interfere with its liberalization. American troops should be withdrawn and bases dismantled. Again, a certain vagueness is evident. No time limit is set for these operations. No special status for Taiwan is permissible; the island is a province of the People's Republic of China.

The Americans for their part urge a peaceful settlement of the situation and pledge that while events move toward a settlement they will withdraw all their military personnel from the island: "In the meantime [the United States] will progressively reduce its forces and military installations on Taiwan as the tension in the area diminishes."

The implication is that the United States will withdraw as long as the mainland Chinese avoid overt military gestures toward Taiwan. Or does the passage quoted above mean that the

Americans also expect the People's Republic of China to refrain from military actions elsewhere in Asia?

Both governments were acutely interested in Vietnam. The Chinese endorsed the program of the Provisional Revolutionary Government of South Vietnam, which among much else called for an end to American support for President Nguyen Van Thieu's government. The Americans opted for a political settlement in Vietnam without outside interference but repeated their position that even if such a settlement proved unobtainable, the United States would ultimately withdraw its forces from Vietnam.

The Chinese at that time were unworried by fears that the United States might withdraw part or all of its forces from South Korea. They are now, of course, extremely worried about the probable departure of the Second Infantry Division. However, in 1972 the Chinese were content to give a ritualistic endorsement of North Korea's proposal for peaceful unification of North and South Korea. This would have involved American force withdrawals and the abolition of the UN Commission for the Unification and Rehabilitation of Korea. The Americans restated their backing for South Korea and for its highly ambiguous attempts to reduce tension in the peninsula.

Japan is the fifth element in the power balance in northeastern Asia. At Shanghai the Chinese were equally ritualistic about Japan. They were opposed, they said, to Japanese militarism. This would be understandable if Japanese militarism existed or if there appeared to be any prospect for a revival of Japanese militarism. The facts, with which the Chinese are well acquainted, are that the Japanese spend less than 1 percent of their GNP on defense and give no sign of making a substantial increase. The Japanese government and industry know that the country is woefully ill defended, that Japan lacks modern radar and communications sytems, adequate antisubmarine warfare weapons, and modern fighter aircraft. But nothing is done, although there is a great deal of talk. As the Chinese saying goes, "Lots of noise on the stairs, but no one enters the room." The

American response to the Chinese statement on Japan was that the United States placed the highest value on its relations with Japan and would continue to cultivate them.

While the Chinese statements on Taiwan appear to represent current attitudes in the Hua Kuo-feng era, there are marked differences between their positions on Korea and Japan in 1972 and today. These differences arise primarily from a heightened fear of Soviet military power in northeastern Asia. Faced with this power, the new leadership has been forced to take a long and, as we shall see, realistic look at China's military resources. A second cause for the differences is the change in U.S. policy toward Korea. A third is the reluctance of the Japanese to take even the smallest step toward the militarism that the Chinese profess to fear.

To the Chinese, the withdrawal of American forces from South Korea destabilizes the military situation in northeastern Asia. This was made very clear in talks with Chinese military and civilian leaders. They did not predict that the North Koreans, armed and supported by the Soviet Union, would fall upon the South Koreans. What worried them was that a small but important factor in the military balance, the American ground forces, would be withdrawn, an action that they plainly believed would favor the other side, meaning in this context both the Soviet Union and North Korea. Basically, the Chinese favor a continuation of the present situation in Korea, even if it involves the presence of American ''imperialist'' troops in the south.

Peking is opposed to Japanese militarism. But often I was told that China understands the reasons for the Japanese-American security treaty. And staff officers, surveying the general military situation in the area, would comment that Japan's security would be greater if there were an investment in defensive weapons to protect the country against attack by sea and air. I inferred, and I believe my inference was accurate, that this reflected their view that in a Far Eastern war, Japan would be unable to defend itself against the Soviet Union if the United

States was deeply involved in a European war and that China would face the Russians without powerful allies in the Far East.

The United States has twice attempted to increase the pace toward normalization of relations with China. President Gerald R. Ford visited the country in 1975 and probed Chinese thinking. Secretary of State Vance went to China in the summer of 1977 for a visit that was widely advertised in Washington before the event as a possible breakthrough in Sino-American relations. Neither mission made headway.

Indeed, Ford's talks were counterproductive in the sense that they clearly confused the Chinese. Early in September 1977, the new Deputy Premier Teng Hsiao-ping said that President Ford had promised to break American ties with Taiwan and establish them along the lines of what is called the Japanese solution. Under this solution, Japan recognized the People's Republic of China and installed a diplomatic mission in Peking and a highly successful but unofficial trade mission in Taiwan. Although this solution has been suggested as a means of settling the dispute over Taiwan between America and China, it really is not applicable to the situation. Washington, after nearly thirty years of military ties with Taiwan, would have to seek assurances from Peking that it would not attempt to occupy Taiwan by force. Given American treaty commitments around the world, and especially in the Far East, no other course would be credible. In any event, Ford declared that he had told the Chinese leaders that breaking relations with Taiwan and keeping an unofficial American presence there was only a possibility.

On the surface, at least, Vance's wooing of Peking produced little discernible movement toward a settlement. Apparently the Chinese rejected his proposal that the American embassy in Taiwan be downgraded to a liaison mission comparable to that now operated by the United States in Peking. There was some hint of flexibility in the Chinese position as it was outlined by Teng. He said that Peking would take into consideration the special conditions in Taiwan. And though he repeated the familiar assertion of the Chinese that their patience about Taiwan was not inexhaustible, he added that he had set no deadline in his talks with Vance. In respect to Taiwan, Teng can be considered a hard-liner in the sense that he appears more convinced than some of his colleagues that the island's forces, well armed by the United States, still constitute a danger to the mainland. He is also realistic enough to recognize that an invasion of Taiwan, so often mooted under Chairman Mao, even if ultimately success-ful would be very costly to the mainland in weapons and man-power.

Normalization quite obviously is not a problem susceptible to early settlement under present world conditions. The options before the United States are clear enough. The first is to meet China's wishes by severing diplomatic ties with Taiwan, with-drawing the military there (now about 850 men), and abrogating the mutual security treaty of 1954 concluded between the United States and the Nationalist government of Chiang Kai-shek. This, the "surgeon's knife" option, has the virtue of simplicity. It is almost certain, however, that it would create a political crisis within the United States and, at the same time, frighten American allies in Europe as well as the Far East.

A second option envisages an expansion of American military sales to Taiwan, enabling the Taiwanese to improve their capa-bility for self-defense against any attack from the mainland. The Taiwanese forces at this writing are not unimpressive as far as training and morale are concerned. For a country of approxi-mately 17 million people the forces are above normal in size: an army of 330,000 men, including two armored divisions; a navy of 35,000 men and 75 combatant vessels; an air force of approx-imately 70,000 men and 268 combat aircraft; a marine corps of 25,000; reserves of 90,000; and a militia of 100,000 men. This is a larger armed force than that maintained by Indonesia, with a population of over 113 million.

Its weakness lies in its weapons, although the Taiwanese forces, by and large, are better equipped than those of mainland China. Taiwan has no tank more modern than the American Mark 48 and no aircraft in its thirteen fighter squadrons more

up-to-date than the F-5A/B/E. The Taiwanese do have three surface-to-air battalions, one armed with twenty-four Hawk missiles and two others with the Nike-Hercules. Should the United
States decide to expand American arms deliveries to modernize
Taiwan's defenses, the program would be extensive and defensive. The Nationalists would be in a position to defend themselves, but it is highly doubtful if relations between Peking and
Washington could be maintained at their present temperature.

The third option, lengthy and laborious diplomatic spade-
work, is probably the safest and most effective. Its drawback
from the standpoint of those inside and outside this or any administration is that it will not produce quick results. For example, developing a formula that will satisfy the Taiwanese that
Peking will not use force against them involves a long period of
diplomatic trial and error, especially since the mainland Chinese
will not accept any solution that in any way reduces their claim
to Taiwan as a province of China.

Would Peking accept an American statement ending diplomatic relations with Taiwan but emphasizing Washington's
views that any future settlement between the island and the
mainland would have to be attained only by peaceable means?
As an alternative, would it be possible for the United States,
China, and Taiwan to issue a joint statement to the effect that
Taiwan is a part of China, which, as Donald Zagoria has
pointed out, is a position accepted by both Peking and Taipei,
and further declaring that reunification will be a slow progress
involving concessions by both parties in prolonged negotiations.

Those who argue for a complete severance of American relations, economic as well as political, with Taiwan overlook that
those relations give Washington some advantages in its dealing
with Peking. The continued sale of arms to Taiwan or even the
probability that the United States would sell arms in a military
emergency may lead to a relaxation of Peking's all-or-nothing
bargaining stance. And the mainland Chinese could also expect
that should the movement toward a union with Taiwan proceed
on amicable lines, American arms sales could be reduced.

There are literally dozens of diplomatic and economic approaches to the problem. Selig S. Harrison has suggested that oil be used to lubricate the process, in this case the rich oil resources in the eastern China Sea whose ownership is disputed by China, Taiwan, and Japan. Harrison proposed that the United States make a transitional move toward normalization of relations with China by disassociating itself from Taiwan's claim to the oil and natural-gas resources in the eastern China Sea. Taiwan's claims, he pointed out, represent an assertion of jurisdiction over the area in defiance of Peking's claim to be the only legitimate Chinese government.

China's potential as an oil producer has political as well as economic aspects. The expectation of Harrison and several other experts on China's oil resources is that the country will attain an annual production of 400 million tons of oil, about 8 million barrels a day, by 1990 through the exploitation of existing fields and the still-untapped eastern China Sea resources. The political impact of this production, on the Far East at least, is best measured by the projection that China's oil output in 1990 will be roughly equivalent to the 1974 output of Saudi Arabia, the major Middle East oil producer. It may be that China will need all, or nearly all, of its oil production to meet its domestic demands. But when considering the policies of an authoritarian state, it is well to remember that resources can be diverted to serve political aims, whatever the demands of the internal economy.

Whatever the Chinese decide to do with their oil, the point remains that if Washington withdraws support for Taipei's claims, Peking could interpret this move as acceptance of the People's Republic of China as the sole legitimate champion of Chinese claims to the field in the disputes with Japan and Taiwan.

Harrison and others would go further. They suggest that the United States should make it clear that it does not recognize Taiwan's title to exploration in areas located within fifty miles of the mainland. Here again the objective is to disassociate the

United States from what in Peking appears to be blind support of the government in Taipei.

There obviously are multiple diplomatic obstacles to normalization of relations with Peking. There are also on both sides psychological obstacles to establishing the friendship that Peking's orators invoke whenever they discuss relations. Those acquainted with authoritarian governments will understand that Chinese obstacles will wither on the Chinese side, publicly at least, if relations are normalized. But, being deeply rooted, the obstacles will remain, and if Americans do not wish to immerse themselves in another era of misunderstanding, the obstacles and their bases should be recognized.

Since the triumph of the Communists in 1950, government propaganda has consistently portrayed the United States as the patron and paymaster of Chiang Kai-shek's forces in what Peking calls the war of liberation. Vast sums—vast by Chinese standards, at any rate—have been expended to produce movies that portray the Nationalists as American hirelings. In one such film, *From Victory to Victory,* the Nationalists travel in American jeeps, use American tanks, and wear American uniforms. Even if, and when, relations between the two countries are normalized, Americans must understand that they are dealing with a people that has been taught that its foremost enemy in the struggle for "liberation" was armed by the United States.

To the majority of Americans, the Korean War is an almost forgotten episode. But not to the Chinese. This was their first confrontation as a united nation with the forces of "imperialism," and since theirs is an authoritarian society, the Chinese could not have been defeated. I spent a long hour in the regimental museum of China's 319th Infantry Regiment, then stationed outside Nanking. A good forty minutes of the time was spent in listening to the exploits of the regiment in Korea. There was a statue—a pretty bad one—of the soldier who had leaped upon an American tank and tossed a grenade down the open hatch. No one bothered to answer when I wondered idly why a tank would go into action with the hatch open. There were drawings and diagrams of various units of the regiment dispatching entire American divisions. To me there was a sense of déjà vu; it was uncannily like the Russians' portrayal of their part in World War II.

Is this exaltation of the Chinese role in Korea, and the blatant omission of the price they paid when they ran into the massed artillery and tanks of the Americans, ridiculous? Of course it is. But what is important in human attitudes, unfortunately, is not what is true but what people believe to be true. Often, that becomes part of the truth. Yet we are dealing with a people I consider highly intelligent and basically sophisticated.

Although there exists no accurate account on the Chinese side, China's losses in Korea must have been appalling. I met one man who said that he had gone into an attack against the Americans with a full battalion and that 119 men had emerged alive and unwounded. Another said that in one attack on the British Commonwealth division on the Imjin River, only 113 men had returned from a frontal attack. These are casualties comparable to those suffered by British, French, and German battalions in the Somme and Verdun offensives of World War I.

If friendship, or at least cooperation, is the aim of both governments, the United States will not make real progress unless it recognizes both the Chinese memories of American "imperialism" and the equally strong American heritage of antagonism toward the Chinese, born not only of unrequited love but of the antagonisms and suspicions that have endured from 1950 until the present.

The process of normalizing relations with China, begun by Nixon and Kissinger, followed by Ford, and now being implemented by Carter and Vance, must take into account what I perceive as national political prejudices. Admittedly, there has always been in the United States a small, vocal, and often gifted group advocating normalization. There has also been, and still is, a larger, more muted body of opinion that holds that the Chinese have proven to be our enemies after we had showered them with aid and that any administration that sups with the devils in Peking must use a long spoon.

No statesman can afford to forget this group in his efforts to reach an accommodation with Peking. An American president seeking this goal would do well to base his case on the realities of power politics. He need not fear that his case will not be understood; the American public is much more intelligent, although much less informed, than its leaders believe.

The case rests on one of the fundamentals of American international policy. The Soviet Union has been, is, and will be the major potential enemy. But the Soviet Union is an Asian, as well as a European, power. Anything that the United States can do to bolster politically, economically, or militarily the position of China in Asia will continue the diversion of some of the tremendous resources the Russians have hitherto devoted to the Group of Soviet Forces in East Germany.

This sort of support for China should not—and in the present atmosphere in Peking, cannot—approach an alliance. What it will do is increase the complexity of the strategic problems that face the Soviet high command. For example, young fire-eaters at Stavka may argue that the NATO countries are in disarray, as they are a good part of the time, and that this is the moment to attack. But the voice of prudence, probably coming from some grizzled staff officer, asks, What if we do and the Chinese, supported by the Americans, march against the Soviet Maritime Province and Vladivostok, and what if the U.S. Seventh Fleet, supported by the Chinese and the Japanese, sends their aircraft to destroy Russian industrial resources in Siberia? I would guess that such questions already are being asked in the Russian general staff and that they will increase in importance if relations between Peking and Washington are normalized.

The Chinese have an ax to grind. They tell any American willing to listen that détente with the Soviet Union is a ruse on Moscow's part, that the Russians have not abandoned their aggressive aims, and that they will fall on NATO Europe first.

A certain ideological flexibility is evident; less than twenty years ago the Chinese were berating the Russians for not being sufficiently aggressive toward the West.

Occasionally, I sensed that the Chinese officials who predicted so confidently the Soviet attack on Europe had not considered all the repercussions of such an act. The Soviet Union, like the United States, is a Pacific power, and a war involving the two states could not be confined to European battlefields. The Chinese belief that the West is inviting a war in Europe, and only in Europe, is not in accord with their manifest uneasiness about the program for American troop withdrawals from Korea and Japan's modest defense forces.

Does China's preoccupation with the Soviet military threat mean that when, and if, relations with the United States are normalized, China will seek immediately substantial American military and economic aid? My feeling is that China will not. We must remember the present pervasive influence in China of Mao's creed of self-reliance or independence. For more than a century the Chinese have been dependent on foreign powers for economic aid and technological assistance. This is shaming to a people who regard themselves as the earth's elect. The withdrawal of Soviet help only reinforced the Chinese belief that they must depend on themselves, economically and militarily. This hasn't much to do with Communism. A Chinese people as free as the Norwegians would, I am sure, take the same line. The sentiment represents an authentic, broadly based nationalism that was not invented by Sun Yat-sen, Chiang Kai-shek, or Chairman Mao.

Today, nationalism must be accounted as powerful a world force as Communism. So, I submit, it is in China. After the great earthquakes of 1976, which killed thousands of people and devastated large and important industrial areas, the Chinese did not ask the rest of the world for so much as a single bandage. Why? Because they, the government and the people, were determined to reconstruct and rehabilitate on their own. Given the importance of the devastated areas, which covered some of the richest coal reserves in China, this might have been foolish. But there is a certain grandeur in this fierce self-reliance.

The United States and China are moving slowly toward normalization of relations. This will come unless there is an unexpected turn by the Chinese leadership back toward the Russian alliance. If the Soviet Union should attack China after relations have been restored to normal between Washington and China, could China effectively resist the Russians without American aid?

No hard-and-fast answer is possible. The American people, in their mood of disillusionment born of the failure of the Vietnam War, are unlikely to sanction any military assistance in Asia that hints, even obliquely, at the involvement of Americans as technicians or advisors. Aid to China in a war with the Soviet Union would have to be on a mammoth scale, for China's military deficiencies, as we shall see, are enormous. Moreover, U.S. military aid to China would at best end all prospects of continued détente with the Soviet Union over strategic-arms limitation in Europe and at worst might provoke Soviet aggression against the NATO states.

The road to normalization of relations with China is long and hard. Even when it is accomplished, if it is, the problems that will arise are as difficult as those that now impede normalization. Granted the present military strength of the Soviet Union in both conventional and strategic nuclear forces, the most prudent course for Washington lies in adopting a cautious policy of political support for China in eastern Asia, accompanied by a willingness to sell, not give, defensive weapons. Such a policy would strengthen, rather than weaken, China's interest in a true détente with the Soviet Union.

We have been living since 1950 in a period in which two great military blocs, NATO and the Warsaw Pact, established a global strategic balance. Now China, potentially a great military power, has entered the arena. The question hanging over America's future relations with China is not what is good for American interests there but what favors American interests in a world that daily becomes more complex and more dangerous.

The Chinese, too, see complexities and dangers when they look beyond their frontiers. Many of the former probably arise from what is the second most important policy problem facing the country: how to deal with the United States. The first, certainly, is policy toward the Soviet Union. It is evident that from the first Nixon visit through the death of Chairman Mao, two views on relations with the United States existed at the upper levels of the Peking government.

On the one hand, there were those, including possibly Chairman Mao, who opposed rapid normalization of relations with the United States. More friendly relations than those of the past might serve to make the Russians more cautious. But beyond that? The Americans are a superpower, the Americans are imperialists, the Americans support the government on Taiwan and oppose its liberation. Their opposition was ideological and, to some extent, emotional. The group included, among others, Chiang-ching.

In the three years immediately preceding the chairman's death in 1976, the radical Gang of Four managed to impede any progress toward an improvement of relations with the Americans. As Harold C. Hinton has pointed out, lack of progress in this field also was caused by the debates within the administration on the speed at which the United States should approach normalization. As a result of these developments, members of the American liaison mission in Peking found their contacts with government officials restricted. Visas for Americans were issued more sparingly. The Chinese government became a good deal more sensitive about the nation's position as a Communist power. For example, China insisted that news reporters from Taiwan, South Korea, South Africa, and Israel be barred from the preview of an archaeological exhibition to be staged in Washington. A tour of the United States by a concert group was canceled because Peking would not agree to the omission, requested by the State Department, of a song about the liberation of Taiwan.

Petty incidents of this type began to disappear late in 1976 when Chairman Hua took power and the persecution of the Gang of Four became government policy. This should not be taken to mean that Hua or Teng Hsiao-ping, China's third-ranking leader, are any less nationalistic or, in the basic sense of the word, Communist than their predecessors. My conclusion is that it did mean that the new leadership did not intend to have its relations with the United States disturbed by trifling incidents.

It is clear even to me, an American of no official position, that the American system of government mystifies the Chinese. The views about the United States of the military men and diplomats with whom I came into contact were fragmentary, dated, and—in some instances—wonderfully ingenuous. One reason is that there were no formal diplomatic exchanges between China and the United States for nearly a quarter of a century. Another was that although there are many Chinese—scholars, editors, former diplomats—who know a great deal about the United States, most of them are in exile or were thrown out of their jobs during the Great Proletarian Cultural Revolution.

Those Chinese with whom I discussed the subject were utterly unable to understand President Nixon's fall or the national uproar over Watergate. This was only partly because they had approved of Nixon; a "realist" was the way they described him. It was also, I thought, because the charges and countercharges associated with Watergate and the dismissals and imprisonments gave the impression of instability in a country that they had regarded as the leader of the West and, consequently, the leader of the forces arrayed against the Soviet Union. It was useless to point out to people with no knowledge of the democratic process that Watergate was an example, albeit an extreme one, of the manner in which democracies cleanse themselves. But we should not be too hard on the Chinese. Watergate confused a great many foreign peoples with far greater knowledge of the American system than the Chinese, including some of our close allies.

James R. Schlesinger, who as secretary of defense had taken

a hard line toward the Soviets, was popular. The Chinese were puzzled and worried over his dismissal by President Ford. Secretary of State Henry Kissinger was less esteemed. The Chinese thought him too devoted to détente, a condition they considered impossible to attain with the present Soviet leadership.

Jimmy Carter's campaign was in full swing when I reached China, and his election took place during my visit. My impression was that the Chinese would have preferred a more outspoken opponent of the Russians and a stronger advocate of the military. By then they knew a little about President Ford and, like foreign officials everywhere, particularly in the Communist countries, preferred the man they knew to the man they did not know.

Looking toward the future, the Chinese must be somewhat dubious about American policy in Asia and, as a natural corollary, their own attitude toward that policy. They are privately unhappy about the proposed withdrawal of American ground forces from South Korea. They welcomed the American withdrawal from South Vietnam, but my impression was that the North Vietnamese triumph over Saigon in 1975 did not arouse any great enthusiasm.

The Chinese attitude toward a united Vietnam, now the most powerful state in Southeast Asia, owes much to China's pretensions to political and ideological leadership in Asia. This is a policy area in which there does not seem to be any great difference between Chairman Mao and his successors. It follows, therefore, that the establishment of a unified Vietnam with considerable military power may be seen in Peking as a barrier to China's drive toward leadership.

Finally, both the proposed withdrawal from South Korea and the enforced retreat from South Vietnam raise doubts about American resolution in the western Pacific. These doubts are clearly related to the Chinese fear of what the Soviet Union would do in a destabilized political situation in that area. Now and again Chinese propaganda will accuse Washington of seeking hegemony in Asia. Such accusations do not represent the true feelings of the present government. What the Chinese want is a stronger United States policy and presence in the western Pacific.

Yu Chan, quoted at the beginning of this chapter, made it clear that he did not believe the United States was doing enough to contain the Soviet Union in either the Pacific or Europe. Soldiers and lower-ranking diplomats said the same. Some students of China have suggested that Peking's dissatisfaction with American policy toward Moscow may in time prompt the Chinese to seek an accommodation with the Soviet Union. Such a policy is always a threat to the present political and military balance in Asia and the world. When I was in China, such a reversal of policy seemed very distant. But the threat will remain in the background as China and America fumble toward a new relationship.

A great deal has been made in the United States about the psychological problems facing the American people in a movement toward détente with China. They are obviously deep and abiding: the pledges to Taiwan, the memories of Korea and Vietnam, the frequent and unbridled attacks by Chinese leaders on the United States in world forums. There are many in official life and among the military who still regard China as a potential adversary and as a present threat to the freedom of America's allies in Asia, principally Japan and the Philippines.

It would be surprising if the Chinese did not harbor their own suspicions about the United States and be slightly disillusioned about the value, present and potential, of friendship. They, too, fought in Korea. They, too, were involved in Vietnam, although on a far smaller scale than the United States. They, too, have been subjected to attack by American leaders. A more important cause for Chinese discontent with the American connection, however, probably is that the connection has done nothing to restrain the Soviet Union.

No Soviet forces have been withdrawn from the areas near the Chinese frontiers. On the contrary, the level of equipment of those forces has been raised. The United States offered no resistance to the last Russian overseas adventure, the Cuban-Soviet incursion into Angola. The Carter administration, like its predecessors, appears to be seeking a more solid détente with the Soviets, something that the Chinese consider impossible to achieve. And the Chinese mission in Washington must have informed its masters that there is in the United States a very powerful body of public and congressional opinion that is strongly opposed to withdrawal from Taiwan as the price of normal relations with Peking.

There are other areas where American policy, despite what Peking considers the promises of presidents Nixon and Ford, has not favored China. The Peking government clearly considers Taiwan, the South China Sea, and the oil deposits there part of China. But the Chinese know that American oil companies are prospecting in the area and that there has been no United States effort to support China's claims.

Some of China's resentments and objections to American policy as it has developed since the Nixon visit may seem petty and unconnected with the realities of world events. Allowance should be made, however, for the self-centeredness of the Chinese and their consequent high valuation of their national policies as the only correct ones. This, of course, is common to all authoritarian countries. But the difference between the Soviet Union and China, for example, is that officials in the latter compound their nationalism with an alarming ignorance of the outside world.

If the Chinese are disturbed by American withdrawals and evasions of responsibility in Asia and elsewhere, can America expect more positive assertions of Chinese national interests? I have noted earlier that Peking considers itself the leader of the developing world. How is that leadership to be furthered by supporting wars of national liberation in countries like Indonesia, Burma, and Thailand? Doubtless there are a few leaders who favor this course, a favorite theme of Chairman Mao and Lin Piao in the 1960s.

Two arguments weigh against such a policy. One is that even

minimal support for a liberation movement is not cheap and the Chinese economy is only now shaking off the consequences of the Great Leap Forward and the Great Proletarian Cultural Revolution. China's present inadequacies in weapons are such that little of value could be spared for guerrilla armies fighting elsewhere. China obviously is not going to abandon its claim to lead the Third World in Asia or elsewhere. But at the moment, the Chinese probably must confine their intervention in wars of national liberation to diplomacy and propaganda.

The second argument is that a policy of intervention abroad in Asia would ultimately result in a confrontation with the United States. Peking would then face a choice between alienating the one power capable of maintaining a military balance with Russia in Asia and proving that China, not the Soviet Union, is the fountain of leadership and support for all oppressed peoples fighting against reactionary imperialists.

Some students, notably Hinton, have suggested that China might be forced into a more aggressive policy in Asia by Vietnam's adoption of a comparable policy aimed at leadership in Southeast Asia, especially since the Vietnamese enjoy Russian diplomatic support and a certain amount of economic aid. When I was in China, this contingency seemed remote. But recent events have signaled Peking that China cannot expect to take over leadership in Southeast Asia automatically.

Early in 1978 the Vietnamese, using frontier harassment and an ill-defined border as an excuse, invaded Cambodia, whose revolutionary government is closely allied with Peking, thus exacerbating the rivalry between the Soviet Union and China for ideological and political hegemony in Southeast Asia. The Vietnamese, who are termed the Prussians of Indochina with good reason, knifed through the poorly equipped Cambodians, employing a mélange of American and Soviet weapons.

There were signs of alarm in Peking. Significantly, the first public Cambodian reaction to the invasion came in the form of a Cambodian government statement issued not from Phnom Penh but from the Chinese capital.

The conflict between Cambodia and Vietnam is rooted in the ancient antagonism between the two peoples. But it also owes something to the support given each side by the Communist giants. The Chinese believe that what they term the realities of geopolitics entitle them to leadership in the area. These realities are geographical location, ethnic background, economic development of roughly similar character, and comparable political systems. These realities are linked to the historic fact that imperial China once exercised suzerainty over wide areas of Southeast Asia. In the case of Vietnam, this could be a liability. Vietnamese history's greatest ancient triumph was the successful popular resistance to the Chinese. It may be that today's Vietnamese favor the Russians because the Soviet Union is far away, whereas China is on their doorstep.

The Chinese, too, have another problem. The state of their economy is such that they cannot afford lavish military and economic aid to states like Cambodia. The Russians can. The rebels in Thailand, armed and encouraged by the Chinese, have not been able to make serious progress and are confined to minor guerrilla operations because they lack sophisticated modern arms. The denial of such arms to the Thais or the Cambodians, however, may reflect an abiding Chinese faith in the "people's war" concept.

Whatever Peking's reasoning, it is clear that Vietnamese success against Cambodia will strengthen Hanoi's claim to leadership of Cambodia and Laos and promote plans for a union of the three countries under Vietnamese control. Meanwhile, the Russians, with a small investment in military hardware and economic aid and ostentatious political support, have strengthened their position in Southeast Asia.

My conclusion is that China certainly realizes the dangers to its claim to leadership inherent in the emergence of a militant and ambitious Vietnam supported by the Soviet Union but that under present conditions Peking is not in a position to take any action that will reverse the present tide of events.

Events in the Indochinese peninsula have moved a great deal

faster than was anticipated after the fall of Saigon in 1975. The conventional wisdom then was that it would be a decade, perhaps longer, before the united Vietnam could overcome its economic problems and emerge as a competitor for leadership. Three years later, however, the Vietnamese are on the move.

Vietnamese chauvinism may affect Sino-American relations in the sense that it will make Peking more interested in closer ties with the United States. The Chinese cannot complain that the Ford and Carter administrations have not offered the hand of friendship.

Secretary of State Kissinger assured the Chinese in 1973 that "no matter what happens in the United States, friendship with the People's Republic of China is one of the constant factors in American foreign policy." It is a bold, supremely self-confident man who, knowing history, will make such a statement. The inference is that Kissinger believes that the present relationship of the two countries is irreversible.

Yet the problems confronting the two governments, beyond the central issue of the future of Taiwan, are so numerous and so intricate that a prudent man can envisage half a dozen situations in which Sino-American friendship would cease to be a "constant factor" in American policy.

Sino-American friendship has a good chance to develop beyond its present state but only, I believe, if American leaders and diplomats are as tough as the Chinese. It will not develop as a result of mutual concessions. At the moment, Chinese concessions are unimaginable. Growth is most likely to come over a shared perception of the long-term international aspirations of the Soviet Union, although the mildness of the Carter administration's position toward Moscow in its first year surprised and upset the Chinese. Even if Carter were to be as tough and uncompromising toward the Soviet Union as the late John Foster Dulles, the process will not be easy. The Chinese will demand much from America in terms of diplomatic support and offer little in return. In the development of a friendship fruitful to both Washington and Peking, reciprocity is the key.

4

The Superpower Myth and the Developing Economy

A PENCHANT for hyperbole leads many writers to describe China as a superpower. China is many things: old, varied, populous, virile, industrious. But it is not yet a superpower. The strongest impression I received in three weeks of travel was that after a quarter of a century of prodigious effort China remains a developing country. It is developing, just as Nigeria, Indonesia, and Brazil are developing, toward greater industrial and agricultural production and higher standards for its nearly 1 billion people. The historic fact, which so impresses visitors, that ancient China was the wellspring of Far Eastern civilization, that its leaders were cultured gentlemen fostering the arts and industry while ours were still in the Dark Ages, is really beside the point. That point is that China, for many reasons, not all of them self-generated, is well behind in its development compared to half a dozen other countries in the same class. It was part of the genius of Chou En-lai that he never discounted the basic economic weaknesses of China.

It should always be kept in mind that as long as the Chinese harbor their present fears of the Soviet Union, a sizable proportion of the country's resources will be devoted to defense. The national growth rate, which I expect to increase, will not under that circumstance approach the growth of West Germany in the 1950s or Japan since 1955.

I was invited to China to look at its military establishment.

My hosts insisted that I see something of the industrial base on which that establishment rests. Although it was difficult to connect a trip through an embroidery factory with defense, on the whole the time was well spent. I tramped through steel mills, factories making electrical equipment, textile plants, and agricultural communes. I saw iron ore processed, electric locomotives built, ships constructed, glass blown, and synthetic fiber spun.

My conclusion is that although this is an expanding economy, it is nonetheless a backward one when measured against that of the United States, Japan, or any of the members of the European Economic Community. In some industrial establishments I was reminded strongly of similar Soviet plants in the Donetz Basin immediately after World War II. There was the same improvisation, the same emphasis on essentials, the same carelessness about the finish of the product—it had been produced under difficult conditions, and wasn't that enough?

The mainstay of the Chinese economy is an industrious but technically unsophisticated labor force. The economy uses, particularly in the heavy metallurgical industries, raw materials that would be rejected in an advanced economy. People, abundant and hard-working, meet deficiencies in production.

The Chinese estimate—or, it might be said, hope—is that by the year 2000 the country will have attained a truly modern economy. This strikes me as an outrageous overestimate of the prospects for progress. It is difficult not to admire sweating factory workers when they proclaim that by the target year China's economy will be on a par with that of the United States, the Soviet Union, or Japan. It is even more difficult to convince the Chinese that other economies are not standing still, that the rate of progress in the three countries, accelerated by new technology, is faster than that of China.

In many respects China's is a "catch-up economy," one seeking desperately to overtake the economies of more-advanced societies. The electric-locomotive works at Dairen provides a good example. About nine thousand people, two thousand of them women, work in a factory more than seventy years old that was used first by the Russians and then by the Japanese as a repair shop for steam engines. The factory now produces approximately two hundred locomotives a year, according to the plant manager. Like most advanced industrial plants in China, the factory suffered severely when the Soviet Union withdrew its technicians and plans in 1960. It was then producing steam locomotives. The Russian advisors and technicians departed with their plans for modernizing the factory.

"There was no other course but to sit down and design our own locomotives," the factory manager said. "We built them, but they were not powerful enough. So, during the Great Proletarian Cultural Revolution the workers agreed that we design and build a more powerful locomotive. But first we rebuilt fifteen hundred that we had in the plant. Then we went ahead and produced nearly ten thousand items that we needed for the new four-thousand-horsepower locomotives," he said.

Such statements, supposedly testifying to the ingenuity and devotion of the workers, are standard in China and partly true but partly, I would say, blatant propaganda. The new locomotives are being built. Visitors are treated to a ride in a new one that, according to the guides, is being tested. But information about how much time it takes to produce a single locomotive or how many man-hours are devoted to the job is not forthcoming. Also, it is well to be skeptical about the part that the Great Proletarian Cultural Revolution played in the decision to make the more-powerful new engines. I have no doubt that Chairman Mao and his pet revolution were given the credit. But my conclusion after some hours of talk is that the plans for a new engine were conceived in Peking and brought to the works by engineers and technicians sent by the central government.

One odd aspect of the Chinese industrial expansion is that very few managers—the "leadership cadres," the Chinese would say—appear to think about the future production of the plant. "We do not consider that at this point," a foreman said. "Our task is to produce these new, powerful locomotives."

The impression was that if the provincial government or the central government tomorrow ordered the factory to cease making locomotives and turn out tractors or tanks, the workers would, without argument, devote themselves to the new task. My hosts considered an amenable labor force a strength. So it is, up to the point at which the individual worker's ideas for improving a product are submerged in the mass by the authoritarian approach. The Chinese are an ingenious people, much more so, I believe, than the Russians. But ingenuity is a casualty of authoritarianism in both countries.

An Shan (the name means "Saddle Hill" or "Saddle Mountain" in Chinese) is the center of a major iron-mining area. The place itself has that unfinished, mining-camp look of all centers of basic industry. Men are taking the iron out of the earth. When the iron is gone, the men will go; there is no need for the niceties of civilization. Despite its rawness, however, An Shan—more particularly, the vast iron and steel plant—is important, for in China, as in every developing country, iron and steel are the master keys to progress.

The Chinese have done well in this area of their industrial economy. The Soviet Union helped develop a large number of iron and steel plants in the 1950s. After the Russians departed, progress continued, although at first at a slower rate. There are no accurate figures for production; an informed estimate is that annual production of crude iron and steel is just over 26 million metric tons annually. This makes China the sixth-largest producer in the world. But China, if it is to fulfill the industrial destiny foreseen by Chou En-lai, will have to do better than that. The Chinese admit they have the potential for greater production. But three factors evidently retard further progress.

The first is that although China has plenty of iron ore and coal, both are of a low quality and must be given special treatment. The untreated ore that was being dug in the vast open-face works at An Shan ran about 30–33 percent iron. What is called benefication technology, now used in advanced economies, would enable the Chinese to treat their ores and eventually to expand the steel industry. But the Chinese have been slow to invest in benefication, though they know its value. But here again we encounter one of China's primary problems. Almost every industry, almost every economic department of government clamors for money to be spent abroad for technology that will hasten modernization. The amount of money available is limited. What industry gets priority?

The second factor is that despite heroic efforts, the Chinese had not trained a skilled work force when the Soviets withdrew in 1960. As a result, heavy industry in most cases still lacks the expertise in organization and technology necessary for major increases in production. The Chinese know that technical assistance is available in Japan and in Western Europe. But their stubborn emphasis on self-reliance or independence makes them reluctant to bring in foreign technicians.

Finally, capital shortages have led to an imbalance in the iron and steel industry. The mining sector has been given a minimum of capital and, consequently, has to use labor to an inordinate degree. Yet the demand for steel is growing, and it is likely that the government will be forced to divert capital from other areas to increase production of iron ore and pig iron. Another problem is that finishing facilities have not kept step with crude-steel output. As a result, a large tonnage of finished steel products has had to be imported.

All these problems were present at the An Shan iron and steel plant. The guides knew that the iron percentage of the ore was small. "Would you use it in America?" one asked. They also knew that there were processes for improving such ores and expanding steel production.

They obviously were proud of what had been done "since the Russians left," a phrase used by almost everyone I encountered. But there was a tendency toward exaggeration. One guide said that I would find the plant "fully automated." Later he apologized. What he had meant, he said, was "fully mechanized." There *is* a difference. Even complete mechanization was doubtful. I saw many workers doing jobs that in a modern industrial plant would have been done by machines. An Shan has a work force of thirty-six hundred, including five hundred women. But my guide claimed that when the plant had been at maximum production under the Japanese the labor force had been about ten thousand.

The present ore field at An Shan is expected to last another thirty-five years. When extraction first began, the main hill was 250 meters above sea level. Now the workers at the open-face mine are 50 meters below sea level. The pit itself was about three-quarters of a mile long and a quarter of a mile across. From atop a cliff, I could see the ore trains winding their way to the processing plant. There was an atmosphere of tremendous vigor and energy. Yet the plant itself seemed ramshackle and worn. The impression was one of the spirit of a youth in the body of an elderly man.

The Chinese are attempting to improve their steel industry through what are to them the most difficult means. Modern capital equipment is being imported, although most of the lesser machinery in the plants, such as drills, excavators, and ore-train locomotives, is made in China. It will take several years to install the new equipment and train workers to use it. Foreign experts predict that overall production will rise only marginally through the 1970s. In the 1980s, progress will depend on the ability of the Chinese to produce their own machinery and on their willingness to devote large sums in foreign exchange to pay for steel-making equipment and technology imported from abroad.

Iron and steel, as all Chinese industries, have suffered from the vagaries of government policy and foreign influences. The Great Leap Forward, a sort of blast-furnace-in-every-village experiment, was a failure, and almost all the small iron and steel plants built during that period were closed. Production of steel fell from 18.67 million tons in 1960 to 8 million tons in 1961.

The withdrawal of the Russians was a second blow. The technicians left two major iron and steel plants at Wu-han and Pao-t'ou unfinished and took with them their managerial and technical expertise. The Chinese made do then, and still do to a great extent, with technicians and managers trained by the Russians. These were sufficient to repair the damages of the Great Leap Forward and reintroduce a semblance of order into the industrial structure. The plants at Wu-han and Pao-t'ou were completed after a fashion. Foreigners who have visited them report that the steel-finishing capacity of both is a problem.

After the failure of the Great Leap Forward, the Chinese turned to foreign sources for help in building a modern steel technology. The sources were Western. The Chinese would not consider asking for help from the Russians. Had they done so, it is highly unlikely that it would have been forthcoming. So, at great cost, basic oxygen furnaces were imported from Austria and air-separation plants from Japan. There was a rise in the production of alloy steels, and by 1966, steel production overall had risen to 15 million tons, including 1.5 million from Wu-han and Pao-t'ou.

The Great Proletarian Cultural Revolution caused another recession in steel production and the general economic output. In that turbulent period there was a fall in coal production, and transportation of coal and other raw materials became uncertain. Once reason had returned and the Cultural Revolution was swept under the mat, steel production expanded, reaching 25 to 26 million tons in 1973. Some of this expansion resulted from the reintroduction of small plants, better planned and managed than those of the Great Leap Forward. They used local labor and raw materials to a considerable extent. However, when their demands on the local labor supply threatened to reduce the harvests in 1971 and 1972, the construction of small plants came to a virtual end and resources of personnel and materiel were concentrated on existing plants large and small.

Politics and ideology, however, continued to harass this fundamental industry. Political turbulence again erupted during the campaign against Confucius, surely the most ridiculous aberration ever indulged in by an authoritarian state. There were work stoppages while laborers absorbed the thoughts of Chairman Mao. Production fell.

The industry weathered this trial, which was political in nature. It could not avoid the inexorable laws of economics. The imbalance between the final stages of steel making and the input of iron ore and scrap persisted. This problem continues. The Peking government has increased investment in ore-processing plants, coal and iron-ore mines, and beneficating plants to improve the raw materials moving into the steel industry. There have been some purchases of foreign equipment, but even in this essential industry, the Chinese emphasis is on self-reliance.

The state of the iron and steel industry is critical to the progress made by any society groping toward modern industrial status. Equally critical is the contribution to the economy of the nation's agriculture. The Chinese Communists began their long campaign to improve the country's agricultural resources with the single, essential goal of feeding the people. As industry has increased by stops and starts over the last quarter of a century, the leadership has recognized that it is not enough to meet only the day-to-day demands of the vast population; foodstuffs must be stored to feed a growing industrial population. One result has been the intensive investment in people, as well as machines, in agricultural communes in industrial areas.

The Wu San commune in Manchuria offered a good example of the relationship between the farming and industrial communities. The commune was established in 1953 when it became evident (although my hosts did not say so) that the expanding industrial-worker population of Manchuria, including many workers transported from Shanghai, could not be fed by imports from agricultural regions without enormous strain on transport.

At Wu San and elsewhere a good 70 percent of what the visitor is told can be put down to Communist propaganda. And, of course, here as elsewhere the visitor is shown the best—not the mediocre, not the bad.

Yet Wu San has positive factors in its favor. It sells about

1,500 tons of grain to the state annually. The nearest city, Mukden, receives 10,000 tons of vegetables, 500 tons of fresh milk, 300 tons of chickens, and other foods. These are produced from a commune of about 75 square kilometers tended by 19 production brigades divided into 86 production teams drawn from a commune population of about 35,000 with a labor force of approximately 15,000. The cultivated land within the commune is about 3,100 hectares, or 7,657 acres.

It was a fine frosty morning in November. Farm folk respond happily to the end of the harvest season and good weather. At Wu San that day there was a glowing air of accomplishment. The commune's children, active, sturdy, and sassy, were out to help store vegetables in underground depots carved out of the earth. Any experienced correspondent learns to distinguish between the staged show in which the actors are simply going through the motions and the staged show from which he gets a sense of communal endeavor and achievement. The latter was true at Wu San, just as it was not true in several factories visited during the tour.

Chi We Tao, the deputy chairman of the commune, was full of statistics. He went through the familiar comparison of production on the farms before and after liberation. Before the Communists took over, he related as though reading from a script, production had been very low and there had been a steady influx of refugees from other less happy provinces. However, with liberation, all went wonderfully well. The peasants became masters of the land and were organized for agricultural activities. The farmers had been told by Chairman Mao that only collective agriculture could save the country. Collectives were established. Production increased.

Chi We Tao, as in a well-orchestrated commercial on television, recited the figures: 1.5 tons of grain per hectare in 1950, the year of liberation, and 2.25 tons per hectare in 1956. Nothing is easier to do than ridicule solemn, earnest peasants like Chi We Tao reciting such figures. But ridicule clouds a central fact: he and those like him on other communes and in factories are convinced that their achievements are the results of the Communist policy. They are notable in their own small ponds. And what they say to a visitor is what they tell the commune. We cannot discount the influence of Chi or others like him on a hundred thousand communes throughout China.

The primary problems in Wu San and in hundreds of other communes were irrigation and mechanization. The water was there, but electrically driven pumps were necessary. It took twenty-odd years for the pumps to reach the commune. In the autumn of 1976 approximately 95 percent of the land was under irrigation—for Americans a minor accomplishment; for the people of the commune, who have no standards of comparison with the outside world, a miracle. Farmers seized me by the arm, pointed to an irrigation ditch, and chattered to the interpreter. The message was always the same: thirty years ago, when they were young, there was no water, but now there was plenty. We plodded across the fields to see a pumping station. The water gushed forth, and there were blissful smiles. See, the smiles said, the water really comes from deep down in the earth.

Mechanization came next. Mechanization in agriculture, as in industry, has different meanings for Chinese and Americans. To the people of Wu San, mechanization meant 60 big tractors and 160 of what the Chinese call walking tractors, small, twelve-horsepower machines that are the peasants' mules, machines that can be turned to any task. The strange, unknown deities of the provincial government also had sent forty trucks to take the commune's products to market. There were new machines to plow and to harrow. The commune had built a plant to repair these wonderful gifts, and the peasants were experimenting with building smaller machines.

With the machines came a leap forward in production, or so my guides said. In 1958 the commune produced sixty tons of vegetables per hectare; in 1975 the figure was eighty-two tons. The comparable figures for grain were thirty-five and sixty tons. Chi rubbed his hands as though congratulating himself and drank noisily from his mug of tea.

I asked what the children were storing. Again he was voluble with statistics. The commune stored about thirty thousand tons of vegetables in eighty underground storerooms each winter. These were transported to the city and used by the commune in the cold winter months. There were also hothouses for the cultivation of vegetables in winter, he said. These covered one hundred thousand square meters.

With many a genuflection toward the ghost of Chairman Mao, Chi related how the commune had managed to grow in the bleak cold of Manchuria rice and other vegetables and grains usually native to the tropics. Here he made the obligatory reference to the cold winds sent south by those Russian "polar bears in the north." When he said this, however, he discarded his deferential, humorous manner; he meant it.

Rice had been transplanted into this cold climate, he said, and the work had been done largely by machines. Rice was something Mukden needed along with the other foods provided by the commune. Through the work of this commune and others, Mukden was now self-sufficient in grain and vegetables. And, he pointed out, the commune also provided eggs, pork from twenty thousand head of pigs, and milk. Before the Cultural Revolution, he said solemnly, none of this was possible. I asked why not. He faltered, and an interpreter from the provincial government said smoothly that the Great Proletarian Cultural Revolution had shown the people the way to increased production. Chi smiled and agreed. A weatherbeaten character, he did not seem to be the stuff of which cultural revolutions are made, although I could imagine him grabbing a rifle and going out to fight the Japanese or Chiang Kai-shek's Nationalists.

The question I had asked broke the ideological ice to some extent. There were other communes, Chi conceded, with a higher output of grain and vegetables. Not as much food, especially pork, was reaching the people in the cities as he would wish. There had been an advance in modernization, but much remained to be done. I mentioned the cheerful women I had seen shoveling gravel to make a road and suggested that a grader could do the job in half the time and with a hundredth of the manpower. His head bobbed, and he spoke excitedly to the interpreter: Yes, that was what he had meant by modernization; they needed more machines of that type. He had heard, he said wistfully, about bulldozers and graders. They were American, weren't they?

Chi exemplified the beguiling character of the Chinese. They are so ostensibly honest, so eager to talk about what has been done for them by the Communist government, that the unwary visitor is liable to forget what was done by that same government to others who refused to cooperate—to the landlords, to the shopkeepers.

I asked what a commune is. To Chi this was a strange question. Everyone knows what a commune is. But he explained slowly for the benefit of the ignorant stranger: A commune is a collection of villages, some very small, others larger, with storehouses and workshops. Every citizen of the commune can have a private plot for growing vegetables or feeding chickens and pigs. These plots make up about 5 percent of the commune's arable land.

On and on went the statistics as we moved from farmland to silo, from machine shop to processing plant. In one of the latter the women of the commune were dealing with chickens. They said four thousand were killed each day. With pride Chi said that before mechanization the figure had been two thousand a day. I asked if the chickens were tender. This question seemed irrelevant to him. The chickens were there. They were killed and processed. The people who would eat them presumably had no interest in whether the chickens were or were not tender. Again, that pathetic belief in modernization and mechanization.

The commune was now able to rear thirty thousand chickens. In the building where the chickens were killed and plucked, belts moved the bodies from worker to worker.

"We have many, many forms of mechanization in the commune," Chi said. Soon, mechanization would free the people for other tasks.

I asked if this meant that the women shoveling gravel out on the road would be given less arduous tasks.

Of course it did, he answered.

What would happen to them and to the hundreds bent over the fields when mechanization came? The superficial answer was that they would then be free to help develop the commune in other ways and tend their own vegetable gardens. The communes, an interpreter broke in, offered ample opportunity for capital construction. I asked if the women struggling with the stones on the road could look forward to more of the same, more capital construction.

A short, uneasy silence. No, the women and the men could look forward to more constructive work in their own commune once mechanization was completed. The commune, Chi said, would go from strength to strength, from victory to victory. I believe that he believed it.

The spirit of expansion is contagious. Even when, to the Western eye, the prospects for progress are limited, the devotion to their goal of those involved is impressive. Talking to the Chinese I recalled how years ago in the Donetz Basin in Russia just such people—industrial technicians, factory managers, collective-farm managers—had predicted that next year or the year after, the problems would be solved, the difficulties overcome.

A touch of skepticism is a corrective. In 1946 in Kiev, after a tour that had featured optimistic statements by party officials and mine directors alike, I mentioned to Khrushchev, then the party boss in the Ukraine, that I understood that the mines in the Donbas were working.

"In the sense that we've pumped out the water," he said, "they're working. But it will take another ten years before we repair the damage the Germans have done."

In China I often sensed that behind the avalanche of official, doctored statistics, behind the oral obeisance to Chairman Mao and the Great Proletarian Cultural Revolution there were more realistic minds ready to take up the burden of modernizing China when the political atmosphere cleared.

Unlike West Germany in the early 1950s, there was no emphasis on export. At the electrical-equipment works in Mukden, where, the vice-chairman of the revolutionary committee said complacently, production was 174 times greater than in 1950, there was an offhand reference to the transformers exported to Albania and Pakistan. But the thrust of his remarks was on what the factory could do for China. Certainly there were shortcomings, he said; too much of the work was done by hand, and often the factory failed to meet its commitments to the central government. But the workers would compensate for these failings.

And how would this be done? By making our own machines, he said triumphantly. Look, here is a welding machine we have made ourselves. And those huge cranes that can move fifty to two hundred tons are "all ours, all the product of our labors."

"We will be completely mechanized by the end of 1977," he said.

I have stressed the atmosphere in industrial plants and on communes because it is on this economic base that China's military and political future rests. No nation can build weapons without a progressive iron and steel industry or support its armed forces without an equally progressive agriculture.

The economic future of China in the post-Mao period is less obscure as this is written than it was in the autumn of 1976. This is because the forces of stability and technological progress have been restored to leadership; the Great Leap Forward and the Great Proletarian Cultural Revolution are seen as aberrations that slowed China's growth. The spirit of Chairman Mao is exalted, but the mind of Chou En-lai is the guide.

It was Chou who told the Fourth National People's Congress, albeit with many a gesture toward the leadership of Mao, "that we might envisage the development of our national economy in two stages, beginning from the third five-year plan. The first stage is to build an independent and relatively comprehensive industrial and economic system in fifteen years, that is, before 1980; the second stage is to accomplish the comprehensive modernization of agriculture, industry, national defense, and science and technology before the end of the century so that our national economy will be advancing in the front ranks of the world.''

This call for renewed efforts was issued in an unpromising atmosphere. Much as the Chinese would like to disguise it, their economic progress since 1950 has followed a stop-and-go program. There have been successes. There have been failures, many of them directly attributable to empty-headed political interference. A large number of major economic programs, ushered in with a great rat-a-tat-tat on the propaganda drums, have been left unfinished.

Two key tasks that faced the new government back in 1950 have been fulfilled. First, the government has been able to feed its people. I should note here that nowhere in China did I see anyone who appeared malnourished. This is a sweeping statement. But it includes not only those I met in factories and farms but the cheerful folk I encountered in night strolls in Shanghai, Nanking, and Mukden. The second task was to expand the nation's industrial capacity and production. This I believe has been done, although, as I have indicated, the results are spotty.

A third task, the maintenance of a credible national defense, will be discussed later. Here it suffices to say that without a greater measure of success than that already registered in the industrial sector of the economy, the goal of a national defense capable of deterring Soviet attack is not in sight—unless, of course, the Peking government decides to buy arms abroad, a costly process.

The immediate economic prospects in the period of the fifth Five Year Plan (1976–80) can be assessed with some optimism. Farm production is likely to rise, largely because the fertilizer plants built by foreign capital and expertise will boost agriculture toward the end of the plan. Irrigation coupled with control of natural sources of water will also favor agricultural progress. Linked to these factors encouraging advancement is a large, industrious, and intelligent labor force.

Industrial expansion is more difficult to estimate. The potential for a significant expansion of the steel and petrochemicals industries exists. But realization of the potential rests to a large degree upon the performance of machinery and personnel in the new plants now under construction.

Beyond the windows of a train, hundreds of people could be seen working at the construction of an apartment building for industrial workers. There were few machines in evidence. The building appeared unsubstantial. What could be done to speed that work? I asked an interpreter. He shrugged; nothing could be done now for that project. But the future would provide modern building machinery and new methods; buildings like that would be completed in a fifth the time necessary at present. He was a sensitive, intelligent man who had traveled far for a modern Chinese. He had seen Western Europe. He believed—indeed, as a patriot, which I believe he was and is, he had to believe—that the future would more than compensate for the mistakes and failures of the past and present.

No great nation can live without foreign trade. In Shanghai and Peking the Chinese display the goods they consider exportable. Aside from the textiles, many of which are fine, most articles on display (bicycles, radio sets, kitchenware, cheap porcelain) would open the pocketbooks of few, perhaps a stray Albanian or Zairian.

China's most important potential export is oil. By the early 1980s, exploitation of existing fields, exploration of new ones (such as that in the South China Sea), and improvements in refining and transport should move China toward the position of a major oil producer. The amount available for export is unknown. In the projected era of industrial expansion China itself will drink oil like water. But oil will be the fastest-growing, most available, and most sought-after export. Compared to oil, the shoddy machine-made embroideries and cheap china of the factories are very minor rivals for foreign currency.

The oil industry, like every other industry in China, is subject not to the West's familiar laws of supply and demand but to the vagaries of political leaders. Chairman Mao twice came close to wrecking the economy with his Great Leap Forward and his Great Proletarian Cultural Revolution. No authoritarian society is secure from the arrival in power of other economic dunces.

A problem arising from the second of Mao's attempts to fashion the Chinese economy into a reflection of his ideas is the havoc that the Great Proletarian Cultural Revolution wrought on the work force. As we know, and as we shall see, a great many Chinese now enjoy living standards unthinkable and unattainable in 1950. But these folk live in a static society. They have two rooms now. That's it. Do you want three rooms because two babies have arrived? Not a hope. The third room is unheard of. Can the mother and father earn more in their jobs? There are no cash incentives to provoke them to greater efforts. All authoritarian governments apparently suffer from the failure to recognize that once the people have been given a taste of a better life, they will demand more.

The people will not accept shortages of cloth, kitchen utensils, or radios today as they did a quarter of a century ago when their requirements were simpler. Nor will they accept the barrier to additional income enforced by the static caste system in agriculture and industry. The Chinese people have started up the ladder of rising expectations. It would be surprising if they continued to accept today's gains as the end of their progress. The common man, whether in China, the United States, or the Soviet Union, seldom looks beyond the immediate present. But the percipient Chinese (and they are an intelligent people) should recognize the factors working in China's favor.

The most obvious is that China's resources in raw materials and manpower are those of a superpower, although the development of the material resources has been so laggardly that China today, it should be reemphasized, must be classed as an underdeveloped country.

A second factor pointing toward a long-term expansion is that a series of projects initiated by Peking—water control, irrigation, and afforestation among them—should ease in time the pressure of population growth. Today, the excess of manpower is not a handicap. Only by its efficient employment can the country aspire to the goals set by Chou En-lai.

It struck me that the austerity imposed on the people has had real dividends. There is literally no waste. People live frugally, although they have been told they live on a scale undreamed of by their grandparents. They have been taught to use every bit of equipment to the utmost and to recycle animal and human waste. The Chinese may not have much, but they get the most out of what they have.

There are pitfalls ahead. Although China is an authoritarian state, a great deal of initiative is left to the lower cadres. When and if China moves into the status of an economic superpower, the workers in the factories and the communes will have to accept greater direction from the bureaucrats in Peking. The physical and mental appetites of great industries are such that they must be administered from a center, be it Detroit, Moscow, or Peking, despite pleas for decentralization.

Peking's direction, though present, is not now the immediate guiding force in China. Local—that is, provincial or city—authority is. The anticipated attempt by the central government to assume micromanagement of smaller industrial and agricultural enterprises is bound to cause trouble. One wonders if the invocations to Chairman Mao will lead people to accept this new order of things, or whether the first rise in wages since the 1950s—Mao always opposed material incentives—will do the trick.

China is not now, nor has it ever been, a great potential market for the United States, Japan, or the industrialized nations of the West. China is a country whose economy needs certain imports to expand. But for some years to come, possibly until the end of this century, importation will be selective because of a chronic shortage of foreign exchange and also because the Chinese, the government, the Communist party, and the people prefer a policy of self-reliance. They are willing now and, I should think, for the immediate future to rely on machines they make themselves, no matter how uneconomic and, indeed, primitive some of these machines are, rather than buy them abroad.

There is one development that could conceivably alter this picture. That is the emergence of the country as a world oil power. A great deal of effort and ink has been expended by American and foreign intelligence agencies to prove either that China can develop into an oil center comparable to the Middle East or that China in the future will be able to develop an oil industry sufficient to meet its own needs and perhaps have some left over to sell to the nearest major market, Japan.

The attainment of either goal would smooth the road to superpower status. Yet it is clear that serious technological and political obstacles lie in the way. Here we are discussing China's own oil and not the very important deposits in the China Sea, the rights to which are contested by Taiwan, Japan, and the People's Republic.

The experts have set their sights high: 4 million barrels a day in 1980 and 8 million barrels a day in 1990. Randall W. Hardy, in a monograph written for the Center for Strategic and International Studies in Washington, pointed out that to reach these output figures the Chinese must surmount a series of difficult problems. One, perhaps the most obvious, is a much closer economic relationship with Japan than has existed in recent history, a relationship that will encourage Japanese assistance in the technological development of the Chinese oil industry. Japan should be the chief foreign benefactor from the development of Chinese oil. But differing Chinese and Japanese interests in Taiwan, South Korea, and the South China Sea; Japanese apprehensions over China's claim to be the leader of the Third World countries of Asia; and, not to be discounted, the residual antagonism between the two countries are political obstacles.

There is also a built-in international risk. The Soviet Union can hardly welcome Sino-Japanese cooperation in expanding an oil industry that, once fully developed, could accelerate China's progress to superpower status. As the most powerful state in northeastern Asia, the Soviet Union will be in a position for some years to come to frighten the Japanese out of close cooperation with China on oil or anything else.

In China an expansion of the oil resources depends, as does much else, on a continuation of the period of tranquility that Chairman Hua and his close associates appear to seek. This means that Hua and his fellow technocrats will eschew the eccentric revolutionary tactics of Chairman Mao and devote themselves to economic expansion of a stable society.

In oil, and all else, we encounter the problem of priorities. Investment in oil production competes with investment for the expansion of the coal, iron, and steel industries and of the nation's agriculture. At the same time, competition will arise in a different area. The oil industry will demand trained technicians—geologists, geophysicists, and production engineers—to replace the foreigners, principally Japanese, who will administer the first phases of the oil industry's expansion. But China's resources for technical education are limited. So to some extent is the political willingness to send what would have to be a considerable number of students abroad to learn foreign technology.

Hardy has much on his side when he argues that "depicting China as a potential oil giant is . . . extremely misleading." His conclusion is that Chinese oil "will be a complicating but not controlling factor in the future geopolitics of Asia."

Oil—indeed, energy of any sort—is such an important factor in international power politics that China's potential must be kept in mind in assessing the balance in Asia. Hardy concludes that the probability that China will reach an output of 8 million barrels a day in 1990 is considerably under 50 percent when all the problems confronting the country are taken into consideration. But the oil is there and with it the potential for political influence for its exploiters.

For example, U.S. intelligence services agree, as much as they ever agree on anything, that Chinese production will reach 4 million barrels a day in 1980 and that, of this, 1 million barrels a day will be available for export. This estimate does not take into account the demands of China's expanding economy. It may be, as the Central Intelligence Agency report on the subject argues, that export may be only between 540,000 and 600,000 barrels a day in 1980.

The CIA, exhibiting the skepticism natural to an intelligence organization when dealing with others' views, discounts other estimates of oil production and exports. Peking may be exaggerating output and exports to divert Japan from venturing into joint schemes with the Soviet Union to develop Siberian oil. There is also a natural tendency among government planners, democratic as well as authoritarian, to overstate expected goals. And everyone is familiar with the willingness of leaders to demonstrate their infinite wisdom in opening such a resource to the people even though its development is distant.

From the standpoint of the Sino-Soviet feud, it is well to remember, too, that the Ta-ch'ing field in northern Manchuria, China's most productive, is highly vulnerable to Soviet bombs and missiles and, in the event of war, would be one of the first objectives of a Russian offensive.

The Ta-ch'ing field was discovered in 1959 and, since the middle of the 1960s, has produced between 40 and 50 percent of China's oil output. The two next most important fields are the Sheng-li and Ta-kang fields near the coast southeast of Peking. These are the fields in which production is growing fastest, but Ta-kang has a special importance. It is close to the Po Hai Gulf, north of the Yellow Sea, where the offshore-oil potential is important and where the Chinese are carrying out intensive exploration. Another important fact about Ta-kang and Sheng-li is that they are far less vulnerable to Soviet attack or seizure than the Ta-ch'ing field.

Other, interior, fields can be exploited as well as the Po Hai Gulf. Intelligence estimates are that the reserves of these amount to about half of China's total. But many of the fields are far distant from China's production centers. They include the Karamai field in the Dzungarian Basin in the country's extreme northwest. The field in 1974 had a production of about 1.5

million tons and in 1975 a production of 2 million tons, compared with 32 million tons and 40 million tons for Ta-ch'ing in the same years. Another productive field is at Yumen, in north-central China's Kansu Province, which produced 1.5 million tons in 1974 and an estimated 2.5 million in 1975.

The production of three other important fields for 1975 is based on estimates: the Hupeh field in east-central China had an output of approximately 3 million tons; the Fu-yu site in northern Manchuria had an output of about 4 million tons; and the P'an-shan field, northeast of Peking near the Liao River, produced 4 million tons.

The Ta-ch'ing field was first exploited during the period of Sino-Soviet friendship, when the Russians acted as instructors and advisors. The Russians' influence on Chinese oil development lasted for years after their withdrawal in 1960, and the Chinese continued to use Soviet and Rumanian equipment. Following the Soviet pattern, the Chinese have concentrated on readily accessible fields, sometimes of limited production, rather than on more remote fields of greater production.

By the 1970s the Russians were long gone and their equipment had run down or become obsolescent. In the meantime, efforts to increase oil exploration and production were intensified, leading China to what for her was a considerable investment in U.S. equipment—$80 million. The funds were spent on seismic exploration equipment, including a computer, blowout safeguards, and other apparatus connected to the expansion of fields on land.

Yet it is China's development of offshore oil that excites the interest and perhaps the avarice of foreign producers. As Hardy points out, one reason is a geophysical survey produced by the United Nations in 1968 which stated that the "continental shelf between Taiwan and Japan may be one of the most prolific oil and gas reservoirs in the world." As noted earlier, Western companies, including Gulf, Amoco, and Shell, have carried out exploratory drilling in this area, which China, because it claims Taiwan as a province, considers its property.

But before they overcome the political and technological barriers to exploitation of the South China Sea field, the Chinese are likely to concentrate on production in the Po Hai Gulf. This field has several advantages. It is near major industrial areas. Transportation from the field to the mainland or to the potential principal foreign importer, Japan, is relatively simple. The gulf is shallow. The weather is calm, a great deal calmer than that in the North Sea, from which Britain and Norway are extracting large quantities of oil. Moreover, the expansion of the Ta-kang fields near the gulf promises rich deposits under the sea.

By comparison, exploitation of the South China Sea field will be far more difficult. The ocean floor is five hundred feet below the surface—that is, beyond China's present capabilities for exploitation.

Many factors will combine to inhibit rapid and extensive exploitation of the Po Hai Gulf field. The costs will be three to five times as great as onshore development costs. Sophisticated foreign technology will have to be bought abroad. Even if the funds are found, experienced American oil men believe it will be from five to seven years before substantial production is attained.

The costs of imported foreign oil-extraction machinery will tax Chinese foreign-exchange resources. Since 1972, the Russians have spent $3.1 billion on less-advanced equipment to open their Siberian fields. If the Chinese decide to spend comparable sums on the exploitation of the Po Hai field, investment will have to be diverted from other industries.

To repeat, China's basic economic decisions are in the field of priorities. Although Chairman Hua's economic policies are in the development stage, there can be little doubt that the new government intends to concentrate on basic industrial and agricultural production. But where does the money go? For oil, for steel, for railways and highways, to the communes?

The new leaders' economic policies cannot be separated from politics. Given the length of Chairman Mao's rule and the number of his supporters, it is prudent to assume there is a latent opposition to his economic ideas and methods. Yet it seems likely that economic progress and, consequently, improved living standards will prove more attractive to the masses than further revolutions and disturbances and that planning will win over blind leaps into the future. The Chinese leadership will march into a period of industrial expansion. The people will follow. Ultimately, China and Chinese Communism will change. Change will not be rapid. It will not be easily discernible. But it will come.

Change can take many forms. Some authorities believe that continued industrial expansion in China will create a society rather like that of the Soviet Union, in which an elitist group of party bureaucrats, industrial technicians, and military chieftains becomes the most favored class, developing into a socialist bourgeoisie insulated from the people by their comfortable living. This, of course, is what Chairman Mao professed to see happening in Russia. His vision encouraged him to believe that the purity of the Chinese revolution could be maintained only by constant revolutions, which in effect meant a state of perpetual chaos.

China may develop in that direction. But progress toward such a society, if it comes, is likely to be very slow. The Soviet Union, even after the destruction caused in European Russia in World War II, had the basis for rapid expansion of the industrial economy. The Chinese are only now constructing the basis for expansion; the existing industrial infrastructure will suffice only to keep China going as a medium industrial power. China is where Russia was in the late 1920s and early 1930s.

Another factor argues against China rapidly becoming a mirror image of the Soviet Union. China still has a frontier to the west, vast areas undeveloped and waiting for men and machines to explore and exploit their resources. Central and southern China contain districts where agriculture and industry lag well behind that of the rest of the country. The development of these areas is probably possible only in a spirit of pioneering egalitarianism, one that resists the stratification of society.

But it is evident that the beginnings of a social order more akin to that of the Soviet Union than to the revolutionary China of the 1950s do exist. No foreigner really knows how the senior officials of the republic live in Chungnanhai, their closely guarded compound in Peking. But there is some evidence that senior officials of various ministries are able to buy Western products seldom if ever seen in the Friendship Shops open to foreigners. And it would be beyond human experience if a senior official of one ministry who is building a new house did not find the construction aided by access to scarce materials granted by officials of other ministries for whom, in time, he will perform similar favors.

Ross H. Munro, the perceptive correspondent of the Toronto *Globe and Mail,* noted a wall poster at Peking University that may or may not have reflected a general restlessness over official privilege. It said in part, "Senior officials can buy commodities at cheap prices and can also obtain commodities that are scarce."

Any state that supports an enormous bureaucracy, as China does, sooner or later finds that it harbors what the British call the "old-boy net," the communication between equals that gets things done, acquires commodities in short supply, does favors for family members, and discreetly covers up omissions and mistakes. There is no reason to suppose that such a network does not exist in contemporary China. Yet even if it does, the conviction of the few foreigners who have had a glimpse of the life of the country's leaders is that their lives, by the standards of Western or even Soviet society, are remarkably austere.

5

An Enduring,
Endearing People

In the early morning in the autumn the green roofs of the For-
bidden City floated like rafts on the mists. As the sun rose, its
rays touched the mountains to the north and west near the Summer Palace and the Great Wall. Below the hotel balcony on the
streets, tens of thousands of people pedaled their bicycles as
they headed for work. Buses pushed through the bicyclists like
sharks through schools of small fish. For a great city, Peking is
quiet by Western standards.

The visitor is taken to see the Winter Palace with its storied
and fabulous treasures. The guides are oddly embarrassed when
they describe this jade carving or that elaborate imperial head-
dress; the viewer must remember, they say, that these were
made by downtrodden people for the amusement and adornment
of imperialist rulers. An American, gazing awestruck at an elaborately carved jade piece, asked who cared. The workmen responsible were immortal; no one except a few scholars remembered the names of the emperors.

Aside from showpieces like the Winter Palace, Peking has a
certain grim attraction. It is a working city and a city of workers. Life pulses down every street and through every square. In
the autumn evenings the streets were full of ordinary folk shopping for food or ending the day's work with a beer in a modest
restaurant. The ceaseless movement on foot, by bicycle, and by
buses has an inexorable rhythm of its own. The visitor feels as

though he is standing beside some mighty river. There is an almost overpowering vitality.

When night comes, the city is dead. From the hotel balcony the streets appear empty except for a few stray bicyclists. Only once was there discernible activity. That was on the night when there had been a minor earthquake. Then, from the balcony, people could be seen gathering in little knots discussing, perhaps, whether the shock had been the precursor of a greater quake or whether nothing more need be feared and they could return to bed. In the early morning there were no indications that the quake had started fires. The green roofs performed their daily miracle of emerging from the mist, the bicyclists flowed through the streets, and Peking began another day.

The face of contemporary China shown the visitor is that which the government hopes will be accepted as the reality. Here is a busy China intent on greater industrial and agricultural development, a land of mines and factories and mills, of tidy farms and flourishing communes. All these are part of the reality but are not the whole of it.

The teeming roads of China show the foreigner other aspects of the country and its development. There he may glimpse not the completed society but a people who, however eagerly they reach for the new, have not progressed to the point where they can discard the old.

Once the traveler leaves the city limits of Peking or Nanking or Shanghai, he enters a less modern but in some ways more interesting world, speeding backward in time toward glimpses of another China curiously untouched by the drive toward modernization. It was reminiscent of leaving Stalingrad in 1946, a city being furiously rebuilt, and crossing the Volga and entering a central-Asian world of small, poor villages on the edge of the vast land mass stretching eastward to the Pacific.

Traffic is heavy on the outskirts of any Chinese city with buses and trucks, most of the latter sturdy, utilitarian vehicles built in China, although a few are battered relics of the days of Soviet friendship. But as one leaves the suburbs and follows the arrow-straight roads to this division or that air regiment, the traffic changes. The buses and trucks give way to small motorized vehicles with three or four wheels hauling carts full of wood, coal, vegetables, or rice. Sometimes the cargo is chickens or pigs. Often one or two men lie sleeping atop the loads, their bodies jolted by each pothole. But vehicles drawn by animals or humans soon predominate.

Carts are drawn by odd combinations: a donkey and a horse with a foal running loose alongside; a camel and a donkey moving at a stately pace; three men, harnessed, pulling a load of cabbage; a woman and two men on a similar rig; a pretty, laughing girl pushing a wheelbarrow in which reposes an indignant trussed pig. And the inevitable bicyclists and hundreds of pedestrians all moving with a serene purposefulness.

In the cold autumn wind the drivers huddle in their quilted greatcoats. The ear flaps of their fur hats stand out at right angles to their heads. Just so, you imagine, the men of Genghis Khan and Tamerlane must have looked when they conquered not simply countries but continents. These men smoked curved-stem pipes. They grinned at the foreigner and the guides.

A village breaks the monotony of the journey. Brown stucco, windowless walls face the road. A glimpse of a courtyard with horses unharnessed, some men huddled around a brazier. A general store beside the dwelling houses, adorned by a picture of Chairman Mao. Two soldiers waiting for a bus. A mongrel dog trots briskly alongside the car for a moment, the first dog seen in a thousand miles of travel.

The land has a certain gaunt beauty. Beyond the Great Wall the mountains march to the north, and through a pass there is the gleam of a lake. From the hills around Nanking the great plain broken by minor rivers stretches to the horizon. Manchuria is cold, austere, and utilitarian, as forbidding as Pittsburgh in the old days and with a touch of the same local chauvinism; its people know it is not pretty, but "here we do things."

Pollution is an evident but unmentioned problem in China. The mists that hang over Peking are partly natural, partly industrial. From a fifth-floor window of the Peace Hotel in Shanghai the junks and ferries on the Whampoa River are almost invisible in the morning fog. When the sun rises, one of the great river-scapes of the world lies at your feet. The mind's eye recalls the Hudson River a generation ago; here were the same liners and rusted freighters, the busy ferries, the tugs. The only difference was the junks, moving with a certain slovenly majesty behind their sails, through the traffic down the blue and silver river.

The recent past is ubiquitous in Shanghai. One route to the ferry takes the visitor past block after block of gray stone ware-houses built by the British, the French, and others in the old days. How many gentlemen of England now long gone retired on profits from those warehouses? How many eager young Americans stood beside them, rubbed their hands, and dreamed of half a billion customers?

The ferry dodges traffic crossing the river. Moored along the bund is a gaily decorated steamer, a "hero ship" of the War of Liberation still sporting an ancient three-inch gun. Farther up-stream, a modern destroyer lies alongside the quay; on the fore-deck, seamen are repairing the housing of a gun. The crowd on the ferry glances at the foreigner and resumes its chatter.

Poverty, propaganda, and perhaps a desire for uniformity have forced the Chinese into what is now a national uniform—a close-buttoned blue jacket and blue trousers for both sexes. Sometimes one glimpses the collar of a bright blouse above the jacket of a pretty girl, but generally only the children are gaily dressed. They scamper about in bright shirts and trousers of dif-ferent colors. One or two are dressed as soldiers of the PLA, their "uniforms" topped by white imitation-fur hats adorned with red stars. At the memorial for Sun Yat-sen near Nanking, the elders march decorously up and down the long stone stair-cases. Their children frolic and, on the way down, slide shriek-ing with mirth down the stone balustrades, to the concern of their parents.

Travel by air offers pleasant surprises. Around Shanghai the land is cut by innumerable canals. These, winking in the sun, seem strings of precious stones encircling the city. Travel by rail is curiously reminiscent of train travel in the United States in World War II. The stations are jammed with travelers: families burdened with bundles and cheap suitcases, soldiers with eyes for a pretty girl, self-important officials bowed to their seats by underlings. Stations along the way are vibrant with life: family groups waiting for a returned soldier, bewildered visitors fingering a ticket, a man with a crate of piglets arguing with a conductor, a grandfather with two small boys wide-eyed at the sight of the train.

I complain to my hosts that their efforts at sightseeing, though welcome, deny the average tourist a view of some of the new China's real achievements. The Summer and Winter palaces, the Great Wall, and the Ming tombs undoubtedly are impressive, but no more so than the Valley of the Kings in Egypt, the Acropolis, or the Taj Mahal.

No such sights express the spirit of modern China. The great bridge across the Yangtze at Nanking does. It is a cold and windy day. A pretty young woman recites breathlessly the statistics connected with the bridge: 6,722 meters of railroad bridge, 4,534 meters of highway bridge running above the railroad, an investment of approximately $550 million, volunteer labor that on some days ran as high as fifty thousand workers. But no figures can match the impact of this great span thrown across the great, rolling yellow river. In comparison, the Ming tombs, the palaces, and the Great Wall seem faint echoes of an irrelevant past. A train rumbles across as we stand on the bridge. The engineer spits and waves a hand at the group.

It is impossible to generalize about a people as numerous and as varied as the Chinese. China's races vary as much as Swedes do from Portuguese, Eskimos from Frenchmen. But some impressions of the national character do register even from a short and busy visit. Such impressions are by no means comprehensive. I saw only a handful of a new and, to me, infinitely fascinating people.

The first and most lasting impression was of friendliness. I do not mean that the officials who greeted me or those who accompanied me on my various trips were friendly, although they invariably were. It was the others with whom I came in contact, often by chance, who were willing to sit down and discuss not simply the industrial output of such and such a factory or the produce of this commune or the other, but their own hopes and aspirations for themselves and their children.

Their courtesy was enormous. I was an imperialist. But I was also a guest. And, of course, I was someone from another world. The Chinese may consider themselves the greatest people on earth, the citizens of the Middle Kingdom around which the earth revolves. But in conversation, no Chinese reflected this; they did not talk as though they were the elect of the earth. Instead, they wanted to know how people fared in other lands—in America, in Japan, in Europe.

Their friendliness was tangible. In a museum, before the guide had a chance to speak, Chinese sightseers would fall back away from the exhibit to allow the foreigner a better view. When I struggled out of a train in the cold dawn of a November Sunday a passerby, unencumbered, leaped forward to help me with my bags. When I visited a dispensary in a commune, the local doctor was sorely disappointed when I told him that I had no ailments and needed no shots.

Curiosity was a large ingredient of friendship. How did the steel mill compare with those I had seen in America, England, and West Germany? The answer was that it was ten or fifteen years behind the times. No offense was taken. Instead, my hosts wanted to know where they were deficient. When told, they would consult for a few minutes and then return to announce that, yes, this was probably true, the authoritative cadres had told them that the mill was behind the times.

One night at dinner in Mukden, a woman official questioned me about America's northern frontier with Canada. Was it fortified? Could people cross it? Were there police at the crossing points? I explained as best I could that there were no fortifications, that I could go almost as easily from New York State into Canada as I could from New York into Connecticut.

"No formalities, no customs?" she asked. None but showing my driver's license, I answered. She conferred with the official on her right and then with the one on her left. The international relationship between Canada and the United States, she said, must be an easier one than that between Russia and China.

Curiosity is fed by a vast ignorance of life in foreign countries, especially the United States. I do not mean by this that only the peasants driving their carts to market are ignorant of the United States but that aside from a handful who have spent some time in America, the great mass of officialdom is ignorant. Senior officials of the great ministries of state asked childish questions about the American electoral process. An interpreter at the Shanghai industrial fair interrupted her talk to ask if the Americans made television sets. A senior officer of the PLA was convinced that all American army officers were graduates of West Point.

Ignorance of facts betrays no lack of intellect. Whenever I was able to supply facts, the result was a long and detailed discussion. What I said was examined, shaken out, compared with personal experience, and then fed back in a series of interminable questions. Here were people who wanted to know, to examine, and compare.

The peasants in the communes had the manners of grandees. Skeptics will say those were not peasants but "plants" sent to this particular Potemkin village. I am afraid some such unworthy thoughts entered my head. There is one way to be sure. Look at the hands. The hands of those who found me a shelter away from the biting wind and the snow and who helped me up and down the ladders in air-raid shelters were not the hands of bureaucrats on temporary duty but the hands of men who lived and worked in those places.

There is nothing superficial about Chinese courtesy; there is a gravity to it. Nor is it that the Chinese give so much—they have little to give—but that they give what they have with unstinting generosity.

On the surface, the face that China turns to foreigners, life is austere. There is enough food but no frills, no inequality. But I sensed that in China, as in any other society under stress, arrangements are made on the "you do a favor for me and I'll do one for you" basis that ensures a somewhat more flexible distribution system than is called for by state plans. The fisherman who has an extra carp would be only human if he did not swap the fish for a chicken raised by his brother-in-law on the poultry side of the commune. Such trades of favors, extending into the education of children, the assignment of industrial jobs, the location of homes, undoubtedly form a substructure in Chinese life. No money changes hands, so there is no question of corruption. What the Chinese are practicing is a system that was old when imperial Rome was something new in politics: brother (or comrade), you scratch my back and I'll scratch yours.

Circumstance has made the Chinese a rather austere people. From the manner in which sundry guests at dinners to which I was invited wolfed down the food, austerity is imposed by economic conditions, not chosen by the population. But, although it was unusual to see a fat Chinese, it was even more unusual to see one who appeared ill nourished.

Nor do they appear to be heavy drinkers, although the climate of Manchuria would seem to impel men to the bottle as the climate does in Scotland, Sweden, or Russia. I did not see one drunk in China, which was in sharp contrast to Russia, where on any given night you can spot a score or more drunks being hauled away by the Moscow militia. The Chinese, however, have an amusing sectional chauvinism about their beer. And very good beer it is, too. In Mukden I was told that their beer was the best in China and that it would be a nice change from the slop served in Peking. In Nanking my hosts made disparaging remarks about the Shanghai beer, theirs, they asserted, being the best beer in China. I found the beer uniformly good. But then a life of travel has led me to conclude that good beer, unlike good wine, can be found around the world—in India, the Philippines, Mexico, or Israel.

Chinese table courtesies extend to mao tai, a colorless liquid made from sorghum. The Chinese are not amused when a foreigner compares it to vodka. It is drunk in tiny glasses to the toast "Gambei," "Bottoms up." The host and guest then hold their glasses out to show that the drink has been finished. The most popular toast is, "To the friendship of the Chinese and American peoples," but once this had been drunk, my hosts showed a marvelous ingenuity in thinking up various other toasts. At one dinner they began with President Ford and were working their way down the order of precedence—and the bottle—until, at the point where we reached Speaker of the House Tip O'Neill, an elderly colonel passed out and the meeting was adjourned.

The potency of mao tai, I should add, is deceptive. After a farewell dinner, I was writing notes in my room at the Hotel Peking when I felt the floor tremble. This was the sort of mao tai effect my hosts had warned me about. I continued to write but, glancing up, noticed that the chandelier was swaying like a starlet in a discotheque. It was an earthquake, not mao tai. However, the stuff has a good deal of what the Indians called "make brave" in it, and so I continued my notes.

The Chinese are a good-humored people, a characteristic that seems to set them off from other authoritarian people. There is a great deal of laughter in China, not only in the streets and in restaurants but also in factories and communes. There is a lot of horseplay among old friends, and harmless practical jokes. It may be one of China's strengths that though the people take their country and its future seriously, they do not insist that they be taken seriously.

But one also has an instinctive feeling that a strain of violence coexists with the humor and the courtesy. In this the Chinese do not differ from other Asian peoples. How does one reconcile the exquisite formal grace of Japanese ceremony with what happened in Bataan and in Malaya? Are the placid, smiling Burmese that one sees in the Arakan pagoda in Mandalay the same people who will suddenly seize a sword and cut down whole families? This is only to say that a Chinese, like an American, a Dane, or a Kenyan, is not one man but many.

The Chinese can be whipped into a state of violent emotion. One cold November night in Mukden I watched from the hotel window while long columns of workers, accompanied by the clamor of drums and firecrackers, marched shouting down the street. What, I asked the interpreter in the morning, had all that been about? He replied that it was a demonstration expressing the people's relief that the Gang of Four had been vanquished and that Chairman Hua had succeeded Mao in showing the way to the Chinese people. This, he assured me, had been a spontaneous demonstration. Would the workers be back in the factories and communes in the morning? Of course, they would work even harder to express their joy.

A people's capacity for violent emotion can be transformed into an international danger. Hitler played on it to weld the German nation into the mightiest force this century has seen. Could the Chinese be so moved? Undoubtedly, they could be roused to a pitch of extreme national sacrifice against the Russians. But the Russians are on their frontiers. Could the same feelings be roused against a distant enemy, the Americans or the Japanese, for example? I doubt it.

Like all authoritarian peoples, the Chinese are at the mercy of an enormous bureaucracy. It seemed to me—a privileged traveler, I concede—that it was a less officious bureaucracy than I had seen in the Soviet Union or even in France under de Gaulle.

I stood in line at Peking to present my passport for clearance. Several Chinese were in line in front of me. The official glanced at their papers, yawned, and stamped them, and stretched out his hand for my passport. I might have been at Kennedy Airport taking the night flight to London.

The way people live and, more importantly, the way they think they live are useful, but not entirely satisfactory, guides to the state of a society. I do not pretend I was shown the worst slums of Shanghai or the meanest homes in a fishing commune. What I did see convinced me that the hard workers and/or the faithful party members and adherents have reached a life-style that would have been unthinkable for men and women of their station a generation ago.

Against this, however, must be weighed the fact that their ascent to these tiny pinnacles of affluence has been made possible by the elimination of hundreds of thousands of others equally industrious, ambitious, courteous, and friendly.

One I visited was Mrs. Wu Fong-tseng. She looked sixty and was forty-five. She lived in a fishing commune outside Shanghai and still worked with a "brigade," especially in the crabbing season when the brigade works at night with lights and nets.

Do people do this in America? Of course, crabs are a delicacy. The interpreter translated. She did not get it. To her, and millions like her, any food was a delicacy. Why?

As Mrs. Wu told it, she and her parents, and their parents before them, had lived on fishing boats. At five she had gone to work on a fishing boat on which the family lived throughout the year. Shoes were too expensive. All went barefoot. There was one quilt for the family and one pot for cooking. The family's possessions could have been put in one basket.

She was not angry. She spoke of it as an American would of a spell of bad weather or a slow period at the plant. This was the first time, Mrs. Wu said in a matter-of-fact tone, that the family had ever lived ashore. Would I come in and see her house?

As far as I could see it was no different in size or shape from the seven other apartments in a long, low building that ran from the canal, where the fishing boats were moored, toward a cabbage field. But to Mrs. Wu, of course, it was special. There were two bedrooms and a kitchen. The bedroom in which we sat was reasonably clean. The centerpiece was a large elaborately carved four-poster bed covered with an embroidered sheet. There was the obligatory picture of Chairman Mao on the wall. Beneath it was a glass-topped table. Under the glass were snap-

shots of Mrs. Wu and members of her family, pictures taken at
the Great Wall or in Peking or Shanghai. Mrs. Wu pointed out
her daughter laughing with the Great Wall in the background.
Beneath the bed was an ornamented chest. On a shelf was a
small radio. There were no books. The room measured twelve
feet by eight. Beyond the two bedrooms was the kitchen, con-
sisting solely of a wood-burning stove and a sink set in rough
concrete with a single cold-water tap.

There were four in the family, Mrs. Wu explained—herself,
her husband, her daughter, and her granddaughter, Wei Lee,
who was playing outside.

We walked out into the harsh sunlight toward the canal.
Would this be a good year for the fishing commune? Mrs. Wu
looked puzzled. She looked back at her house, then snatched up
her granddaughter, and said something rapidly to the interpreter.

"She says that now in these times all years are good years,"
he said.

The fishing commune sells most of its catch to Shanghai:
110,000 kilograms in 1974 and 120,000 kilograms in 1975.
Mrs. Wu and her family have an annual income of about 2,000
yuan, or about $3,800, if the yuan is figured at the official rate
of 1.90 to the dollar. They pay 12 yuan a year for maintenance
of their house. Would maintenance rise, I asked the interpreter,
recalling horror stories told by friends in New York. Of course
not, he said; as conditions improved, Mrs. Wu's maintenance
would be reduced. Suppose she wanted another house? He was
surprised at the question. Why should she? Isn't she clearly satisfied with this one?

The Chinese are supposed to be satisfied. To the party, dissatisfaction can have no cause other than subversive thoughts.
Mrs. Wu had quite evidently reached the summit of her ambitions—a house and a bouncing grandchild. Shanghai and Peking
were far away. Her world was here.

The visitor is led to ponder how long others will remain satisfied with their rewards of years of toil. Take Lu Tsu Rong, who

works in the Number Three steelworks in Shanghai. Lu was clearly more sophisticated than Mrs. Wu. He operates a crane at the steelworks, and as a laborer in one of China's most important industries, he would be classed by a foreigner, but never openly by a Chinese, as a member of the industrial elite. He was a talkative, bright-eyed man whose apartment was on the third floor of a housing development about a mile from the center of Shanghai. By mistake I had entered an apartment on the second floor. No surprises; the furniture and decorations were very similar to those in Lu's apartment upstairs.

He sat on the edge of the bed and told us about his life. His wife works in a blanket factory nearby. There were three children. The eldest, a daughter, was a student in the shipbuilding school in Shanghai. One son was working in a chemical works in the city. The second son was a student in the middle school. I asked if he was a good student. Lu thought that the boy was improving after a slow start. When he said this, his face wore the same look of worried incomprehension common to fathers all over the world when they discuss their sons. But, he added briskly, his daughter was doing very well.

Lu's apartment was an improvement on the home in the fishing village. There was a balcony looking out on a courtyard surrounded by the other apartment blocks of the housing development. In addition, the family had twenty-eight square meters of living space in two large rooms. Lu evidently lived a little higher on the hog than Mrs. Wu. His furniture was of better quality, although the pieces were the same—the large beds, the chests, the neon lights, the radio. Against one wall was the table, with its glass top holding family photographs. There was also a large ornate mirror.

The family, he said, makes about 160 yuan a month. Food from the market around the corner costs about 15 yuan. The family pays 1 yuan for electricity, 3 yuan for cooking gas, and .5 yuan for water per person each month.

I thought the expenditure for food ridiculously low and said so. Lu pointed out that he and his wife ate at least one meal a day at their factories, and sometimes two, and that these were very cheap. And food itself was reasonable, he said.

Later, I visited the shopping center where he and his wife bought their provisions and found that the food was indeed cheap. The Chinese were crowding the counters to buy vegetables, chiefly Chinese cabbage, at what I worked out to be about 5 cents per kilogram, meat at 1.70 yuan per kilogram, eggs at the same price, apples for .5 yuan per kilo, and biscuits for less than .5 yuan per kilo.

Consumer goods were more expensive. Chinese were buying silk at 4.50 yuan per meter and cotton at 1.50 yuan per meter. The shop was crowded, and I noticed that no one seemed to be there simply to look. Everyone was a customer, good natured and friendly but still a customer. Children ran from counter to counter munching biscuits.

What, I asked Lu, did he do for entertainment? He seemed surprised at the question. In the United States, I explained, a steelworker might fish on his day off, see a ball game, or simply sit, drink beer, and watch television. And, I added, he would own his apartment or house in many cases. Lu's apartment was assigned to him by his factory committee.

Well, Lu said (I thought his manner somewhat defensive), there was plenty to do in the housing development. He thought for a bit and then brightened. There was a theater. And on his day off he could listen to lectures by Communist party officials. Sometimes he and his wife went for a walk along the bund or in the parks. There was, he said, a great deal to do. Then, looking at his hands, he added, "There is always the important work we are doing."

These are but two people out of nearly a billion Chinese. How is this whole vast mass of humanity held together? What inner compulsions lead these two to accept lives that despite the improvements of the last two decades would seem to Westerners to be lives of endless drudgery?

There is a cement in Chinese life more powerful than party

ideology, more insistent than fear of the Russians, more pervasive than any state plan. If I read it aright, this cement is the timeless communal sense of the Chinese, an almost primitive clannishness that holds the individual in his own group, in which he or she can express hopes, fears, and aspirations and can attack neighbors for sloth or even ideological deviation.

The visitor stumbles on evidence of this group feeling without really looking for it. Driving back to Shanghai in the twilight that same night, I saw a row going on outside a store. An interpreter rolled down the window and listened. Someone, he said, had stolen something and accusations were being made. Would the police be called? No, that would not be necessary. Neighbors would deal with the thief. How would they deal with the thief? They would talk to him; point out the social error of robbery; and if he recanted and apologized and, of course, returned the stolen goods, he would return to his job. What if he did not and stole a second time? Then a People's Court would listen to his case, and if he were found guilty, he would have to do extra work and forego certain rights, perhaps even be given some reeducation. What if theft were combined with murder? The interpreter appeared genuinely puzzled. Only lunatics murdered, he said. Of course, a lunatic would have to be handed over to the police.

In all of the authoritarian countries I have visited or lived in, some form of secret police has been omnipresent and omnipotent: the Gestapo in Nazi Germany, the KGB in the Soviet Union, and the Savak in Iran. There is a secret police in China, the Ministry of Public Security, which combines the functions of the CIA, the FBI, and the Secret Service in the United States. Its chief is Wang Tung-hsing, a man of sixty-one who is one of the four vice-chairmen of the Communist party.

The ministry's employees are far less apparent to the foreigner and, I expect, to the average Chinese than, for example, the KGB in Russia. In that sense, China is not a police-ridden state. The secret police are employed widely and emphatically against what the government considers outright enemies of the regime. In 1976 the Gang of Four and its followers were so classified. But the ministry does not appear to supervise on a day-to-day basis the lives of the masses. It is known, however, to keep under surveillance those in senior government posts whose loyalty may be even remotely suspect. But my conclusion is that Mrs. Wu and Mr. Lu go through life without contact with the ministry or its employees, content in their belief that orders, discipline, and internal stability come naturally from the same fountain, the Communist party of the People's Republic of China.

How do we account for the present unity of China? There are three basic considerations. The first is the Soviet threat. As we shall see, the Chinese have plenty to be fearful about when they consider their immediate future. But their current apprehensions are reinforced by racial memories. There are plenty of Chinese alive who can remember Japan's rape of Nanking and the long agony of the war with Japan. Their elders or their history books have painted for the young a dire record of European and American "imperialist adventures" thrusting into the heart of China, a process that, in most Chinese eyes, did not end until the Korean War and will not end until the United States abandons Taiwan and watches that island's absorption by the People's Republic. The folk fear of the Soviet Union, therefore, is exacerbated by the memories of a turbulent two centuries in which Chinese found themselves opposed and, by their thinking, oppressed by Japanese, Russians, British, French, and Americans.

A second reason for China's present national cohesiveness may lie in a widespread recognition that order and stability are necessary if the country is to progress out of its present position as a developing power to become one of the world's superpowers. It would be an error to assume that this sentiment is confined only to the planners in Peking and provincial capitals, to the technicians who implement the planners' ideas, or to the pragmatists, headed by Chairman Hua, who now lead China.

My impression is that rather humble men and women on

communes and in factories recognize this need for order and stability. Far removed from the summit of power, they understand, surveying their own small kingdoms, that forward movement is impossible if China is to be torn apart again by new ideological and political disputes. These, the people with whom I had the most to do, are intelligent men and women. They do not need a Goebbels to ram an evident truth down their throats or a Beria to frighten them into cooperation with a national plan. Finally, of course, they know that the titanic task of moving China into the twenty-first century cannot be accomplished by a disorderly, fractious society.

But the most important force on which Chinese unity is based is much older, much more deeply imbedded in the people's history. Security presents itself to the average Chinese not as something that is imposed from above or by outside influences but by the organic character of the society as a whole. Cell grows upon cell. A half-dozen fishermen and their families, under any government, coalesce into a community for greater security, economic or political. The group becomes a brigade, a commune—call it what you will—but it merges into a more substantial structure.

Within these groupings there is a strong sense of internal discipline. Each group deals with its own sinners. Since there are no written statutes of law, the group must impose its own judgment. And the standards that may be applied will reflect to some degree the current state of the whole Chinese society. Thus, though the motivation for a judgment comes from deep in the recesses of the group character and folk experience, the judgment itself may reflect in its severity or leniency the situation of the hour.

When in 1976 the conservative wing of the party, headed by Hua, took power on Mao's death, the vilification and abuse of the Gang of Four reached extremes that it was difficult for the democratic mind to take seriously. The reason was not solely that two bitterly opposed groups had fought for power and that one, having been defeated, must be reviled. It was that the

Gang of Four or any other group considered disruptive endangered the tasks that the masses considered to have priority—the expansion of all production, agricultural and industrial, and the strengthening of the state against outside pressure.

Of Chairman Mao's many injunctions to his countrymen the one that strikes deepest into the Chinese is this: "Practice Marxism and not revisionism; unite, and don't split, be open and aboveboard and don't intrigue and conspire." As China develops, the appeals for unity and openness and the warnings against intrigue and conspiracy are likely to be considered the most important, whereas simultaneously, revisionism will be practiced under the sacred name of Marxism.

My surmise is that China's chances of accomplishing an economic miracle in the years before the end of the twentieth century depend on the government's ability to exploit the powerful national urge for rapid improvement in the position of the individual and on the role of China in the world. Essentially, it does not really matter to the masses under which political system progress is made—communist, fascist, or capitalist. What matters to Mrs. Wu and Mr. Lu is that their group, fishermen or steelworkers, rises in the world and, rising, helps the remainder of this tightly integrated society to rise. This is not the lure of rising individual expectations that has infected so many countries in the past twenty years but the attraction of progress by a whole society.

This will not be an easy task, as I have indicated in the discussion of China's economic problems. Success will lie not in the sayings of Chairman Mao but in the perceptions and energies of a vigorous and highly intelligent people for whom, I believe, Communism is simply the contemporary means of advancing the interests of those millions upon millions of humans we call the Chinese. I am not saying that China is not Communist. It manifestly is. But there are stronger, older motivations in the Chinese people than the teachings of Marx and Lenin or Mao. Properly encouraged and channeled, these will provide the power for China's expansion. Those very human desires for another room in the apartment, a higher wage at the factory, a longer visit with the old people in the south, a better bicycle— these are the motivations, for the Chinese are among the most human of peoples.

6

Siberia: Russia's Last Frontier

THE wind from the north bit deep. The colonel, huddled in his quilted greatcoat, looked angrily across the wastes that separate Manchuria from Siberia. "From the north," he said, "from the north, always from those polar bears in the north." (The "polar bears," of course, are the Russians.)

The colonel was only expressing what might be called China's universal Siberian syndrome, the obsession with a Soviet attack on Manchuria out of Siberia's Far East or a combination of attacks into China all the way from Kazakhstan in the west to Vladivostok and the Soviet Maritime Province in the east.

This is the Chinese side of the story. There is another.

In 1972, for reasons now obscure, I found myself in Vienna for the opening of the East–West Conference on Mutual and Balanced Force Reductions in Europe. One day I had lunch with a jovial Russian colonel whom I had known years before in Paris. The only time he discarded his ruthless geniality was when I mentioned the Soviet forces in Siberia.

"Nothing at this conference will affect those troops," he said. "They are there to protect Siberia. Siberia is our future."

He and other Russians are sensitive about Siberia. It is the area of the Soviet Union that would be immediately involved in any Sino-Soviet war. More important from the Russian standpoint is that it is the largest untapped reservoir of natural resources in the whole of that vast country. From the Soviet position it is essential to maintain powerful forces along the Chinese frontier for defensive, rather than offensive, purposes.

Whether we, informed Western societies, believe that the Chinese threaten Siberia is essentially irrelevant. What counts in the political-military balance is that the Russians believe it. I had a good friend, a Russian colonel from Siberia, who at our meetings never failed to voice his concern over his mother and father, who then lived in a tiny village near the Chinese frontier. He finally, at some strain on the family resources, got them out to European Russia.

In considering the Sino-Soviet confrontation, Siberia must be accounted Russia's most valuable and vulnerable real estate. Understanding the military equation in northeastern Asia is difficult unless we consider what Siberia is and could be. The other factor in the equation is, of course, what Manchuria represents to the Chinese—and to the Russians. The differences between Siberia and China are enormous and significant.

We have seen that China today is struggling against serious obstacles to attain the status of a great industrial power. It has the largest population of any country in the world: a billion by the end of this century or even by the end of the 1980s. And to the north lies Siberia, rich in natural resources, poor in people.

Siberia includes more than half the Soviet Union. It runs from the Ural Mountains (the dividing line between Europe and Asia) eastward to the Pacific and from the Kazakh Republic, Mongolia, and China north to the Arctic Ocean. The Russians, for economic purposes, divide Siberia into three areas: West Siberia, East Siberia, and the Far East. West Siberia extends from the Urals to the Yenisey River. East Siberia runs from the Yenisey to the Pacific watershed, a line that straggles around the beak of a bend in the Amur River north of China; along the western boundary of the Yakutskaya Republic north of Lake Baikal; to the Laptev Sea near the eastern end of the Taymyr Peninsula. The Far East encompasses the remaining territory stretching to the eastern sea.

Even to Americans, the areas concerned must seem enormous. The three areas of Siberia cover an area 63 percent larger than that of the continental United States. The other side of the coin, however, is population. This vast area has a population of only approximately 27 million.

The importance of Siberian resources to the Russian economy has been recognized since czarist times. But it was not until World War II and the transfer of many industries east into Siberia that governments in Moscow began to take serious action. Action was taken, it must be remembered, in many areas that the Chinese claimed. To the Chinese the development of Siberia, actual or planned, represents both a menace and a flaunting of their age-old claims.

To Moscow it must be apparent that the continued growth of the Soviet economy and of the East European economies that are dependent for many raw materials on Russia rests to a considerable degree on how fast and how far Siberia's resources are developed. Consider these factors: (1) About 80 percent of the energy used in the Soviet Union is consumed in the European part, but 80 percent of the reserves of primary energy are in Siberia. (2) The Soviet Union supplies most of the energy required by the East European satellites, largely from reserves in European Russia. (3) Energy reserves in the western Soviet Union are becoming depleted and more expensive to exploit. (4) Oil production from the extensive reserves of western Siberia is slowing down and additional reserves must be found and exploited farther east.

The Russian economy is at present in a critical situation from which only exploitation of Siberia's riches can save it. It has to import Western technology: $3.1 billion in American oil-extraction equipment since 1972 alone, some metals, computers, and, occasionally, wheat. The deficit in trade with hard-currency countries in 1975 was approximately $6.2 billion.

Why is Siberia the savior? Primarily because exports of Siberian oil, gas, timber, gold, diamonds, platinum metals, and, in the future, other metals can finance imports from the West.

Secondarily because the development of chemical complexes and other types of industry based on Siberian electric power and raw materials, a development still some years in the future, can reduce the Soviet Union's dependence on some imports from the West. In the end, Russia will be as near self-sufficiency as is possible in an era of economic interdependence.

This, then, is the Russian dilemma. Siberia lies there, rich in resources, poor in population. And to the south is a restless, populous China avid for more raw materials and for living space. I do not believe that contemporary China has any imperialist designs on Siberia. But as my Russian friend who was worried about his parents asked, what will be the situation ten years from now?

How much can the Russians do in a decade? An American would assume they can do a great deal. After all, consider the development of the United States west of the Mississippi in the decade after the Civil War. But Siberia is not the American West. A large part of Siberia, especially the western area, is swamp and lakes. In the north, Russian pioneers have from the start had to battle with the permafrost zone, with watery soil that freezes and thaws, buckles, and heaves. As a result, construction of roads, airfields, and buildings is extremely difficult. In the east of Siberia the conditions are even worse. The permafrost in the Yakutsk Basin is about 4,900 feet deep. Temperatures vary from $-80°$ to $90°F$. In some areas the winter winds gust up to ninety miles an hour.

These conditions explain why both the czarist and Communist governments have had to offer special incentives to draw workers to Siberia. At present, these incentives include higher wages, longer vacations, increased pension rights, and privileges in education and housing. They do not suffice. Years ago a Russian friend told me that his elder daughter, a chemist, had "volunteered"—he used the word with a sardonic smile—to go to Siberia to run a bakery. And when would she return? As soon as they will let her, he said.

The harsh fact is that the totalitarian Soviet government has not been able to attract and hold a skilled labor force in Siberia. The Ust'Ilinks pulp and paper combine in the Irkutsk region of eastern Siberia was built with Bulgarian, East German, Polish, and Rumanian help with about two thousand of the twenty-six thousand workers, and those the most skilled, coming from those East European countries. Under these conditions the development of Siberia as an economic entity within the Soviet Union has been slow and uneven. In 1940 the share of the eastern regions of Siberia in Russia's total industrial production was about 8 percent. By 1974 it had risen to a shade over 10 percent. However, the annual average growth in Siberian industrial production during the period from 1960 to 1974 was 8.8 percent, a bit ahead of the national average of 8.2 percent.

Although about three-fourths of the timber resources of the Soviet Union are located in Siberia, the area's lumber output has grown very slowly. There are extensive coal fields, but here again, output has been disappointing. The steel and chemical industries, which showed signs of growth in the immediate postwar years, have slowed down. Capital investment has increased since 1965, up by 16 percent in 1974, but the results are not what Moscow expected. It is not surprising that Chinese technicians, well aware of Siberia's resources, believe that they could do better.

In the last five years the Russians have accelerated capital investment in Siberia. This change of pace, some Western intelligence services believe, is related to the deep-seated and, to me, irrational Russian fear of the Chinese. Obviously, Siberia would be a more defensible country if its communications and transportation were improved, if its industrial centers could provide equipment for the Soviet forces in its Far East.

Another reason for the Soviet drive for Siberian economic development must be, however, a realization that Russia cannot grow economically and cannot supply its allies in East Europe without major economic developments in Siberia. I have mentioned what intelligence sources call the 80–80 factor, meaning that 80 percent of the energy in the Soviet Union is consumed in

European Russia and 80 percent of the fuel and power resources are located in Siberia. Russia in Europe has about reached the end of its energy potential. The Siberian potential must be developed. It is either that or, as a French oil-company executive said in Damascus, "The Russians must go for the oil in the Middle East."

In exploiting Siberia's energy resources, the Soviets will face the same problem encountered by the Chinese—heavy capital investment. But it is not enough for a minister in Moscow to ordain that such and such an oil field be exploited. The quality of the resources may be better, and the quantity greater than in European Russia, but equipment, materials, and consumer goods must be hauled thousands of miles; roads, housing, and services must be established at great cost; and, when the resources are tapped, their movement to users will be appallingly expensive. A study by Alan B. Smith for the Congressional Joint Economic Committee quoted Michael Pervukhin of the Soviet State Planning Committee as saying, "Outlays on the extraction of Tyumen gas are 6.6 rubles per ton of standard fuel, but when the gas is transported to Sverdlovsk, the figures rise to 13.1 rubles, [and] if it goes to Moscow, outlays are 15.3 rubles. The shipping of Kuznetsk Basin coal increases outlays per ton of standard fuel from 8.6 rubles at the place of extraction to 14.1 rubles in Sverdlovsk and 18.5 rubles in Moscow."

Nevertheless, the energy reserves in the east are of immense importance to Moscow and its allies in East Europe. Their exploitation could be of advantage to fuel-hungry Japan. For the Chinese, a booming Siberian economy based on oil means that in time China will be faced with a modern industrial entity, one capable of supporting a major military effort, on its northern frontier.

Siberia's production of oil and natural gas today is far from fulfilling these dreams. But the reserves are there, and they are very large indeed. Soviet government figures say that Siberia's explored reserves of natural gas are roughly two-thirds of all explored reserves in the Soviet Union. Most of these are in northern Tyumen near the Ob Gulf. The Urengoy field, the world's largest, has reserves estimated at 4 to 6 trillion cubic meters. Drilling for the development of this field began in 1975. The Russians, perhaps optimistically, planned to begin commercial production in 1978.

The Soviet Union does not publish statistics on its oil reserves. Intelligence analysts, however, are confident that the Siberian reserves are very large and that their development is being maximized by the government, which recognizes that the older fields in European Russia and central Asia have passed their peak. Most of Siberia's oil production comes from the Samotlor field in West Siberia, which has reserves estimated at more than 2 billion tons, or approximately 2.5 times those of Alaska's North Slope.

The Soviet Union did not begin intensified production of Siberian oil and gas, or indeed of other products, until the mid-1960s. The original production targets for West Siberia were 125 million tons of oil and 44 billion cubic meters of gas in 1975. Oil production reached nearly 150 million tons that year and was nearly 30 percent of the total Soviet output. The position in the development of natural-gas resources was less satisfactory. The installation of pipelines and the development of the fields themselves has gone slowly, and production for 1975 was about 38 billion cubic meters, well below the planned goal.

The Twenty-fifth Congress of the Communist party of the Soviet Union, which met in Moscow in March 1976, adopted plans that illuminate Russia's hopes for Siberian energy production. The target for 1980 was set at 300 to 310 million tons of oil, approximately half of the anticipated national production in that year.

As every student of Soviet economic growth knows, wild discrepancies often occur between targets and realities. By all accounts, the rate of development in the Siberian oil fields has not continued at its earlier, headlong rate, and construction continues to be impeded by the cost of materials and shortages of skilled labor. It may be that the Siberian fields will do well to produce 230 million tons by the start of the next decade.

To a considerable degree the same difference exists between planned production of natural gas, 125 to 155 billion cubic meters in 1980, and the realities of the production situation. There is no doubt that the gas is there. There is a great deal of doubt over the Russians' ability to overcome the obstacles of climate and terrain and current shortages of large-diameter pipe.

As are other advanced industrial states, the Soviet Union is in a situation in which oil production and consumption move faster than the discovery of new reserves. For the Russian oil industry to move ahead at a rate commensurate with production and demand, oil fields larger than those of West Siberia will have to be developed. In consequence, the Soviets have begun a giant exploration drive in East Siberia, where, of course, the weather and the terrain are, if anything, worse than they are to the west and where the logistic problems appear almost insurmountable without foreign help.

The natural-gas situation is slightly easier. In the Vilyuy Basin, proved and probable reserves of 700 billion cubic meters of gas have been found, although oil has not been discovered in marketable quantities. This is an area where foreign assistance is urgently needed. In March 1976 the Soviet government signed agreements for $25 million each from a consortium of U.S. companies and from Japan, to cover exploration over the basin in the following two or three years. The Americans and the Japanese have discussed with the Russians the export of approximately 10 billion cubic meters of gas a year from East Siberia to the West Coast and to Japan. To fulfill such a commitment, the Soviet Union would have to conquer the serious logistic problems in the area.

Massive problems of extraction and transportation also face the Russians in implementing their schemes to exploit oil reserves off the Siberian coasts. The offshore reserves off the Sakhalin Peninsula have been estimated at close to 3 billion tons, in water up to 330 feet deep. The Russians are also believed to have located substantial reserves offshore in the Kara, Laptev, East Siberian, and Chuckchi seas. The last two, incidentally, may be extensions of the Alaskan North Slope deposits.

If Russia intends to exploit these resources, a heavy investment in Western (chiefly American) equipment, technology, and experience will be necessary. Until now the Soviet experience with the exploitation of offshore oil has been in the relatively shallow waters of the Black and Caspian seas. But, as American oil experts emphasize, the Russians need Western technology to speed the search for, and the exploration of, onshore as well as offshore reserves. The Soviet Union lacks sufficient supplies of sophisticated geophysical tools, such as modern seismic equipment and computerized field units.

According to a report to Congress, ''Without such equipment, Soviet capability to locate deep structures is limited. Poor quality drill bits, underpowered mud pumps, and shortages of good quality pipe for drilling and casing [to say nothing of large-diameter pipe] are factors contributing to inefficient operations in this field.''

Between 1972 and 1977 the Soviet Union purchased approximately $3.1 billion in oil equipment in the United States. If the Siberian fields are to be exploited, then the Soviet Union will have to find the foreign exchange necessary for further purchases.

China, as we have seen, hopes not only to feed its expanding industrial economy with its own oil but also to export fuel. Similar hopes are held by the Russians, based mainly on their expectations of future production from Siberian fields. For Moscow, oil exports are the largest single source of hard-currency foreign exchange. In 1975 the Soviet Union exported nearly 39 million tons of oil to hard-currency countries, mostly in Western Europe, and earned close to $3.2 billion in the process. Total Soviet crude-oil and petroleum products exports that year amounted to about 130 million tons—60 percent to other Communist countries and 40 percent to non-Communist states. The East European Communist states, with the exception of Rumania, which is self-sufficient, rely heavily on Russian oil.

The Soviets also are counting on natural-gas exports as a source of foreign exchange. In 1975 about 19 billion cubic meters were exported, 11 billion to Eastern Europe and 8 billion to Western Europe. The sales of the latter earned nearly $210 million in hard currency.

Oil and natural gas clearly are the most important Siberian products both as part of the Asian geopolitical equation and as a key element in the Soviet Union's industrial development. However, Siberia has other resources that not only feed the advanced industries of European Russia but also earn the hard currency that the Soviet Union needs. Wood and wood products, gold (gold reserves, like those of oil, are a state secret), and diamonds are other "earners." Moscow has ordained a major expansion of the copper and nickel industry in the Norilsk area. By the middle of the 1980s, production in this area could exceed 300,000 tons annually, or about 20 percent more than the 1977 output of Canada, currently the world's largest producer.

One other important Siberian resource is electric power. Siberia, with roughly 40 percent of the Soviet Union's surface-water resources, has an enormous hydroelectric-power potential. Once exploited, it can be used not only to help develop Siberian industry but as a source of cheap energy for much of European Russia. According to a congressional study, the Angara-Yenisey region of East Siberia alone contains one-fourth of the Soviet Union's total hydroelectric resources. The Russians estimate that this can be developed economically to produce almost 300 billion kilowatt-hours of cheap electricity annually.

Development has been rapid. The plant at Bratsk on the Angara River, with a capacity of 4,100 megawatts, was the world's largest hydroelectric plant when it was completed in 1966. Since then it has been overtaken by the 6,000-megawatt plant on the Yenisey, the Soviet Union's largest today. The installed capacity of hydroelectric power plants in the Angara-

Yenisey region, now approximately 12,880 megawatts, is expected to reach 20,000 megawatts by 1985 and possibly 60,000 by the end of the century.

The last in this estimate of Siberian resources is coal. Over 60 percent of the Soviet Union's explored reserves of coal are in Siberia and the Far East. Present plans call for the use of this coal for the production of thermal power. A complex of thermal-power plants is to be fueled by cheap coal from the Kansk-Archansk deposits, which lie for several hundred miles along both sides of the Trans-Siberian Railroad east and west of the Yenisey River at Krasnoyarsk. This basin has not yet been completely explored, but Russian government experts estimate that it contains no less than 1.2 trillion tons of coal and that by 1980 it will be producing approximately 350 million tons annually.

Siberia, then, is a land of almost limitless resources. But, to turn potential into reality, transportation and communications are essential. The Soviet experience in World War II resulted in the establishment of a series of airfields across Siberia and the improvement of the northern and eastern ports, but internal land transportation continues to be a major problem.

The Baikal–Amur Mainline (BAM) Railway is probably the most important project undertaken by the Soviet government to overcome this problem. The railway will run nearly two thousand miles from Ust-Kut on the Lena River to Komsomolsk on the Amur River. At Komsomolsk the line will connect with the railway running to Vladivostok via Khabarovsk. The length of the railway is roughly 2.5 times that of the Alaska pipeline, and the line is being built under comparable conditions of climate and terrain. When completed in 1983 the line will cross seven mountain ranges, a number of large rivers, and more than thirteen hundred miles of permafrost.

BAM's importance to the Siberian economy will be immense. The area between the new line and the Trans-Siberian Railway will be opened up, allowing the copper deposits of Ukodan, with a potential of 400,000 tons of refined copper annually, to be exploited. Asbestos in Buryatskaya, timber for pulp and paper in the Far East, iron ore from the Aldan area, and coal from the South Yakutsk Basin are all resources whose exploitation will be facilitated by the completion of BAM.

Ironically, BAM was first planned for the transport of oil from West Siberia to the Far East, where it would be refined and exported. But permafrost is a major problem over nearly three hundred miles of the railroad. The Russians concluded that, instead, pipeline must be laid to insure a steady flow of oil to the coast.

By any standards, BAM is one of the major construction works of this century. It also is the principal means by which the riches of Siberia can be made available to both the Soviet Union and the countries bordering the Pacific. BAM also will contribute significantly to the development of Siberia itself.

Over five years, 13,000 skilled workers and 4,280 college graduates are scheduled to be trained and then induced to settle along the route. According to *Gateway to Siberian Resources: The BAM*, by Theodore Shabad and Victor J. Mote, the inducements will be higher wages, lump-sum payments to families moving into the area, and special loans.

Building the railroad has involved the construction of earthworks of 222 million cubic meters. The builders deployed 7,440 eight-ton trucks, 1,200 excavators, 835 cranes, and 950 mobile compressors. The railway has consumed each year 80 million bricks, 400,000 tons of road metal ballast, 11 million cubic feet of rock, and 40,000 tons of lime; 5,000 tons of corrugated iron will be used annually during construction to build water pipes. The total cost on completion in 1983 is estimated at $1.5 billion, although in Siberia, as elsewhere in the world, cost overruns are expected. Part of the cost is being financed by credits from Japan for the purchase of equipment, building materials, and ships. These are to be repaid by future deliveries to Japan of Siberian coal, natural gas, and timber.

For the Chinese, BAM has great political and military significance. Politically, it allies Japan, the major industrial power in

East Asia, with the Soviet Union in a project that, once completed, will speed the economic development of Siberia. Militarily, it will facilitate the lateral movement of Soviet forces over a railway more distant from China and less vulnerable than the Trans-Siberian. This, in theory at least, increases the number of Soviet options for possible routes of attack on China.

The popular Soviet view is that the Chinese, when they look at Siberia, see a vast, underpopulated, underdeveloped area into which they can pour their excess millions. This was not my impression after talks with military and diplomatic officials in China. Their emphasis was on the tremendous economic potential of Siberia and the implications for China's future of the area's development. They recognize that the Soviet Union is today well ahead of China in industrial development. The successful exploitation of Siberia's resources—and the opening of BAM will expedite that process—could mean that China would be unable to catch up to its main rival in the Communist world in the industrial field. The Chinese vision of a nation that in the year 2000 is the economic and military equal of the Soviet Union and the United States would be dashed.

These are long-term considerations. To the officers huddled in their greatcoats near the frontier and to staff officers in the Ministry of Defense in Peking, Siberia is the area from which a Soviet attack is most likely to be launched. The Pacific ports shelter the fleet that could drive Chinese naval and merchant shipping from the seas. The industrial complexes of northern China are within range of the missile sites and airfields built across Siberia in the last decade. The armored and mechanized divisions beyond the frontier represent the most powerful ground army that China has ever faced.

7

Soviet Military Preparations

UP to this point, the focus has been on the Chinese, on the PLA gazing apprehensively north toward the great land mass of Siberia. What is the view from what Wellington called "the other side of the hill"? What forces have the Russians amassed along the long frontier? What would be their strategy and tactics in the event of war? What are the problems to be overcome by Russian forces seeking victory?

The demographic and geographic conditions in any Sino-Soviet war impose certain strategic imperatives on each side. Although the Russians have fortified their positions, the Soviet armed forces' tactics for a war in Europe call for a blitzkrieg of greater strength and velocity than the great German offensive of 1940. It is highly unlikely that the Soviet tactical approach to a war with China differs from their European blitzkrieg concept in any important respect. What can be anticipated is that an offensive against China would be even more violent in the sense that it would involve a greater use of missiles with nuclear and conventional warheads than an invasion of Western Europe.

A Soviet offensive against China, it is reasonable to assume, would be localized. Relatively cheap victories could be won by qualitatively superior forces in Mongolia or farther west. But the principal target for an offensive would have to be the Peking area and Manchuria. Wars are won by going for the jugular.

The northeastern quarter of China, including the Peking area and Manchuria, in the words of a CIA report, is "the most important industrial region of the country and a nationally significant and still developing center of agricultural production." A very high proportion of China's population, including most of the technologically advanced workers; the best railroads, highways, and waterways; and much of the heavy industry, including armaments plants, are located in this area. The Russians know that successful thrusts into the Peking area and what is called the Manchurian Plain would cripple China. This does not mean that all resistance would cease. The theory and practice of successful guerrilla warfare are deeply rooted in Chinese military thinking. It does mean that success in these areas would rob the Chinese of the bases, both industrial and geographical, for fighting a modern war against the invaders.

The idea of a Russian offensive into the Manchurian Plain and the Peking area awakens a curious echo of the past. In 1941, Adolf Hitler and his generals, contemplating an invasion of the Soviet Union, planned along similar lines. Storm or isolate Leningrad, seize Moscow, drive southeastward into the Donetz Basin and the oil fields, and the war would be won. What would it matter if Stalin transferred the government to some remote central-Asian refuge? The areas of Russia that could generate great military power would be in German hands.

As they are now constituted, the Soviet forces facing China are more formidable than those that would be required solely for defense against Chinese attack. This is especially true when the Russian capabilities in missiles and modern aircraft are considered.

Deployed around Chita, Khabarovsk, and Vladivostok is a sizable force of SS-12 surface-to-surface missiles with a range of five hundred miles and a warhead yield of about one megaton. Along the eastern stretches of the Trans-Siberian Railway, the Soviets have deployed about two hundred SS-4s with about twice the range of the SS-12 and a comparable yield. Farther west lie another 150 or more SS-9s, intercontinental ballistic missiles (ICBMs) with ranges of seventy-five hundred miles that can be armed with up to 18 nuclear reentry vehicles. It is quite probable that in the event of a war with China, and China alone, the Russians would reprogram some of their ICBMs in European Russia to hit targets in China. The SS-9s and the heavier weapons farther west are deployed in hardened silos.

Air power is the most mobile element in any national armament. Assessment of Soviet air power along the four thousand miles of frontier with China must include the probability that Russian air strength would be doubled in a very short period, provided—and it is a major proviso—that the Soviet Union was not faced simultaneously with a war in Europe.

The minimum figure for Russian aircraft deployed in Asia is nine hundred. Some estimates, perhaps influenced by the Chinese, run as high as fourteen hundred. Whatever the quantity, there is no doubt that the Russian high command has steadily improved the quality of the Far East air force. There are three to four squadrons of MIG-23s in the Vladivostok area, an equal number of SU-19s, the best of the Russian ground attack fighters, and at least two squadrons of the high-altitude MIG-25 reconnaissance-interceptors. There is some photographic evidence that the TU V-G bomber, known to the West as the Backfire, has visited airfields in the Soviet Maritime Province. Whether the visits were proving flights or presaged the establishment of a powerful long-range bomber force in East Asia is not known. But under war conditions, the Backfire could fly to East Siberian airfields from European Russia in less than a day.

The Russians shield their forward airfields and missile bases from Chinese attack with an air defense system at least 130 miles in depth running east and west, north of the frontier, from the Pacific almost to the Caspian Sea. The system is intended to protect the Trans-Baikal and Far Eastern military districts from Chinese air attack. Chinese bombers would have to penetrate a three-tier radar curtain directed and controlled from Khabarovsk and avoid hundreds of surface-to-air missile sites, most of them stocked with SA-6 missiles.

The Soviet preparations for offensive missile warfare, nuclear or conventional, and for defensive warfare against Chinese missiles or bombers must be reckoned as reasonably complete and efficient. But the ground army is the dominant force in Russian military politics, and it is the ground army that would be the cutting edge of an invasion of China.

The frontier runs from Sinkiang east to the Pacific. Although the Chinese are rich in manpower, they are poor in modern arms; it is, thus, manifestly impossible for them to maintain a strong defense everywhere along the frontier. The Soviets, then, with a superior capability to concentrate and strike, have a choice of invasion points.

They are restricted by what, to Russians, appears a shortage of manpower. The Russians have forty-three divisions in the Central Asian, Trans-Baikal, Siberian, and Far East military districts. About half of these, including five armored divisions, are in what the Russians call Category I; that is, they have all their weapons and equipment and are at between 75 percent and 100 percent of war strength. Of the remainder, about half are in Category II, or at between half and three-quarters strength in personnel complete with all combat vehicles. The remainder are in Category III, or at about one-third of war strength and equipped with largely obsolescent fighting vehicles.

The Russian armored divisions each include approximately 315 tanks, T-54s or the more modern T-62s. The newest Soviet tank, the T-72, is deployed in increasing numbers in Central Europe, but there is no hard evidence that it has appeared on Russia's eastern front.

The Soviet mechanized rifle divisions, which make up most of the remaining divisions, have, like their counterparts in Central Europe, taken on added tanks, guns, and manpower. The Category-I divisions now have approximately 260 tanks and 370 armored personnel carriers, which provide Russian infantry with greater mobility.

In the event of a war that did not involve operations in Central Europe, the Siberian Far East front could be reinforced by the transfer of some of the twenty-four Soviet divisions in the North Caucasus, Trans-Caucasus, and Turkestan military districts. At the same time, reservists resident in the Far East would be called to fill the ranks of the Category-II and Category-III divisions in the area.

The ground forces can be expected to receive the T-72 tank, once European requirements have been met, and the new self-propelled artillery pieces, which are a departure from the truck- and tractor-drawn guns of the past. Some of the guns now deployed can fire nuclear ammunition. The principal surface-to-surface missiles supporting the ground forces are the Frog 4s, 5s, 6s, and 7s, with ranges of up to 70 miles.

Two airborne divisions with their own light tanks, artillery, and transport and a combined strength of about fifteen thousand men are stationed near Khabarovsk. Until about 1974, Western intelligence analysts assumed that the most modern Soviet ground-forces weapons and equipment would be sent to the group of Soviet forces in Germany and that comparable equipment would not reach the Siberian divisions until all the European requirements had been met. Recent events, including the testimony of Lt. Victor Bilenko, a defecting Soviet MIG-25 pilot, that aircraft of that type were now stationed in the Maritime Province have altered the intelligence view. It is now regarded as probable, although not certain, that some of the new Russian T-72 tanks have been deployed in the armies in the Far East.

Superficially, the Soviet military position is strong: missiles from ICBMs to SAMs that are more sophisticated than anything the Chinese are likely to deploy, a qualitatively superior air force operating from well-protected bases, a Pacific fleet of one hundred submarines and sixty major surface combat units, and armored and mechanized rifle divisions equipped with weapons far superior to those of the Chinese.

There are, however, glaring weaknesses in the Soviet position. The Trans-Siberian Railway is vulnerable to guerrilla attacks. When BAM is completed, it, too, will share this vulnerability, although once in operation, BAM would move the main military lifeline farther north and increase the logistical capacity of the Siberian railroad system. Completion of the BAM line is essential to the Russians. They cannot now maintain their forty-three divisions in the Far East on the service of the dual-tracked Trans-Siberian Railway alone.

Forty-three ground divisions with their essential headquarters would amount, once fully mobilized, to well over half a million men. The daily support requirement for a force of that size, by American estimates, would be between forty thousand and fifty thousand tons of supplies of all types. In World War II many of the Russian divisions smashing through Poland into Germany got along on half of that tonnage. But they were moving through, and unrestrainedly looting, relatively rich areas. There will be very little to live off in Siberia or Manchuria.

The Russians are not going to fight unscathed. One American estimate puts Soviet casualties at just under five thousand each twenty-four hours. Some, perhaps half, of these will be able to return to action within two weeks. Even so, nearly thirty-five thousand soldiers would have to be replaced during that period to maintain the ground forces at the initial attacking strength.

As presently operated, the railroad system in Siberia, using this term to cover the lines serving the entire battlefront, cannot meet these demands. American experts calculate that the Trans-Siberian Railway can handle thirty trains moving twelve thousand tons of supplies a day in each direction. In a long campaign even sixty trains operating out of the Pacific bases would probably be unable to support operations, especially if the rail lines were subject, as it is reasonable to assume they would be, to guerrilla and even airborne attacks by the Chinese. The answer, already grasped by the NATO allies in Western Europe, is the stockpiling of supplies in the Maritime Province for distribution in time of war to the various fronts or, in my opinion, the one major front, Manchuria. Stockpiling, of course, is wasteful; weapons, ammunition, food, and fuel deteriorate in storage.

The alternative is supply by sea to Vladivostok and other

ports. The Russians, of course, recognize this alternative. But recognition and accomplishment are vastly different. Winston Churchill once said that the Russians are land animals. They have no experience in transporting large quantities of troops and military supplies by sea as do the Americans and British. The obstacles to swift and regular replenishment of the ground and air forces in Siberia would be formidable.

The weather is uncertain and at times forbidding. The Russians have little experience with, or equipment for, the unloading of large cargoes of materiel. And finally there is what Field Marshal Alexander called "the unassailable enemy"—distance.

Philip A. Petersen, an American expert, has pointed out that it is roughly fourteen thousand nautical miles from Murmansk or Leningrad to Vladivostok via the Cape of Good Hope and nine thousand nautical miles from the Crimea to Vladivostok through the Suez Canal. Given a sailing rate of twelve knots, which is very good time for a convoy, the journey from the Black Sea would take a month and from Murmansk or Leningrad almost fifty days.

Moreover, Vladivostok is not operational as a port the year round, and even Odessa on the Black Sea is closed by ice for about two months each winter. Then, it is estimated that it would take six and a half twenty-four-hour days to unload the normal cargo ship carrying perhaps 5,600 tons of supplies. Petersen estimates that to meet all the requirements of the forty-three divisions in Siberia, the Russians would have to allocate 460 cargo ships to the supply effort, hoping that at least 46 merchantmen would be in port and unloading at any given time.

All this would have to be accomplished in the teeth of what could be expected to be an unrelenting attack by those Chinese submarines that had survived the initial Russian attack on their bases. Even when we grant the technological advantage of the Russians in antisubmarine operations, it is reasonable to assume that some Chinese submarines would get through. Whatever the defensive measures, some bombers, submarines, or tanks *always* get through.

There are other, equally problematical, ways of attacking the Soviet logistical problems for a war in Siberia. One, and perhaps the most farfetched, is to combine sea and road transport. Supplies and reinforcements could be brought from Murmansk and Archangel across the Arctic sea lanes, icebound in winter, to the Lena River. From there they could move as far south as Yakutsk. Transport thereafter would have to be by road, a hazardous journey, because Yakutsk is not connected by railroad with the Sino-Soviet frontier areas.

Another means of supply is by air. The Soviet Union has an air-transport force of about fifteen hundred planes, the majority of them to be conscripted in war from Aeroflot, the national airline. Resupply and reinforcement by air presents an attractive picture. It is fast. If the receiving bases are safe, it is secure. It is also of minimal use. The most recent example of massive resupply by air was demonstrated in the Arab-Israeli war of 1973. The two greatest air powers in the world, the United States and the Soviet Union, launched massive airlifts. What was the outcome? The United States moved 22,395 tons of supplies in 566 round trips, and the Russians approximately 15,000 tons in 934 round trips, in neither case enough to support the Soviet Siberian forces for a day. These flights were not harassed by hostile air forces or guerrilla operations against the receiving airfields. Such conditions could not be assured in a Sino-Soviet war. Americans will recall what happened to some of the airfields in Vietnam. The threats to a Soviet airlift into bases along the frontier or in China itself would be serious.

The Soviet advantage in a war with China is probably greater at sea than in the air or on the ground. The Soviet Pacific fleet is second only to its northern fleet, based on Murmansk, in size and modernity. The core of the fleet is a force of 100 submarines, of which about 30 are ballistic-missile boats and about 60 major surface combatants of a thousand tons or more. There are also approximately 140 minor surface combatants, of which some 40 are armed with missiles, about 90 are minesweepers and minelayers, 20 are amphibious landing craft, and 200 are auxiliaries. The Pacific fleet, like the other Soviet fleets, has its own naval air force and attached naval infantry (i.e., marine) units.

Since the mid-sixties the Soviet Pacific fleet has relied for ships on vessels built in Siberia. Occasionally, a unit is transferred from other Soviet fleets. In 1976 a Krivak-class missile destroyer and two Ropucha-class landing craft joined the fleet from Europe. The Arctic route along the north coast of Siberia also has been used for the transfer of naval craft, including submarines, during the short ice-free period in summer.

Vladivostok is the main Pacific-fleet base. Located at the southern end of the Muraiev Peninsula, it is close to the mouth of the Ussuri River and within one hundred miles of the Chinese and North Korean frontiers. Vladivostok is not only fleet headquarters but also has a large submarine school and building yards. A newer base is at Sovetskaya Gavan, three hundred miles east of Khabarovsk on the coast inside Sakhalin and, consequently, less vulnerable to attack by Chinese aircraft. The Pacific fleet uses the base for submarines, destroyers, and light, fast patrol craft. There is a small shipbuilding yard, repair facilities, and a submarine school on the base. A minor base has been built at Korsakov at the southern end of Sakhalin, chiefly to service a recently enlarged naval air station located there.

The Pacific fleet's other major naval base, in addition to Vladivostok, is at Petropavlovsk, on the northeast coast of the Kamchatka Peninsula. This base, which can accommodate major surface combatant vessels and submarines, is ringed by a number of naval air stations.

Soviet naval power in the northwestern Pacific is far superior to that of the Chinese or Japanese. In the event of a war, its mission would be to drive the Chinese fleet off the seas and establish a blockade from Vladivostok south to Vietnam. The second phase of the scenario would see the Russians using their naval power to attack China's coastal air and naval bases and civilian ports. One estimate is that the Soviets would need about two weeks to eliminate the Chinese fleet as a fighting element, drive China's commercial shipping off the seas, and close the great ports of China's east coast.

Adding and subtracting military assets is an interesting exercise. But geography has almost as much to do with strategy as do the force levels on each side, just as weapons to a large extent dictate tactics. Considering geography, force levels, and the distribution of China's industrial bases, a Soviet attack on China would be most likely to concentrate on Manchuria. Such a strategy would not exclude feints elsewhere along the long frontier to pin down Chinese reserves. But the principal objective would be Manchuria. There, although the geography is forbidding, conquest offers the richest prizes in terms of raw materials and established industry, much of it built by the Russians. Moreover, Soviet ground and air forces established in Manchuria and supported by the Pacific fleet would be in a favorable position to launch a second offensive.

In the west, north, and east the Manchurian frontier is covered by mountains. Such areas pose difficulties for invading armies, because they raise formidable logistics problems. Mountainous regions also favor guerrilla activities, on whose success the Chinese place great faith. But no mountains are impassable. And south of the mountains lies the Manchurian Plain, covering most of the central part of the province. Beyond it is the Liaotung Peninsula, with the thriving industrial areas in and around An Shan and Mukden, the naval port of Port Arthur, and the busy commercial port of Dairen. Across the base of the peninsula there is more open ground leading to Peking, Tientsin, and China's most populous industrial centers. This region is protected to the north and west by mountains and by the Great Wall, so that the axis of attack into it would probably be westward along the coastal plain.

Interestingly, even today the Chinese count on the Great Wall as a security factor. This may be the result of their ignorance of the power of modern conventional explosives. A good demolition team could, in a morning, blow gaps in the wall through which an armored division could pass by nightfall.

The open ground leading to the Peking–Tientsin region is not all easygoing. There are tidal swamps along the coast and to the west and south of Tientsin. However, the easiest avenue of approach, and the one likely to be most heavily held by the Chinese, is that which runs southwestward from the Vladivostok area across the base of the Liaotung Peninsula into the Peking–Tientsin sector. Moving north of the Yalu River, the Russians would be in terrain suitable for large-scale tank operations, the very type of attack that they have emphasized in the majority of their training exercises. But, to repeat, this is the area that the Chinese, who can read a map as well as the Russians, are most likely to defend in strength and in depth.

Some American specialists have emphasized that the Amur River would present a formidable obstacle to the Soviet army. The Russians, however, faced with river barriers in Western Europe (the Elbe, the Rhine) and in the Far East (the Yalu), have invested millions of rubles in devising machinery and tactics to cross rivers. The Egyptian army, for example, crossed the Suez Canal in 1973 employing equipment and tactics that had been devised by their Russian tutors. And the Egyptians did it against the Israelis, who are brave, ingenious fighters.

Every attack opens the way to a counterattack, if not in the immediate area, then somewhere else along a battlefront. Clearly, there are abundant opportunities for the Chinese to divert Soviet reserves from an attack from the Vladivostok region on the peninsula and Peking by launching their own offensives from northern Manchuria.

Geography and tactics are two of the factors in any military equation. The other two, no less important, are morale and generalship. Like all generalities, this is open to historical refutation. The morale of Lee's tattered Army of Northern Virginia in the last months of the American Civil War was accounted equal to, and in some respects superior to, that of the better-armed, better-fed bluecoats of the Army of the Potomac. Napoleon and his marshals were one of the great commands of all time; it was unthinkable that they could be beaten in a battle in which the numbers and weight of metal were approximately equal. But in the end they were whipped at Waterloo by a straight-thinking fox hunter named Wellington, who was never mesmerized by dreams of glory.

What of Russian morale in a war with China? There is no reason to suppose that Soviet morale would be as bad as it was during the opening months of the German invasion in 1941 or that it would approach the sorry state of American morale, particularly in the supply areas, during the last months in Vietnam.

Lt. Gen. Samuel V. Wilson, until recently director of the Defense Intelligence Agency, summarized the basic rationale for a Soviet attack on China. His assessment also supports the belief that the Russians would fight as well in that invasion as they have done innumerable times in defense of Mother Russia.

General Wilson said, ''What I am trying to get across is the conviction which I hold that the Soviets' bad dream is a China, Communist China, ten years from now with a nuclear capable force able to reach major Soviet European cities, and a force on the ground which has steadily been improved to the extent that a conflict between the Soviet Union and China would become a fairly awesome proposition. . . . I think it weighs very heavily in their [Russian] military and strategic considerations.''

Lt. Gen. DeWitt C. Smith, Jr., then head of the Army War College, gave another assessment of the Soviet army in Siberia. ''It is an army that has been built without any reduction of Soviet forces in the west,'' he pointed out, ''a fact that cannot be ignored by either NATO or China. It is nearly as modern as the [Soviet] armies in the west. It is, as are all Soviet-built armies, an offensive instrument, but now in dug-in defensive positions. It is deployed astride the major avenues of advance into northern China and Manchuria. It appears to be an army which is both equipped and postured to execute classical armored thrusts deep into the Chinese homeland as well as to defend the Soviet motherland with its critical cities, ports, and rail lines which lie close to the border. It seems the Soviets are sending a very clear signal to the Chinese leadership.''

The presence of this army, General Smith pointed out, "tells the Chinese that they must not look to force as a means of settling any of the outstanding issues, ideological, political or territorial, between themselves and the Soviet Union, that any indication of an attempt to do so *can be and will be preempted by violent Soviet attack*" (author's emphasis).

He continued, "Next it cautions the Chinese leadership against any temptation to use force to influence China's southern neighbors against Soviet interests in that region. Finally, it warns the Chinese against any close military relationship with either the United States or Japan or both.

"If it is the Soviets' political objective to neutralize the People's Republic of China, to isolate her from natural allies, to reduce her influence outside her borders, the Soviet eastern armies appear to be making a major contribution to the accomplishment of that objective."

To these reflections must be added the immense and growing importance of Siberia to the Soviet economy and the fears of its inhabitants about Chinese invasion. The Soviet Union is a rigid, totalitarian state. But no state, no matter how totalitarian, can fail to listen to the pleas of its people. The inducements offered to settlers in Siberia, especially technical workers, may well be outweighed by the fear that their lives may be forfeited to the Chinese hordes in the south. The Russians have good reason to fear the future China and, consequently, a rationale for contemplating a preemptive war.

It would be prudent to assume that the morale of Soviet army and air force troops involved in a war with China would be high. But morale, although important, is only part of the equation on which military effectiveness is based. Training is another factor in that equation, and the Soviet training system is considered the weakest part of Russia's enormous military establishment.

Manpower for the Soviet army is provided by a system of universal military service. Under the current law, which went into effect in 1968, men are conscripted at the age of eighteen for a minimum of two years of active service. The earlier system called up men of nineteen for a three-year period. The change was apparently the result of pressure from the economic ministries for more men to be made available for training for the civilian economy. It was strenuously opposed by the Soviet military chiefs, who saw the reduction as leading to lower training standards in an era when more-sophisticated weapons were being deployed by ground forces.

One result was a significant expansion and intensification of training programs before the conscript joins the colors. Much of the responsibility has been given to organizations outside the regular military establishment. Young men from sixteen to eighteen undergo compulsory military training at their schools, factories, and farms. The programs are run largely, but not entirely, by the All-Union Voluntary Society for Assistance to the Army, Air Force, and Navy, known in the Soviet Union by the acronym DOSAAF. Even by Soviet standards, DOSAAF is huge. Forty million people working through some 300,000 primary institutions are the core of the system. Reserve officers act as instructors. The curriculum includes drill, familiarization with small arms, knowledge of military regulations, and map reading. The standard program is 140 classroom hours plus two weeks of field exercises each summer.

Big though DOSAAF may be, it is unlikely that it offers an adequate substitute for the third year of service provided by the old system. Intelligence estimates are that the program does not provide a sufficient number of trained soldiers, largely because the reserve officers and, in some cases, noncommissioned officers who act as instructors are out of touch with contemporary developments in weapons and tactics. What the DOSAAF system does do is relieve the active army of the burden of preliminary training, or what the U.S. Army calls basic training.

Once a conscript is in the service, he moves into advanced training plus, of course, the ideological indoctrination common to all authoritarian armies, including the Chinese. The question raised by experts is whether this postinduction program really improves the combat readiness of the conscript. The emphasis on ideological indoctrination, for example, reduces the time available for instruction in increasingly complex weaponry.

Another weakness in Soviet training in all the services is the failure to use in training the actual equipment that would be employed in war. Soviet pilots fly far fewer training missions than those of the United States and its NATO allies in Western Europe. A high percentage of the vast armada of Russian tanks in Central Europe and Siberia are in storage, and, except for major exercises, it is unusual for more than a fraction of the tank strength of an armored division to be deployed for maneuvers. Similarly, Soviet warships, especially submarines, spend about one-third as much time at sea as their American counterparts. It is reasonable to believe that in the event of war the Russian soldier, sailor, and airman will be less well acquainted with his weapons, especially those of extreme sophistication, than his American counterparts. These training problems are believed to be even more acute on the Siberian front, where the winter is more severe and protracted than in Central Europe.

As was Germany in the 1930s, the Soviet Union is today obsessed by fear of a two-front war—one in Europe and the other in Asia. The Russians understand what many Americans have chosen to overlook: a European war involving the United States automatically becomes a Pacific and Asian war because both America and the Soviet Union are Pacific powers. There are thus grounds for assuming that if the Soviet Union is to fight the Americans and their allies in Europe, then China, whose bases and manpower would figure largely in a conflict in the Far East, must be neutralized, if not defeated, first. Here we are making another and more questionable assumption—that if war occurred between NATO and the Warsaw Pact powers and spread to the Pacific, China would cast her lot with the Western imperialists. There can be little doubt, however, that the Soviet high command is deeply concerned with the military problem posed by the PLA.

The most striking change in Russian military deployments, an increase much greater than that in Central Europe, was the strengthening of the forces in the Far East between 1967 and 1974. Where there were just over twelve divisions in 1967, there were forty-five in 1975. The reasons for this buildup are obscure. One school of intelligence analysts believes it is in preparation for an invasion of Manchuria, which, as we have seen, is the action that offers the quickest and most valuable return. Another group believes that the Soviet forces have been assembled for a foray against Chinese nuclear installations. Another, more low-keyed approach is to assume that the Russian divisions are there merely for the defense of Siberia against the Chinese forces in back of the frontier. Granted the present inadequacy of Chinese weaponry and logistics, acceptance of this theory involves a good deal of wishful thinking.

A more convincing reason for believing that the Russian forces are prepared for defense rather than for attack is the composition of the forces. Initially, only 20 percent of the divisions were armored ones, compared with 52 percent of the Soviet forces in Eastern Europe. That, however, was a preliminary estimate. More recent information is that the number and quality of the tanks, armored personnel carriers, and surface-to-surface and surface-to-air missile systems moving to the Far Eastern armies has improved. Moreover, whereas only ten of the forty-five divisions were at full strength in 1974 when the Far Eastern deployment was completed, the present estimate is that twenty are now in that category. The divisions of Categories II and III, like those in interior Russia in the same classes, lack their full complement of advanced weapons and trained manpower. There is a steady stream of evidence reaching Western intelligence services concerning the continued building of barracks and housing for families, and of highways, railroad spur lines, and permanent training grounds in the Far East.

To some, the evidence above points to establishment of a Soviet garrison rather than to preparations for offensive war in the Far East. Others point out that the Soviet force now deployed there may be considered as the spearhead for a much larger force moved east from the central regions of the Soviet Union to participate in a one-front war against China.

Whatever the rationale behind the Soviet buildup in the Far East, Russian military doctrine includes one pervasive element—wholehearted devotion to the offensive. Russian military writers stress that victory can be achieved only by vigorous and resolute attack and that, in consequence, the offensive is the only proper type of operation for Soviet troops. This is, as we shall see, dramatically different from the defensive cast of thinking in China or among American military planners.

A. A. Sidorenko, one of the Russian military establishment's best known and most widely read writers on doctrine and tactics, in his book *The Offensive* declared that "victory over an enemy is achieved only by a resolute attack" and consequently "the offensive is the main type of combat action of [Soviet] troops." Defensive operations, although recognized as sometimes unavoidable, are regarded as a forced and temporary form of war because "a side which only defends is inevitably doomed to defeat."

American and European students of Soviet doctrine conclude that the tactics planned for an invasion of West Europe, a blitzkrieg of great momentum and speed through West Germany to the sea, would be those adopted for an attack on Manchuria, where the axis of attack in the successful Soviet invasion of the Japanese puppet state of Manchukuo in 1945 would be followed by the new invaders.

In 1945 the Soviets launched three independent thrusts. General Meritskov entered eastern Manchuria from Vladivostok. General Purkayev struck south across the Amur River. Marshal Malinovsky, the most noted of the commanders, later to become minister of defense, led the attack on Manchuria's western areas.

Soviet military writers have since made a great deal about this lightning campaign (the offensives began on August 9, and on August 15 the Japanese surrendered), and viewed entirely from the statistical side, the Russian progress was remarkable. The

Sixth Guards Tank Army penetrated 510 miles into Manchuria in ten days. The average daily rate of advance was 51 miles, and Soviet writers never fail to emphasize that this is a higher figure than the 12 miles per day registered by Guderian's German Nineteenth Corps in 1940, or the 12.1 miles per day of Patton's Third Army in 1944.

The campaign is held up as a model for future Soviet offensives. What the Russian military authorities omit from their articles is that the Soviet forces had an enormous advantage in manpower and weapons over the Japanese Kwantung army in Manchuria. Jeffrey Record of the Brookings Institution reports that the numerical balance of forces at the start of the Russian offensive was as follows: divisions, 3.3 to 1; independent brigades, 4.2 to 1; armored fighting vehicles, including tanks, 4.5 to 1; artillery and mortars, 3.9 to 1. As we know from subsequent Japanese accounts of the campaign, the Kwantung army's equipment was obsolete and most of the divisions were well understrength.

In this cold statistical light, the Soviet offensive is less impressive, especially when it is noted that the Sixth Guards Tank Army encountered *no* resistance for the first four days of its offensive. Whether the invasion was a prolonged picnic and drunk or whether it was, as Russian military historians contend, a miracle of offensive warfare, there can be little doubt that it is a central focus for studies in the Chinese staff.

Such studies must take into account the future Soviet use of tactical or strategic nuclear weapons to support a general offensive against China. Acquaintance with Soviet doctrine leads to the conclusion that the Russians today are committed to use tactical nuclear weapons, for, as Sidorenko says, "nuclear weapons are the basic means of destruction on the field of battle" and "strategic and tactical nuclear missile forces are the basis of the firepower of the land forces for defeating the enemy.

"Nuclear weapons are the most powerful means for the mass destruction of troops and rear area objectives," Sidorenko holds. "Among all other means of combat, they possess the greatest force for physical and moral-psychological influence and therefore have decisive influence on the nature of the offensive. . . . Their employment in the battle and operation permits inflicting large losses in personnel and equipment on the enemy almost instantaneously, destroying, paralyzing, and putting out of action entire regiments and divisions and even corps, and thereby changing the relation of forces sharply in one's favor and destroying structures and other objectives as well as enemy centers of resistance and frustrating his counterattacks and counterblows."

These are the conclusions of a distinguished Soviet military theoretician. Would they be implemented in a war against China? Clearly, the major Chinese advantage over the Russians (perhaps their only advantage) lies in manpower. And if nuclear weapons can destroy regiments, divisions, "and even corps," then the obvious Soviet means of reducing Chinese superiority in numbers lies in the use of such weapons.

But the Russians would not be invading China, specifically Manchuria, to kill Chinese. Rather, their goals would be Manchuria's industrial structure. Would this survive a nuclear attack of the type envisaged by Sidorenko? It seems unlikely, granted the Soviet penchant for overkill, whether the weapons are rifles, field guns, or ballistic missiles. A ruined, radioactive Manchuria would be no use to the Russians. It would be years before its industry could be linked to that of Siberia.

My conclusion is that should the Soviets follow their proven scenario and invade Manchuria, they would refrain from using nuclear weapons against cities and industrial complexes and would limit the number of tactical nuclear missiles used against Chinese troops and supply and transport centers. Not, I might add, because of any concern for the butcher's bill but because they would wish to limit what the U.S. Air Force calls collateral damage to urban industry. Of course, if the Chinese at the outbreak of war employ their rather limited nuclear weapons resources against the Russians, the Soviet response would be in-

stant and devastating. But in that "worst possible case," a Soviet conquest of Manchuria or of all eastern China would produce very little beyond ruined cities and industry. And that is
exactly the situation in which Chinese guerrillas would be able
to operate with high effectiveness against the conquering Soviet
forces.

"Surprise is the master key to success," Basil Liddell Hart
wrote. Both the Chinese and the NATO armies are aware of the
importance given surprise attack in Soviet military doctrine. The
reason for this emphasis is understandable.

In June 1941 the Russians were surprised by Hitler's invasion
of the Soviet Union. This was almost inconceivable. The U.S.
and British governments had warned Stalin and Molotov, the
foreign minister, that the invasion was about to be launched; the
British even identified the German armies, corps, and divisions
that were to be employed. Stalin and the group of military
dunces and political time servers who surrounded him paid no
attention. The consequence of Russia's unpreparedness was a
series of humiliating defeats that brought the Wehrmacht to the
gates of Moscow.

The Soviets will not be surprised again. The boot is on the
other foot; they intend to launch the surprise. Current Russian
doctrine argues that the deployment of nuclear weapons has
increased the role and importance of surprise because, to quote
Sidorenko again, "delay in the destruction of the enemy's
means of nuclear attack will permit the enemy to launch . . .
nuclear strikes first and may lead to heavy losses and even to the
defeat of the offensive. The accumulation of such targets as
nuclear weapons and waiting with the intention of destroying
them subsequently are now absolutely inadmissible."

A Russian strategy based on surprise, as the present one
clearly is, not only raises visions of incalculably more disastrous
Pearl Harbors for potential opponents but prompts the question,
When does a surprise attack become a preemptive attack?.

A Radio Moscow broadcast in 1970 dismissed the idea that
the Soviet Union could ever become the victim of the kind of

protracted conventional war that Chinese military doctrine prefers. The broadcast declared that ''in a nuclear war an enemy can deal very powerful nuclear strikes on the most densely populated areas of a target country at the outbreak of war without sending troops to invade it. Can this [Chinese] military theory based on a defensive and deceptive action to lead an enemy into an unfavorable position provide any answer to such military operations by the enemy? No, it cannot.''

Russian military writings emphasize that ''the side which first employs nuclear weapons with surprise can predetermine the outcome of the battle in his favor,'' that ''surprise blitzkriegs with nuclear weapons, aviation and tank groupings may be irresistible,'' and that ''preemption in launching a nuclear strike is . . . the decisive condition for the attainment of superiority over the enemy and the seizure and retention of the initiative.''

These are, or should be, very clear warnings to potential adversaries of the Soviet Union in Asia or Europe. Their seriousness is heightened by evidence that in an international crisis it will be the Soviet government that decides at what point the situation has deteriorated to one in which a preemptive strike is necessary. The Soviet Union takes the position that it never begins wars but only reacts to threats upon it from its imperialist enemies. But it is the Soviet government—or, more precisely, the Politburo—that fixes the magnitude of the imperialist threat and its danger to the motherland and, consequently, the means (nuclear or conventional or both) that are required to resist, by preemption, this threat.

Any assessment of the prospects for a Soviet attack on China must include five basic factors: the Russian advantage in modern weapons, missiles, aircraft, tanks, artillery, submarines, and surface vessels; the proximity of the Soviet armies, air forces, and fleet to the rich industrial area of Manchuria; the knowledge gained in 1945 of the proven routes of invasion; the doctrinal emphasis on surprise; and the strong possibility that in the event of a real or imagined Chinese threat, surprise would become preemption.

There is, however, one condition, mentioned earlier, that is necessary if a Soviet invasion of China is to be considered feasible. That is a stable military situation in Europe. From 1968, when détente first raised its alluring head from the debris of the Cold War, there have been those analysts in Europe, usually a minority, who argued that the true objective of détente was to tranquilize the situation between the Warsaw Pact powers and NATO to the point where the Russians could launch an attack on China without undue concern over their western front.

Again there are those who argue that the consequences of a prolonged Sino-Soviet war would be of advantage only to the West, just as there were influential people in the United States and Britain who contended in 1941 that it would be best not to help the Russians too much; let the two totalitarian giants destroy each other.

Under present conditions, the odds are in Russia's favor. The problem is familiar to intelligence services the world over. Troop, aircraft, and naval dispositions and weapons are known. Plans of attack can be guessed with considerable accuracy. The central element that is lacking is a clear knowledge of Soviet intentions.

Winston Churchill's words, uttered nearly forty years ago, about Soviet policy still hold good: "I cannot forecast to you the action of Russia. It is a riddle wrapped in a mystery inside an enigma."

8

*The Human Sea,
the People's War,
and Other Dreams*

EVER since the establishment of the People's Republic of China, the PLA has been the subject of scrutiny by foreign governments and military experts. Assessments vary with the temperature of the times and the political coloration of the experts. During the Korean War and the disputes over Taiwan and over Quemoy and Matsu, it was fashionable in Washington to portray the PLA as a ravening horde armed with the latest Soviet weapons, which was then at least partly true, and prepared to conquer all Asia if not tomorrow, then sometime next week.

Today it is possible to look more objectively on the PLA of yesterday and tomorrow. The Chinese military threat to Taiwan in the 1950s never developed, if indeed it ever existed. The chaos caused by the Great Proletarian Cultural Revolution ended, or should have ended, American, Japanese, and Russian fears about the effectiveness of the PLA in the decade between 1966 and 1976. The revolution seriously weakened the PLA, just as it weakened almost every institution in Chinese society, and the armed forces of the post-Mao era are recovering slowly from the effects of the Cultural Revolution.

Chairman Hua and the other new leaders have begun the long, expensive task of tailoring the PLA to what they perceive as China's principal policy objectives. These objectives have never been identified in a policy paper. The Chinese, when they can be induced to discuss them, talk in generalities. But it became apparent that a consensus exists on five goals for China in the post-Mao period. They are not drastically different from those pursued under Chairman Mao and Chou En-lai. The differences will be in the means. These objectives may be summarized as (1) the maintenance of national security, (2) the attainment of independent great or superpower status before the end of the century, (3) the achievement of political leadership in eastern and southeastern Asia, which implies the exclusion of the Soviet Union, (4) the rectification of China's frontiers, including the claims on the Sino-Soviet border areas and on the islands of the South China Sea and the assimilation of Taiwan as a province of China, and (5) the ideological leadership of Marxism-Leninism throughout the world. The first four objectives, obviously, cannot even be approached without a modernized, effective PLA; a wide gulf thus exists between ends and means.

At the summit of the Chinese military establishment is the Military Commission of the Chinese Communist party's Central Committee. The commission is now headed by Chairman Hua, who is supported by a group of vice-chairmen and a standing committee. This commission exercises command and control of the entire establishment, which is administered by the Ministry of National Defense, headed by the minister, at this writing Yeh Chien-ying, who is assisted by two vice-ministers.

On almost the same level and of maximum importance in the current drive to modernize the PLA is the National Defense Scientific and Technological Commission, which supervises weapons research and development. Associated with this commission is the National Defense Industries Office, which apparently coordinates the military and civilian sectors of the economy. Also near the top level is the administration of the military training schools, a mission performed by the Ministry of National Defense, which is responsible for the Academy of Military Science, roughly approximating a combination of the

Command and General Staff School and the three service war colleges in the United States. The three service arms of the PLA—army, navy, and air force—also supervise their own specialized schools.

Directly below the Military Commission and the Ministry of National Defense in the chain of command are three departments. The General Staff Department performs the staff and operational functions of the PLA and, in effect, is general staff headquarters for the army, navy, and air force. The General Logistics Department provides logistic support for the three services. Finally, there is the General Political Department, responsible within the PLA for all political affairs. The headquarters of the various arms and services carry out their specific operational functions as directed by the General Staff Department. There are eight specialized arms and services: air force, navy, armored corps, artillery corps, engineer corps, capital construction engineer corps, railway engineer corps, and the second artillery, or strategic missile, corps.

In the event of war or a perceived threat to national security the PLA most probably would organize its forces into "fronts." These fronts would not be of standard size but would be manned and equipped to conform with the danger. They would include not only the active forces of the PLA but the militia and supporting elements. Six major fronts have been identified.

The northeastern front includes the Manchurian military region facing the Soviet Union. The northern front, including the Peking and Lanchou military regions, is aligned against the Russians and their Mongolian allies. The western front, based on the Sinkiang military region, also is deployed to face the Soviets and the Mongolians. The southwestern front, based on the Chengtu military region, confronts India. The southern front, contiguous with Indochina, comprises the Kunming and Kuangchou military regions. The eastern front, opposite Taiwan, includes the Nanching, Fuchou, Tsinan, and Wuhan military regions.

A further complication arises from China's division of the

ground forces into the main forces and the regional, or local, forces. This division, like so much else in the PLA, springs from the experiences of the War of Liberation against Chiang Kai-shek and the teachings of Chairman Mao.

In 1945 Mao wrote, "This army is powerful because of its division into two parts, the main forces and the regional forces, with the former available for operations in any region whenever necessary and the latter concentrating on defending their own localities and attacking the enemy there in cooperation with the local militia."

Main-force troops, then, are regular army troops under the strategic command of the PLA's general staff. They include combat units: infantry, armor, horsed cavalry, border defense, internal defense, and garrison units. The airborne units, which are under the command of the air force, also are classified as main-force troops.

The regional or local forces are regular PLA troops stationed in, and assigned the mission of defending, a particular geographic area, including the coastal areas and land frontiers. There are three distinct types of regional-force units in the PLA.

The most important type of regional-force unit in the present situation is the border-defense unit. These are stationed along and are responsible for the preliminary defense of frontier areas. They are essentially light infantry forces whose mission in war would be to register and report border violations and provide the first line of defense in the event of invasion. The largest organization of this type is a division, but it is somewhat smaller in numbers than the standard infantry divisions of the main force, which have a strength of twelve thousand.

Another type of regional-force unit is the internal-defense division. Also lightly armed, these divisions have the responsibility of maintaining law and order in the areas to which they are assigned and, in the event of war, conducting limited defensive operations and guerrilla activities.

Finally, there are garrison divisions deployed in static, reinforced positions along the coasts and on offshore islands. These units are armed mainly with artillery and have little mobility.

For administrative purposes the PLA is divided into eleven military regions and twenty-eight military districts. Their importance varies with the general strategic situation; the Peking and Manchuria military regions currently are regarded as the most important.

All these commands and subcommands and geographical divisions and subdivisions are required to administer the largest military force in the world. The total regular services of China have a manpower strength of 3.95 million, compared to 3.68 million for the Soviet Union. In addition, there is an armed militia believed to be about 7 million strong and organized into seventy-five divisions, urban militia of several million, the Civilian Production and Construction Corps of about 4 million, and a basic militia whose strength is estimated at between 75 and 100 million. Members of the basic militia have received some basic military training but are not armed.

The main forces, however, are the heart of the PLA. They are formed into 12 armored divisions, 121 infantry divisions, 3 airborne divisions, 40 artillery divisions (some of which are antiaircraft units), 15 railway and construction engineer divisions, and 150 independent regiments. Supplementing the main force are the regional forces of 70 infantry divisions and 130 independent regiments. The overall strength of this massive land army is 3.25 million.

Under the present deployment of the main forces, 55 divisions are stationed in the Manchuria and Peking military regions; 25 divisions in the Tsinan, Anking, and Fuchou military regions; 21 in the Canton and Wuhan military regions; 15 in the Lanchou military region; and 26 in the Sinkiang, Chengtu, and Kunming military regions.

Here is an array of raw manpower unequaled in this or any other age. Small wonder that Chinese military leaders swell with pride when they contemplate these legions and the vast reservoir of hardy, brave militia. It is understandable that, deploying this tremendous numerical strength and encouraged by what they interpret to be the lessons of the past, Chinese planners should put their trust in men and the People's War formula for victory. But is this formula applicable in China's present situation?

Under present conditions, the opening phase of a People's War—agitation and propaganda among the peasants and workers—would be superfluous. The safest assumption about a Sino-Soviet war is that Peking could count on the mass support of the population. The second phase would center on guerrilla operations and the establishment of secure bases for operations. Again, contemporary conditions would call for guerrilla operations, but only in conjunction with the operations of the main-force units. The third and final phase is, according to Mao's teachings, a major offensive by regular units.

The People's War concept, to repeat, is deeply rooted in Chinese military thinking. But it is questionable whether the strategy is really relevant to China's position vis-à-vis the Soviet Union under present conditions. The exception would be Soviet preemptive nuclear strikes destroying much of the main force and its equipment and bases and forcing the Chinese back to their basic strategy.

The People's War will not be forgotten by political leaders. It will be exalted as a symbol of national resistance, the instrument that achieved the triumph of Communism. But there are reasons to assume that the military leadership, while paying lip service to the People's War, will move as rapidly as resources allow into a new period of Chinese military development.

The army, navy, and air force at present are strikingly deficient in everything but manpower. This weakness in modern weapons is accompanied by a grotesquely dated approach to modern war even if we forget the verbal kowtows to the People's War. Chinese leaders are firmly convinced that a Russian attack on China will take the form of a general invasion and that the invaders, to use an often-repeated phrase, "will drown in the human sea."

The Chinese, in other words, expect the Russians to do exactly what the Chinese want them to do in war. One of the gravest mistakes a high command can make is to expect that potential enemies will adopt a strategy that accords with its own plans. The French, students of military history will recall, committed this error not once but twice. In 1914 they expected the Germans to attack the fortress line in eastern France and be routed by the valor of French soldiers inspired by Colonel Grandmaison's doctrine of the uninhibited offensive. The Germans came through Belgium and within a throw of the dice of winning the war. The French in 1939 believed that the Wehrmacht would dash out its brains on the new Maginot Line. Once more, the Germans struck in the north, turned the Maginot Line, and defeated the French in the field.

The rationale for the current Chinese confidence that they will be able to defeat a Soviet invasion is the product of the experience of most senior commanders. They may also be making a virtue out of a necessity. Recognizing their inferiority to the Soviets in weapons, the Chinese may consider that their only hope in the event of war is a prolonged half-conventional, half-guerrilla resistance. Listen to Wu Hsiu-chen, the deputy chief of staff of the PLA, during an interview in Peking:

As to war, we have our own experience. For instance, we fought more than ten years of Civil War [with the Nationalists] and after that the Japanese for eight years and the War of Liberation [again, with the Nationalists] for four years. In those wars we defeated enemies with better weapons. Probably you know Chairman Mao's saying, "In the past wars we wiped out an enemy with better weapons with [our] militia and rifles." After the liberation of the new China there have been great changes and basic things still remain. I have told you that weapons are a most important factor in war. We are not neglecting the im-

provement of weapons. We are adopting the policy of
using present conditions and present techniques to equip
the army as best as possible. To compare the weapons
China is using with the weapons of other countries shows
China lagging behind. But to compare present weapons
with China's old weapons, there is a lot of improvement.

Of course, the arms situation has improved if the present
weapons are compared with those available in the 1930s at the
start of the war with Japan. But the present weapons cannot be
compared with those in the hands of the Russians—or the South
Koreans and the Japanese.

"According to the concrete conditions in China," the general
continued, "we do not only lay stress on the improvement of
weapons. We would also lay stress on the *man factor*. Weapons
are to be used by men. So in the Chinese army we have the
principle, 'We fear neither difficulties nor death.' In wartime
this army could overcome any type of difficulties and, if necessary, sacrifice their lives. Because every soldier knows what a
better life their parents and families have lived after the Liberation and will protect the benefits which have been gained. We
have deep confidence in the political feelings and the fighting
spirit of the Chinese commanders and soldiers."

He bristled defiance as he sat there, sipping tea and repeating
these military platitudes. One could almost hear the drums of
Valmy, Saratoga, and other revolutionary victories in the background. It is difficult to judge the age of a Chinese, but I would
say he was nearer seventy than sixty, courtly, experienced, and,
to my mind, hopelessly optimistic.

His was—and, I believe, will, for political reasons, continue
to be—the public approach to China's military capability in the
event of an attack by the Soviets. But another, quite different attitude toward China's basic military problem can be sensed
among younger officers in the provinces. There one encounters
an uneasy acceptance of the inadequacy of present arms; an
eager curiosity about the new weapons being deployed in the

NATO and Warsaw Pact armies, particularly remotely piloted weapons; and a third attitude more difficult to define. This combined a sturdy belief that the Chinese army, or at least that officer's unit of it, could get by in war with the weapons it now had with an evident wish that their men, too, could be equipped with the new antitank and antiaircraft weapons now common to the armies of East and West in Europe.

But they were relatively junior officers in an organization that, like all armies, is hierarchical in character. What they thought and occasionally said weighed little against the pontifical comments of the deputy chief of staff.

"Of course, there are many friends in the Western countries showing great concern as to how we are going to deal with modern war," General Wu said. "They are showing great concern and goodwill about how the Chinese will deal with a war in which tanks are used. We are also paying attention to that point. According to our concrete conditions, we are working hard on it. Generally speaking, we are confident of wiping out all aggressors."

A war of Soviet aggression could happen, he said.

"There's a saying, 'You fight in your way and we fight in our way,' " he added. "We do not regard ourselves as more stupid than the enemy."

By the time I had seen the deputy chief of staff near the end of my visit, I had concluded on the basis of what I had been shown and what I had seen and learned elsewhere that the PLA was sadly behind the Soviets, or indeed any Western army, in arms and equipment.

"We admit that weapons are a very important factor in war," the deputy chief of staff said, "but we do not consider them the decisive factor. We hope that man is the decisive factor. As to the equipment and technology in the army, I can tell you that the Chinese army is lagging far behind the equipment used by the West and the Russians. We admit that, but we lay more stress on the man factor. . . . The industry of our country is another element. Here, I can tell you frankly, we are also lagging behind. We do not have the first-grade steel to make modern weapons.''

The last sentence expresses both the inadequacies of Chinese weaponry and their engaging frankness. I cannot conceive of a Russian or an American general making the same confession of national weakness.

If the Chinese lack the means of producing the best steel to go into the weapons we were discussing—tanks, antitank guns, and conventional aircraft—how is their nuclear power to be assessed? Officers and officials were not outgoing about the Chinese nuclear arsenal. They admitted it existed. Once or twice there was a comment to the effect that the means of delivery rather than the nuclear devices themselves were the problem. There was nothing extraordinary in this. Modes of delivery—from land, from submarines, from the air, by cruise missile or individually targeted warhead—are problems for all nuclear powers. But I surmised that in China, with its relatively unsophisticated industrial base, the problem of delivery is far greater than it is in the United States, the Soviet Union, or even Britain and France.

China's development as a nuclear power began during the bright days of Soviet-Chinese friendship in the mid-1950s. The Chinese, benefiting from Russian technical advice and assistance, exploded their first nuclear device in 1954. When Sino-Soviet friendship went down the drain, China devoted an increasing amount of investment to the nuclear research and development program. Initially, this was concentrated at Lop Nor in Sinkiang. Recently, most of the advanced work has been shifted to installations in western and central China.

The Chinese exploded their first hydrogen bomb on January 17, 1967. There have been twenty-three nuclear tests since then, the majority from air drops from one of the air force's elderly TU-16s. One rocket test was fired in a modified Russian SS-4 missile at the new missile-testing range in Heilung-kiang. The tests have ranged from those of twenty-kiloton fission warheads through H-bomb triggers to a four-megaton nuclear device exploded on November 17, 1976.

This warhead, Western intelligence sources report, is intended for the Chinese derivation of the Soviet SS-9, which has a range of seventy-five hundred miles, or quite enough to hit almost every important target in the Soviet Union. The SS-9, however, is in the twenty-five-kiloton range, and it is considered unlikely that the Chinese missile will have the same killing power.

The Chinese strategic forces by Western calculations include thirty to forty CSS-2s, an intermediate-range ballistic missile (IRBM); a similar number of medium-range ballistic missiles (MRBMs); and about eighty elderly TU-16 bombers of medium range and payload. The Chinese MRBMs are liquid-fueled and transportable by road, with a range of approximately six hundred miles. The NATO intelligence consensus is that these weapons are highly inaccurate, with an estimated target area, or "circular error probable" (CEP), of four kilometers, compared with the 0.5 CEP of the U.S. Minuteman III ICBM.

The newer missiles, the IRBMs, reportedly have a range of fifteen hundred miles and are now being deployed on hardened sites in Sinkiang and Manchuria.

The Chinese are also believed to have available about 150 tactical nuclear weapons with warheads ranging from thirty kilotons to one megaton. But there are no reports of atomic land mines being available, and no portable nuclear launcher comparable to the American Pershing, Lance, or Honest John has been reported as deployed.

The Chinese are deficient in the offensive sectors of strategic nuclear warfare, but they have made considerable progress in passive defense. As we shall see, the country's system of underground shelters against conventional or nuclear attack represents a tremendous investment in capital and labor. The system's effectiveness in nuclear war is questionable.

This consideration of China's overall military strength, strategic and tactical doctrine, and nuclear weaponry reflects the country's desperate need for modern weapons. Hua's government has three choices: China can buy the most urgently needed modern weapons in the West, hoping that these, in combination with her homemade weapons, will suffice; the government can follow the line of strict independence of foreign suppliers and make its own weapons; or the PLA can make a desperate choice, believing that the serious reverses probable at the start of any war with the Soviets will be outweighed in the end by national triumph in a People's War.

Signs multiplied in 1977 that China's leaders, including the newly rehabilitated Teng Hsiao-ping and the aged defense minister, Yeh Chien-ying, have come around to the view that to provide an effective PLA, arms must be bought abroad. This means a retreat from the idea of a China independent of foreign arms supplies. From the standpoint of economic development it complicates the planners' task by giving priority to nonproductive imports and insuring the diversion of funds from investment in the oil industry and heavy industrial plants and from improvements in the national transportation system to arms purchases.

Military spokesmen have continued to genuflect to Chairman Mao's idea of a People's War. But they have also voiced views on modernization that would not have been heard under Mao's leadership. Reviewing the threat posed by the Soviet Union, one military spokesman said, ''We must effectively grasp scientific research and industrial production for national defense so as to gradually overcome our inferiority in weapons and equipment. . . . We stress People's War and human factors, but this does not mean that we do not want to improve weapons and equipment or want to improve our technical conditions.'' Another military leader, cited in the Peking press, declared that modernization must reach the point where ''we will not only have what the enemy has but also what he lacks.''

One final comment seemed to sound the death knell for the Chinese reliance on pure manpower: ''The decisive factor for victory in war is man—man with weapons in hand.''

Chairman Hua told the Eleventh Party Congress that the government was determined to increase both military research and development and the production of military equipment. This emphasis on military modernization may reflect the stronger position of the military within the central government. Three military officers were added to the Politburo after the Eleventh Party Congress. With ten military figures now serving on that body, the services enjoy greater representation there than at any time since Defense Minister Lin Piao was the second power in the state in the late 1960s.

By November 1977 the Chinese were weighing the usefulness to them of the British Harrier, a very short take-off/landing (VSTOL) fighter. The Harrier already has been bought by the U.S. Marine Corps and the Royal Air Force. In the course of a visit to France in the same year, a Chinese military mission inspected some of the new French antitank and antiaircraft guided missiles. Interest in these is natural. The Chinese, like the NATO powers, would face a Soviet armored force vastly superior in numbers. The Western nations, notably the United States, Britain, France, and West Germany, have developed effective new antitank missiles and guns to compensate for this quantitative inferiority. China has not.

Arms purchases from Britain or France are likely to cause less ideological trouble for the Chinese leadership than any from the United States. Although Chinese officers, senior and junior, express a high regard for American military technology, both they and their civilian colleagues regard the United States as an imperialist superpower. There consequently is an obvious reluctance to depend on a supply of weapons from such a power. Here is an echo of the break with the Soviet Union. That superpower betrayed the Chinese. Why should they trust another superpower? The British and the French, although clearly capitalist societies in Chinese eyes, at least are not imperialist superpowers. Traffic in arms with them is permissible because there is little possibility that London or Paris will attempt to exact political rewards in addition to the sales price.

In Peking and in Western capitals the reporter encounters the diehards, the officers (usually elderly) who believe that China can make her own modern weapons. They are those who also believe that the Russians, if they have the temerity to invade China, will drown in the human sea. In discussion they will admit that Chinese industry does not yet produce the lightweight heat-resistant metals required for the manufacture of modern jet engines. They concede that China has not produced a tank as reliable as the now elderly American M-60A or as effective as the British Chieftain or the West German Leopard. They know that in tank battles their T-59, a simplified version of the obsolescent Russian T-54, would be no match for the Soviet T-62 or the new generation of faster, more agile T-72s. China, they insist, must make her own modern weapons. This is a patriotic sentiment, a reassertion of the Maoist idea of independence. But it has precious little relevance to the increasingly complex world of modern military weaponry.

Let us assume that the Chinese set out to design, produce, and test an antitank missile comparable to the contemporary American TOW or the British Swingfire weapons systems. A modern industrial society, such as Britain's or America's, needs at least seven years for research and development, design, testing, and production of such a weapon. The Chinese, if they began today, would be fortunate if they were able to provide the PLA with such a weapon in a decade. But what of the Americans, the British, and especially the Russians in the interval? In ten years their research and development organizations and their engineers and production chiefs probably would produce antitank weapons far superior to those now deployed. The Chinese, however, would be left with a weapon that would have been capable enough in the 1970s but was now inferior to the new Western weapons.

This is the prime weakness of the stubborn and often admirable Chinese determination to make their own weapons. They have started so late in the armaments race that their only chance of catching up lies in purchases abroad.

Undoubtedly, there is great interest in Peking in the Harrier, which would be highly useful for coastal defense, and in other Western weapons. The acquisition formula for the Chinese is likely to follow the pattern of the Rolls-Royce Spey engine deal. Under the terms of their contract with the British, the Chinese bought 150 Spey engines. They also contracted for the erection of a factory with all its necessary machinery by the British and the training of Chinese on machines that would produce more Spey engines. This is an expensive and time-consuming process. But it is less time-consuming and ultimately less expensive than starting from the ground up, which means designing the product and the factory, training the technicians, and building the machinery. If the Chinese want the Harrier, and there are many military reasons for wanting it, the Spey deal may serve as a useful precedent. Such an arrangement should appease the conservatives, who want China to build all its own weapons and at the same time avoid the political stigma of continuing reliance on Western societies for the arms that will enable China to resist Soviet invasion. To what extent and by what methods the PLA's armament is modernized is the most important military question facing the Chinese government.

The present standard of weaponry in the land, air, and naval forces is so low that it is unlikely that the PLA as now armed could hold, let alone defeat, a Soviet invasion of Manchuria. Doubtless, the Chinese forces would fight bravely and well. But bravery and discipline are no match for Soviet forces equally brave and equally well disciplined. And what, the strategist may ask, will happen if the Russians take Manchuria? One much-favored scenario is that the Soviets will sit down, develop their conquest, thumb their noses at the Chinese, and say, "Come and get us." This, in the present circumstances, the PLA will be unable to do.

A senior American diplomat asked me after I had visited the PLA if I thought that in a Sino-Soviet war the United States would support the supply of arms to China. The question really breaks down into two related questions: could the United States supply arms to China, and if it did, would the arms be effective on the battlefield?

Could America supply arms in the face of the expected Russian blockade without risking war with the Soviet Union? World War II in the Pacific, the Korean War, and the Vietnam War encouraged the belief that the United States could provide logistic support for its own or friendly forces anywhere in the world. To do this for a China plunged into a war with the Soviet Union would be infinitely more difficult than any previous adventure, quite apart from the risk of a war with the Soviet Union. This would not be logistical support of a modern, technologically advanced nation like Israel but of an undeveloped country without the technological base or the ports and airfields to assimilate the supplies.

Assuming, however, that the arms are landed—meaning that the Soviets shy away from war with the United States—would they be effectively employed in the war?

At the moment, the answer is no.

The Chinese are a highly intelligent people with an obvious quickness and ability to learn. But what they would need to reverse initial Soviet successes is not rifles, machine guns, and hundreds of tons of ammunition but modern weapons, missiles, tanks, electronic warfare devices, and remotely piloted munitions. To expect forces ignorant of modern technology to assimilate such weapons and to use them is asking too much even of a people as smart and adroit as the Chinese.

China's military position today, when viewed in its broadest aspects, is parlous. The present strategy is unsuitable for the kind of war the Soviets are likely to launch if it comes to war. To me it is unthinkable that the Russians, victors over two invaders, in 1812 and in the year of Stalingrad, 1942, would repeat the errors of their enemies and invade en masse. The Chinese nuclear force, though undoubtedly capable of punishing the Russians for invasion, is not powerful enough to deter it and would in all probability cease to be a serious factor after the Russians had employed their nuclear weapons, which are superior in destructive power and accuracy. There remain the brave, devoted Chinese soldiers, sailors, and airmen. But bravery, devotion, discipline, and physical toughness do not suffice today, nor did they in the past, to overcome inferiority in weapons.

All these Chinese deficiencies, mental and in materiel, may be changed in time. Given time, the infinite internal resources of the people may turn the scale. But do the Chinese have the time?

9

The Unarmed Giant

*Now the resources of those skilled in
the use of extraordinary forces are as
infinite as the heavens and earth.*
—SUN TZU

GEN. Manton S. Eddy, who remains in memory as America's
best divisional commander, once said that what he wanted
from the infantryman was durability, the mental and physical
resources that would survive reverses in battle and logistical
foul-ups, that would weather cold and heat, snow and rain, and
be capable, at the end, of attacking. In China I often recalled
his words. For what the Chinese soldier, sailor, and airman
has is durability. Granted Soviet superiority in weapons and, I
suspect, in operational planning and command, durability may
be China's signal advantage.

Upon the infantryman, the lowest common denominator in
war, rests China's fate in any conflict with the Soviet Union.
The Chinese infantryman is not to be confused with the infantryman of today's mechanized American and Soviet armies,
borne to battle in an armored personnel carrier and armed with a
bewildering variety of sophisticated weapons. He is the marching and, if lucky, truck-carried infantryman, the "straight legs"
of the American army, the "poor bloody infantry" of the British service. He is anachronistic, a throwback to Waterloo, Gettysburg, the Somme. "Give me enough of those," the Duke of

Wellington said, gesturing toward an infantryman, "and we can beat Bonaparte." The Chinese may find solace in this remark, for they have enough.

The PLA for most of its fifty years has rested upon the effectiveness of its infantry. Today's ground forces reflect the past in their training and their operations, just as the strategic thinking of the present high command is overly influenced by battles long ago.

The birth of the PLA came on August 1, 1927, in Nanking, when some thirty thousand Communists and dissidents from Chiang Kai-shek's National Revolutionary Army revolted. The revolt failed. But it marked both the advent of the PLA and the long struggle for the domination of China between the Communist party—and its army—and the Kuomintang.

The new army was blooded in five major "annihilation" campaigns (they were so advertised by the Nationalists) between 1930 and 1934. Better armed and more intelligently led, the Nationalists finally succeeded in encircling the Communist forces. But in October 1934 the First Front Army, commanded in name at least by Mao Tse-tung, broke out and, after joining other forces, began the six-thousand-mile march to a sanctuary in Shensi Province in Yenan, in north-central China.

The Long March is now the glorified centerpiece of Chinese military history. Like all climactic military events, it has spawned legends, some valuable to national morale, others highly dangerous as precepts for modern warfare. It is sufficient to point out that the Long March was made under conditions that have no relation to contemporary conflict. Had the Nationalists had sufficient aircraft, for example, the march would not have covered one thousand miles, let alone six thousand. Unhappily, the surviving veterans of the Long March, including Mao himself, have exercised an unwarranted influence on Chinese military planning and, in many cases, have risen to high rank solely because they happened to be on the march. It is as though every surviving company commander at Dunkirk had been elevated to general's rank because he had survived. It is not so much that "old men forget" but that they remember too well and their memories raise a formidable barrier to new ideas, new methods, and new men.

Japanese aggression into China began in 1931. But the fighting between the Nationalists and Communists continued despite Mao's efforts to reach a truce and unite against Japan. Not until 1937 did the two sides agree to form a united front. The PLA, in theory, at least, was now integrated into the Nationalist army. The Nationalists' reluctance to form the united front was hotly criticized at the time, but subsequent events demonstrated that Chiang had a clearer perception of the Communists' true aims than did his critics abroad.

The Communists spent the next eight years establishing the conditions that would enable them to seize power once the Japanese and the Nationalists were beaten. They concentrated on winning the support of the peasants and the industrial workers, organizing bases for future operations, and integrating political and military activities. They followed two of Mao's prescriptions for a People's War.

They were led by men of distinction—Mao, Chou En-lai, and Lin Piao. They and their lieutenants found this program more congenial than fighting the Japanese, because it was directed toward their ultimate goal, the control of China. Their policy, as it now emerges from all the propaganda claptrap about "the glorious and victorious fight against the Japanese invader," was to conserve the strength of the PLA by avoiding major encounters with the Japanese and thus consolidate their military power in the countryside. The process has been described as 70 percent expansion, 20 percent skirmishing with the Nationalists, and 10 percent fighting the Japanese.

The 10 percent dominates Chinese thinking on World War II. As far as I could judge, propaganda has led otherwise intelligent men to believe that China, in this case the PLA, won the war against Japan. References to Midway, the Philippine campaign, or Iwo Jima brought blank stares. One senior officer obviously had never heard of the long, bloody campaign fought by the

British against the Japanese in Burma. This is annoying. But it is common in authoritarian countries. The Russians, for example, have forgotten the sacrifices of the British and Americans carrying supplies to Murmansk during World War II.

There were areas in which the PLA, in cooperation with local peasants, won victories over the Japanese. I was taken to a village where, with the aid of an elaborate table model, the history of the battle that freed the inhabitants from the Japanese yoke was traced in lights. The battle had pitted the local militia against a Japanese regiment. The elderly survivors of that battle, delighted at a foreigner's interest, expanded upon the engagement until it resembled Armageddon or, at the very least, Gettysburg. And how many men, I asked, did you lose in this battle with a Japanese regiment? Two or perhaps three was the answer. So much for Armageddon! One cannot fault these old men for exaggerating the triumphs of their youth. Old soldiers, those that do not die or fade away, see the battles of their prime in a different perspective. The danger in China is that these battles long ago have become the basis for strategy and tactics in a totally different military environment.

A young colonel asked me if I thought that the village would be able to repel an invading regiment today. The reply was obvious. No modern commander would waste a regiment on a village. He would dust it with napalm, bomb it to ruins, and go on to attack his main enemy, the active field forces. This view did not sit well with the colonel.

After the Japanese surrender in August 1945, the conflict between the Communists and the Nationalists expanded. Under Lin Piao, who in retrospect appears the most capable of the PLA's field commanders, the Communists moved about 100,000 effectives into Manchuria, then as now the most important Chinese industrial area. These troops made contact with the Soviet armies that had accepted the surrender of Japan's Kwantung army.

When the Russians withdrew from Manchuria in 1946, only after some sharp prodding by Moscow's Western allies, the

PLA seized Japanese tanks, heavy artillery, and aircraft. It was now better equipped to pursue its real objective, the defeat of Chiang Kai-shek's Nationalist forces. The PLA for the first time had to plan to fight battles far removed in character from the guerrilla triumphs of the past. The command and the nascent staff now faced problems unknown to guerrillas. Their success in solving these problems emphasizes the flexibility and toughness of the Chinese military mind.

There were negotiations between the two sides, but given the total commitment of the Communist leaders, these never had much chance of success unless Chiang was prepared to accept his destruction. The civil war, known today in China as the War of Liberation, was renewed in July 1946.

Overall, the situation was favorable to the PLA. The Nationalists held the cities and the main lines of communication. The Communists were paramount in the countryside. Their forces, now over a million strong and supported by perhaps 2 million ill-armed militia, were well situated to wage a guerrilla war.

Guerrilla tactics predominated at the start of the war. But the Communists learned quickly. When conditions were right, the PLA planned and fought conventional battles with considerable success. Peking fell in January 1949. Nationalist resistance dwindled. Two months later, the Communists crossed the Yangtze River and took Nanking; a month later, they took Shanghai. The Nationalist government fled to Taiwan, and the People's Republic of China was founded on October 1, 1949.

This victory was won by an army that was composed basically of peasant infantry. The military technology of the day played a minor role. Communist successes, it should be remembered, were often scored over an enemy whose leadership was corrupt and whose forces were halfhearted in their efforts. But the War of Liberation, like the war against the Japanese, had an inordinate effect on Chinese military doctrine, one not wholly corrected by Chinese intervention in Korea.

There the Chinese People's Volunteers, as the interventionist force was called, soon learned that unsupported infantry attacks, the "human wave" tactics, were a prescription for disaster when launched against reliable forces backed by greatly superior artillery and air power. One officer recalled that he had led a company into battle against the Americans and emerged with only six unwounded men. Another, speaking of the attack on the Imjin River, recalled that his entire battalion had been shot to bits. What lessons had they learned? "Don't punch," said one in rudimentary English. It developed that he meant "don't bunch" troops when confronted by superior firepower.

The Korean intervention offered awkward new problems for the Chinese. With their frontier not many miles away they were unable to carry out a favorite maneuver of the War of Liberation and make a strategic retreat behind the frontier, because this would have enabled the UN forces to enter China in pursuit. Korea was the last war for the PLA. Its officers have observed and learned from the fighting in Vietnam and the two Arab–Israeli wars of 1967 and 1973. At least, some of the younger officers appear to have learned.

The lessons of past wars were elaborately preserved at the headquarters of the 573rd Regiment of the 179th Infantry Division, a main-force unit stationed near Nanking.

All armies are alike in their preservation of traditions and totems. Aside from the differences in battle areas and enemies, the regimental museum might have been the museum devoted to the American armored forces at Fort Knox or any one of a dozen British regimental museums. The objective was the same, to glorify past deeds and stimulate contemporary morale.

There was, however, one significant difference. Like all authoritarian peoples, the Chinese find it difficult, even impossible, to admit reverses, political, economic, or military, in public. The division had begun as a guerrilla unit in 1937 and had been developed naturally under the impetus of Chairman Mao's military thought. In the intervening forty years, my hosts said, the division had fought six hundred battles, ranging from small firefights to major encounters, and had "annihilated" 80,000 enemies. I took *annihilated* to mean killed. Given the usual 3:1 ratio of wounded to killed, this meant the division had inflicted approximately 240,000 casualties.

The museum's displays showed that in the war against Japan guerrilla tactics had been the rule, and these had also been used in the War of Liberation when the division lacked tanks and aircraft. The walls were festooned with flags and newspaper clippings to serve, much as they do in American or British unit museums, to remind today's warriors of yesterday's glories. Most of the clippings concerned the division's fighting in the War of Liberation during the period of the war when most of its heavy equipment had been captured from Chiang Kai-shek's forces. An elderly captain explained that since the breech blocks had been removed from some of the captured cannon, his gunners had fired the shells by hitting the base of the projectile with a hammer!

The siege of a minor city in faraway Shensi Province was described in another elaborate series of diagrams, rough sketches, and out-of-focus photographs. It had been a seventy-two-day campaign, and, I was assured, many victories had been won and many soldiers decorated. Decorations in the PLA are honorifics, not medals. Soldiers or officers are rated as Skilled Fighter or Fighting Hero.

Fewer exhibits were devoted to the Korean War. One of the regiment's Fighting Hero awards had gone to a private who had climbed atop an American tank and dropped a grenade down the open hatch. Another had been awarded to a private who had blocked an enemy fire point with his body.

The regiment, like most active PLA units, participated in civilian construction and had organized and run economic enterprises. In recent years it had helped reclaim one thousand hectares of farmland and had cultivated vegetables, which were sold to the state. The major contribution, however, was a pharmaceutical factory in which the labor force was composed almost entirely of the wives and daughters of the regiment.

So spartan is the life of the Chinese soldier that an American infantryman would have difficulty recognizing him as in the same profession. The regimental barracks were one-story buildings rising from a treeless dirt yard. Each platoon slept in a rectangular, unheated room even then, in November, when it was very cold. Along the north wall was a row of double-decked bunks. A neatly rolled quilt was at the foot of each bunk. Rifles, ammunition, and other equipment, and rice bowls and chopsticks were stored along the opposite wall. Two regular officers and two political officers sleep in each platoon room. Next to the room was a communal storeroom. Heavy winter clothing, additional ammunition, and personal clothing, all of it neatly folded, was stored there. There was no lock on the storeroom door, a condition difficult to imagine in American barracks.

The company's mess hall was combined with a club or recreation room. Plain tables and benches for eating meals, a Ping-Pong table, and racks containing newspapers, propaganda leaflets, and what an earnest young major assured me were edifying works. The barracks were austere and monastic; no pictures of naked girls, no television, no stereo sets. The soldiers, I was told, went to bed at 9:00 P.M. during most of the year and got up at 5:00 A.M.

Sunday is the soldier's only holiday. If a soldier learns of a crisis at home—an ailing parent, an unfaithful wife—he can obtain a pass. Military service in the ground forces lasts from two to four years, according to the soldier's military specialty, four years in the air force and five years in the navy. A recruit receives six yuan a month as basic pay. When he progresses to the status of combat infantryman, pay rises to seven yuan. A corporal gets eight yuan and a squad leader (sergeant) ten. An officer, on the other hand, starts at sixty yuan a month.

The infantryman, the backbone of the PLA, begins his service with two months of basic training: military drill, familiarization with army life, and, inevitably, ideological indoctrination. Then he is assigned to his unit, where he begins to learn a specialty as a rifleman, machine gunner, mortar crewman, signaler. There are far fewer infantry specialties in the Chinese army than in the NATO and Warsaw Pact forces, with their more sophisticated weaponry.

Uniforms are simple and serviceable. An officer's uniform differs from that of a private's in only one respect: the officer's has four pockets, the private's only two. In winter both officers and men wear the heavy quilted trousers and greatcoats that have been common to Chinese armies since the Middle Ages. They are bulky, ill-fitting, and, I should think, uncommonly constricting in battle.

In one sense the PLA has no rank system. Officers are not called colonel, lieutenant, or general but are identified by their roles: chief of staff, platoon leader, or divisional commander. Commanders and men mix off-duty. But in the ground forces and the air force, field discipline appeared strict. Salutes were exchanged punctiliously; field orders were carried out at the double.

The firing exercises for the regiment that day were held in a shallow valley outside the post. As the infantrymen jogged to take up their allotted positions, they chanted "be on the alert" and "defend the motherland," exhortations that, though certainly sincerely meant, have an odd sound to anyone who remembers the American infantry going into the Saint-Lô fight singing "Roll Me Over in the Clover" or the British Tommies in Egypt roaring out "King Farouk, King Farouk, catch his bollucks on a hook."

As the exercise unfolded, Chang Feng-ge, the divisional chief of staff, mused on the differences between the PLA and the Russian army. To the latter, he said, "the tank is everything," whereas to the Chinese "the role played by the soldier is decisive." Unconsciously paraphrasing Oliver Cromwell, he added, "The man who knows why he fights and for what he fights will be victorious."

The exercise that day did little to generate confidence that the 179th Division, or any other division so armed and trained, would be able to hold its own in a maneuver battle with a Soviet mechanized rifle or armored division. The heaviest antitank weapons available were some elderly 85-millimeter guns with sights and rangefinders that vanished from European armies in the 1950s. But the antitank weapon on which the division apparently relied was the 75-millimeter recoilless rifle. The accuracy at 370 meters against stationary or moving targets was excellent—as long as one kept in mind the old sergeant's maxim that "you can always hit a target when the other fellow isn't firing back."

But 370 meters? In the Sinai in 1973, tank engagements were fought at between 1,500 and 2,000 meters. American tankers in Germany are trained to fire at comparable ranges. Moreover, it took the Chinese recoilless-rifle teams an average of twenty-five seconds to set up and fire; in the Seventh Army in Germany, tanks and antitank weapons open fire in ten seconds or less. The laser, the thermo sight, the infrared mechanisms, and the precision guided missiles have raised lethality in tank battles to levels that the Chinese cannot approach with their present weapons.

Machine gunners, riflemen, and mortar teams banged away at various moving and stationary targets with commendable accuracy. The enthusiasm and vigor of the various platoons could not be doubted. The exercise was carried out with the snap and precision associated with veterans. Yet, despite all that, it seemed a page out of the military past. This feeling that the Chinese thought in terms of the 1940s was even more pronounced when two platoons engaged in a bayonet-fighting competition. This is an exercise upon which the Chinese spend an inordinate amount of training time, in view of the tiny percentage of wounds suffered in modern war by bayonets. I had a vivid memory of the German panzers tearing up Polish lancers in 1939.

Here, at the divisional level, there was an outspoken recognition that the unit—and indeed the entire ground army—needs more modern weapons. "Much depends on our economy and the development of industry," said Chang Feng-ge. "We have started to pay attention to the modernization of weapons, but for the present we must depend on what equipment is available and make the best use of it. The soldiers are quick to learn, and tough. We know that precision and timing are all-important factors in modern battle. It is just a question of time until modern weapons, like laser sights, are supplied to our forces.''

Here, at the sharp end of the PLA, I heard less talk of the Russians drowning in the human sea. Instead, the officers eagerly sketched a doctrine not far removed from that of the U.S. Army, based on the coordination of all arms, tanks, artillery, engineers, infantry, and air force in battle.

The officers said that in addition to competitive fire exercises such as the one we had witnessed, the division and its units carry out realistic field training, including preparation for bacteriological, chemical, and nuclear war, twice a year, and that smaller field exercises were carried out on a weekly basis.

By chance, I saw the start of one of the latter. There was a steep hill opposite the window of the room I had been assigned in the headquarters. From there in late afternoon I saw a platoon leader and his unit come rushing out of the bushes at the base of the hill and start scrambling up the hill toward the top. The platoon leader, young and active, was first on the summit. He turned and with hand signals directed the infantrymen toward the next objective. They ran, rifles held across their chests as men have held them since the weapon first appeared on the battlefield. The officer followed and was swallowed up by the forest.

After modern weapons, sufficient transport appears the most startling inadequacy of the field army. I asked how the division would move to its assigned sector in a crisis. The chief of staff looked surprised. "Why, by trucks if they're available; if not, on foot." Such divisions would be pitted against an enemy that counts on covering at least sixty miles a day in its version of the blitzkrieg.

Infantry reconnaissance, providing detailed information, is emphasized by Chinese field officers. They see it as a balance to the Soviet lead in aerial and electronic surveillance. The ground forces pride themselves on their scouting ability; the Chinese soldier, they say, can melt into the countryside, lie hidden for hours, and return with a detailed account of the enemy's strength and movements.

"We always knew what the Japanese and the Nationalists were going to do," a general said complacently. "Our soldiers are unmatched in finding the enemy and assessing his intentions." Perhaps. But they may face enemies more alert than the overconfident Japanese and the slovenly Nationalists.

Although the emphasis in the 179th Division was on firepower—the human-wave attacks of Korea apparently have been put aside—a great deal of importance is placed on getting as close as possible to hostile forces, "to embrace the enemy," on the theory that Chinese soldiers are superior to any others in close combat. The problem here is that today embracing the enemy can entail losses unacceptable to any army, even one as large, motivated, and disciplined as the Chinese. For example, by 1983, an American division will be able to deposit 5.2 million pounds of ordnance on a battlefield in thirty minutes. Embracing the enemy in those circumstances would be the kiss of death.

The ground forces' organization in some respects reflects a conviction that initial losses will be very high. All units are divided into first and second echelons. The first comprises the leading assault or main defense elements in the initial phase of an encounter. The second includes the forces required for subsequent phases of the battle.

Chinese officers on the divisional level are acutely aware of the changes that new weapons, particularly precision-guided munitions, have imposed on tactics. But, in their present situation, they cannot do more than theorize over the effect that surface-to-surface missiles or advanced antitank weapons can have on a battlefield.

On paper the ground forces' organization conforms to the structures of other armies in Europe and Asia. The largest tactical formation is the army, which has three infantry divisions, one artillery regiment, and supporting forces. The total force of an army would be about forty-three thousand men, or approximately that of an American corps.

All ground forces around the world are what the mandarins of the Pentagon call man-oriented. This is more pronounced in the Chinese service than anywhere else because of the shortage of modern equipment. A distinction should be made between what the Chinese require today and Western military needs. The PLA, in all its branches, wants equipment that is relatively simple to operate, maintain, and repair, a requirement that results largely from a scarcity of skilled technical personnel and an industrial base barely capable of manufacturing the necessary spare parts.

In the 179th Division there was a no doubt justifiable confidence in the average soldier's ability to improvise with available material. The divisional shops were counted upon to keep transport in service by making the required spare parts or, more often, by cannibalizing vehicles. Such procedures may suffice in peace. Under the stress of active operations in war, they will not be enough.

China has begun tentatively to modernize its forces, partly, at least, through purchases abroad. Even if the present program is doubled in volume, the amount of equipment available to the PLA is unlikely to modernize the units of the ground army in accordance with its standard tables of organization. These tables call for 32 tanks and 10 assault guns for each infantry division. Multiply these figures by the 121 infantry divisions of the main forces and the total requirement is staggering in both numbers and quality.

The Chinese currently are producing major weapons for the ground forces that meet basic needs, such as the Type 62 and Type 63 amphibious tanks and a new armored personnel carrier. Neither of the tanks, however, can be considered the equal of the new Soviet T-72, the British Chieftain, or the West German Leopard II. And despite the emphasis on the new tanks, the standard armored fighting vehicle of the PLA's ground forces remains the T-59 battle tank, which is a simplified version of the elderly Soviet T-54 minus the old Russian tank's power traverse, gun stabilizer, and infrared rangefinder.

The picture in artillery is very much the same. The basic weapons date back to the days of Sino-Soviet friendship. The Chinese have experimented, and only experimented, with self-propelled guns; curiously, the Soviets, until very recently, have also lagged in this field. I saw no indications that the PLA was acquiring the new types of high-penetration antitank ammunition rounds now common in most NATO armies. Finally, although soldiers at the divisional level were familiar with the precision guided weapons that have been developed and deployed in the Soviet, American, Israeli, British, French, and West German armies, there was no indication that the Chinese expected such weapons to be delivered to their units within the next ten years.

The Chinese ground forces today are equipped to conduct large-scale conventional warfare within the borders of China or to engage the forces of neighboring states that are not supported militarily by one of the superpowers. Their capability to conduct large-scale offensive operations against either the Soviet Union or even India is limited by inadequate armored fighting vehicles and transport. It is unlikely that the PLA—air, sea, and ground forces—could mount and carry out a successful attack on Taiwan in view of the present qualitative superiority of the Nationalist forces there. The attempt might be successful, but only after some years of murderously high casualties that would eliminate some of the best field units of the ground forces, much of the air force, and a large part of the navy. It is because the Chinese military recognize the enormous cost of a seaborne invasion, the most hazardous of all military operations, that the emphasis in their policy toward Taiwan in their negotiations with the United States has been on the severance of American military support of the Taiwanese forces.

Evidently, China has a very large, well-trained (within the limits of its almost primitive weaponry) ground force. The officers at divisional and regimental levels are experienced, although in many cases probably a little too old for active combat service in the field in the fast-moving conditions of modern battle. But it is not an army that could beat the Russians unless the latter make the elemental mistake of fighting an enemy under conditions in which he is superior.

The ground forces are the core of the PLA. Many of their strengths and weaknesses apply to the two other, junior services, the air force and the navy.

A staff officer of the Thirty-eighth Air Division, stationed southeast of Peking, confided that the first aircraft he had flown in 1948 was an American P-51 Mustang captured from the Nationalist forces during the War of Liberation. It was, another officer recalled, the first modern aircraft most of the officers had seen, for the Chinese air force was not organized as a unit until 1949. Well before that date, however, in the 1930s, Mao's Communist forces had acquired some Nationalist aircraft. Later the Communists picked up some Japanese planes. But it was not until the Korean War that a real air force was developed, largely through the delivery of Soviet fighters and a few bombers and the advice of Russian pilots and maintenance crews for the new air force. But, by the time of the break with Russia, the Chinese air force was numerically weak and qualitatively inferior. By their own efforts in aircraft design and in production, the Chinese have made up much, but not all, of the ground lost when the Soviets recalled their advisors and technicians.

The withdrawal of the Russians seriously affected all the services, but nowhere was the impact greater than on the air force and the industry that supplied it. According to Richard M. Bueschel, in *Communist Chinese Air Power,* "The Soviets withdrew 1,390 experts, cancelled 343 contracts and left 257 scientific and technical projects high and dry. Russian management and technical personnel at the National Aircraft Factory at Shenyang [Mukden] stripped their offices and even took their blueprints with them, leaving the new Shenyang MIG-19 production lines unfinished and inoperative."

The slowdown was general. For the next three years, production of engines and airframes was at a virtual standstill. Part of this may be explained by the general economic malaise that overtook China after the failure of the Great Leap Forward and an agricultural crisis caused by two bad harvests. A second explanation was the obvious Chinese dependence upon the Russians for technology.

The Chinese air force probably was saved from mass obsolescence by an unexpected Soviet action, according to a report prepared for the Defense Advanced Research Projects Agency of the RAND Corporation. The Russians provided the Chinese with up to thirty-six MIG-21F day fighters and continued to ship spare parts and specialized materials to China. The reasons for this uncharacteristic Soviet action are not known. It may have been that Moscow was upset by Chinese shopping expeditions in Europe. In 1962 the Chinese negotiated with SAAB of Sweden for licenses to produce the J-35B Draken fighter-interceptor and with AFA of Switzerland for the P-16 Mark III strike fighter. Neither negotiation was translated into a firm contract, but possibly they influenced the Soviet decision.

One of the paradoxes of this period is that though aircraft production was retarded drastically, the Chinese were able to make significant progress in nuclear research and production. This may have been the result of a governmental decision to shift the emphasis from the vast conventional forces to nuclear weapons and missile development.

The operational strength of the air force was reduced, however. In these years, aircraft had to be cannibalized to keep some part of the service in the air, and pilots' flying time was cut to less than fifteen hours a month. Consequently, and not surprisingly, morale plummeted.

Help was on the way, however, in the form of a widespread reform of the entire aircraft industry under the guidance of Shen Yuan, vice-president of the Peking Institute of Aeronautical Engineering. The principal target was design, a field in which the Chinese had up to that point been content to take the specifications handed them by the Russians and then design the required aircraft. The designer, the RAND Corporation report noted, was "booted out of his ivory tower down to the production site, where he was expected to assume responsibility both for the feasibility and for the success of his designs."

Next there was a five-year program of self-reliance, beginning in 1964. MIG-19 production was resumed in Mukden, but the aircraft were now entirely of Chinese manufacture and bore the Chinese designation of F-6. By 1965, China was able to export a few of these aircraft to Pakistan and Albania.

Work also was pushed on manufacture of the Tupolev TU-16 medium bomber. If China was to have a credible nuclear arsenal, some means of delivery was necessary. By 1964 China had detonated its first atomic device. Two samples of the TU-16 had been delivered by the Russians before the break. Not until 1967 were the Chinese able to turn out an all-Chinese prototype.

An even more difficult project was production of the MIG-21, which the Soviets had given the air force in 1962. The MIG-21 had a sophisticated Tumanski turbojet engine. Series production did not begin until 1969, and then only in very small numbers. The Chinese assisted their production by a relatively simple, if unorthodox, means. In 1966 a few MIG-21s were lifted off the Soviet arms-supply pipeline to Vietnam, which at that time crossed China by railroad. Manufacture of the MIG-21 with what was considered by the Chinese an advanced engine was further complicated by the demands of rocket-propulsion technology for the missile-development program. The Chinese began intensive test firing of their own version of the Soviet SS-4 MRBM in 1965 and used it to deliver a ten- to twenty-kiloton atomic warhead in their fourth nuclear weapons test, in October 1969.

The impact of the Great Proletarian Cultural Revolution on the aircraft industry was akin to that on other branches of the industrial economy. Turmoil and turbulence plagued the Seventh Machine-building Ministry, then in charge of aircraft production, to the extent that PLA units were sent into the factories to restore order. The industry was quick to shake off the effects of the Cultural Revolution to the extent that the MIG-21 went into production. But greater progress lay ahead.

China's first venture into independent design and production was the F-9 fighter bomber, code named Fantan, first produced in 1969. This aircraft has a speed of Mach 1.56, a range, when fully loaded, of approximately seven hundred miles, and a bomb-load capacity of about thirty-three hundred pounds. These are not, by Soviet or Western calculations, the statistics associated with modern fighter bombers. It is therefore understandable that by early 1977 there were indications that production of the F-9 had been either halted or slowed. There are reports that a delta-wing supersonic aircraft similar to the latest French Mirage types is being designed to accommodate the Rolls-Royce Spey engine.

The Chinese air force is the third largest in the world, ranking just behind those of the Soviet Union and the United States. But a quantitative comparison, heartening though it may be to the comrades in Nanking or Shanghai, is irrelevant. Qualitatively, the air force is well behind the Soviet and American air forces or, in fact, the British, West German, French, and half a dozen others.

The air force could probably provide an effective air defense against any potential Asian enemy with the exception of the Soviet Union. The fighter bombers and tactical bombers possibly could give close air support to the ground forces for a period limited to the time it took the Russians to deploy their vastly superior MIG-23s and MIG-25s.

The willingness to face long odds and to admit deficiencies is one of the most engaging characteristics of the officers and men of the PLA. At the Thirty-eighth Air Division there was no attempt to argue that the division's standard aircraft, the F-6, which in reality is the old Soviet MIG-19, was superior to Soviet fighters. The Soviets, incidentally, halted production of the MIG-19 in 1958.

Talking to pilots, one of whom had been flying for seventeen years, it was evident that they had complete confidence in their aircraft and that they were largely ignorant of the advances in fighter performance and in air defense that have been made in the Western states and in the Soviet Union in the last twenty years.

They were, in fact, like all fighter pilots everywhere. Big, healthy, smiling, they exuded that confidence in their aircraft and their personal combat abilities that is the hallmark of their breed. They spoke Chinese, of course, but it seemed to me, a foreigner, that had I been able to speak the language, I would have caught phrases not much different from those used by the pilots of the Eighth Air Force or the RAF long ago.

The staff officers claimed that with the installation of three 30-millimeter guns and the replacement of the original Russian power plant with two Chinese engines, the aircraft were now superior to the original Soviet version. The pilots said that for ground support, their aircraft were equipped with rockets. So they were, but they were the rockets of the 1940s rather than the precision weapons of the 1970s. Their radar, the pilots said, was more useful by night than by day. As I sat in the cockpit of one of the aircraft, the radar looked rudimentary, the sort of thing encountered in American aircraft of the 1950s.

Most of the pilots who carried out a demonstration of precision aerobatics and a ground attack run—a demonstration that would have been matched by any adequately trained National Guard squadron in the United States—had about six hundred hours flying time. Some of the seniors had over a thousand hours.

The division's primary role in war would be cooperation with the ground forces. Defense of the base would be assumed by the fighters stationed there and by antiaircraft manned by the local militia. In the absence of any sign of surface-to-air missile sites or, indeed, of antiaircraft guns, the base appeared highly vulnerable. I said as much to a cheerful staff officer. His reply was that in war the Russians would never get close to the base.

The regional organization of the ground forces is duplicated in the air force. The organization is based on air districts generally analogous to the military regions. Air force headquarters, in theory at least, exercises direct command. Actually, I learned later, the military regional headquarters have a good deal to say about how air resources are employed in combat. As in the ground forces, strength in the air districts relates directly to the importance of the district; the number of aircraft per district is highest in the Mukden, Peking, Nanking, and Kuangchou districts.

The largest operational unit in the air force is the air division, which generally consists of three regiments of three squadrons.

The basic Chinese tactics for fighters emphasize multilayered flights with two planes in each flight providing mutual support at different altitudes. On paper this is impressive. But wars are not fought on paper, and it is my opinion that, given the superior altitude performance of the Soviet fighters, this multilayered flight deployment would be picked to pieces by MIG-23s.

From what I could learn, the fighters are armed, as their most advanced equipment, with the old Soviet-made ATOLL-type heat-seeking air-to-air missile. The rockets with which the fighters of the Thirty-eighth Air Division were armed were for ground attack only and not much advanced beyond those employed by American and British fighter forces in France in 1944.

Bomber tactics are apparently highly conventional in that they reject the progress that has been made in surface-to-air missiles and radar-controlled antiaircraft guns since the early 1960s.

Attacks on ground targets at low levels would be carried out at varying speeds and altitudes; high-level attacks would be conducted in formation. In the support of the ground forces, the air force is hampered by the absence of any effective air-control system. Sorties by bombers or fighter bombers would be carried out on the pilots' initiative without much, or any, direction from the command on the battlefield.

The absence of an adequate ground-to-air control system, the primitive electronic countermeasures available, and the inadequacy of the Chinese radar weigh more heavily than the vigor,

experience, and enthusiasm of pilots in any assessment of the
Chinese air force. The era of uncontrolled fighter or bomber activity "into the wild blue yonder" is over. Successful air warfare today is as sophisticatedly precise as the engines that power
the planes.

There are about 10,000 pilots in a Chinese air force of about
170,000 personnel. They are the warriors, the products of two
years' training that includes daylight flying under all weather
conditions, night operations, aerial gunnery, fixed-point bombing, plus a thorough grounding in aerodynamics, theory of
flight, and meteorology. But intensive training and individual
enthusiasm cannot overcome the present and acute disadvantage
of obsolescent aircraft. The air force is basically a daylight
force, with only a very small percentage of the aircraft equipped
for all-weather operations.

The bombers include sixty-five TU-16 intermediate-range jet
bombers and more than four hundred IL-28 medium-range jet
bombers. These two aircraft probably would carry out any nuclear strikes. The air defense system is long on numbers (forty-
one hundred aircraft) and short on quality (largely old MIG-17s
and MIG-19s and a relatively few advanced MIG-21s). The tactical bomber force, used for ground support, includes about four
hundred elderly MIG-15s and some F-9s.

The air force is based on approximately four hundred operational airfields. This seems adequate for dispersal until it is
realized that the majority are located in China's most populous
areas, within easy striking range of Soviet bombers in the Maritime Province.

Chinese air force officers have studied the lessons of the Vietnam War. They were aware of the American bombing successes, in the last phase of that combat, against the bridges in
North Vietnam and of the U.S. Air Force's casualties to Soviet-
made surface-to-air missiles elsewhere. They knew that new
types of "smart" bombs—the Maverick, for example—were
being deployed and that there are electronic means for diverting
surface-to-air missiles. They had also studied the air-to-air and

air-to-ground fighting in the Arab-Israeli war, which one colonel called, quite accurately, the first modern air war. But they knew that all these new and deadly toys were beyond them, that they would have to fight the Russians with inferior equipment if war came soon. That they appeared quite prepared to do.

The air force is largely a defensive one. There is the potential for a nuclear strike force. But it is arguable that its outmoded aircraft would encounter great difficulties reaching their targets in view of the superiority of Soviet fighters and the massive Russian deployment of surface-to-air missiles. Like other services of the PLA, the air force seemed to be waiting for an infusion of new weapons that would transform it into an effective modern air force.

Just as the number of aircraft in the air force tend to exaggerate its effectiveness, the number of ships in the navy are a temptation to exaggerate its importance in the military balance between China and Russia in Asia. In numbers, the Chinese navy now ranks second in the world, behind the Soviet navy. Its fleet of diesel-powered attack submarines is the third largest in the world. The Chinese have built one diesel-powered ballistic-missile submarine and a nuclear-powered attack boat. Possibly both are part of a ballistic-missile nuclear submarine development program. But, despite its size, the Chinese navy suffers in comparison with the Pacific fleet of the Soviet Union in types of modern vessels and in the sophistication of its armament. It is also, for a variety of reasons, limited in its missions.

The Chinese navy's principal task is the defense of the republic's coastal areas. It does not have a "blue water" capability at the moment. I asked the deputy chief of staff if China had considered sending a squadron into the Indian Ocean, where the Soviet and American fleets are active. He said no, they had to build the ships first. Moreover, to the Chinese the dispatch of a fleet to distant waters smacks of the gunboat diplomacy practiced by the Western imperialists against China in the days of her weakness. Most of China's tormentors—the British, the French, the Japanese, and the Americans—came by sea. Only two decades ago the activities of the U.S. Seventh Fleet raised a serious (to the Chinese, at any rate) threat of invasion.

So coastal defense receives priority, with the submarine force as the primary weapon. This force's strength lies in more than sixty medium-range attack submarines of the Soviet-designed Romeo and Whiskey classes; the names are those given to the Russian boats by NATO intelligence.

In a war with Russia, these submarines would have the mission of intercepting Soviet naval units as they entered the East China Sea through Tsushima Strait or from the Ryukyus, headed for Shanghai or the entrance to the Po Hai Gulf.

Why depend on submarines when the navy has comparatively large forces of surface combatants: ten destroyers, twelve destroyer escorts, and sixteen patrol escorts plus hundreds of missile-armed fast patrol boats? The answer has been provided by Lt. David G. Muller, Jr., of the U.S. Navy in a penetrating article: the majority of these ships are vulnerable to air attack because they have no shipborne surface-to-air missiles. "Until the destroyer force is given a reasonable capability to defend itself against high-performance aircraft it will be forced to remain within range of shore-based aircraft," Muller argues.

The Chinese apparently are aware of this weakness. They were very optimistic in conversation about the future strength of their navy. But they admitted, with that beguiling frankness that extended to discussion of all their military strengths and weaknesses, that it would be some years before the fleet would be able to take on what they called ambitious missions.

There are reports that the Chinese have built a missile-carrying frigate. If they have, they said nothing about it, and I saw no ship of that type at Shanghai or when flying over Port Arthur, the main naval base in Manchuria. But if the destroyers, which are armed with the Soviet-designed Styx surface-to-surface missile with a range of twenty miles, are to be effective outside the range of land-based aircraft, then they must be armed with some form of surface-to-air missile.

Beyond the submarines, China's second line of defense

would be the flotillas of missile-armed patrol boats: more than 60 of the Russian-designed Osa class and another 60 of the Hoku class, which is a Chinese improvement on the Soviet Komar class. Controlled and operating in attack groups within the cover of shore-based aircraft and in cooperation with destroyers, these fast craft could present a very serious threat to a Soviet force approaching the Chinese coast. There are also more than 240 torpedo boats in the navy's inventory. Most of these are of World War II vintage, but about 100 are hydrofoils capable of up to 55 knots.

In view of the number of submarines and surface vessels available, there is a reasonable prospect that the Chinese navy could take a heavy toll of Soviet warships and transports approaching the coasts. If the Russians were foolish enough to attempt amphibious landings, the cost would be very high. However, here, as elsewhere, the Chinese appear to think that their potential enemy will do exactly what they want him to do. With the obvious superiority in quality of the Soviet army and air force, it is unlikely that the Russians would risk heavy losses in a seaborne invasion.

I sensed in talking with Chinese officers that the navy, for reasons never fully explained, enjoys a privileged position within the PLA. Whereas the ground forces and the air force wear similar uniforms (except that the trousers in the air force are blue), the navy clings to a distinctive naval uniform, blue trousers and white wide-collared shirt and gay navy cap. Perhaps this is because the navy, more than any other segment of the PLA, had a life of its own in the days before victory in the War of Liberation.

The first ships of the navy were those captured from the Nationalists, and many of its original officers were defectors from Chiang Kai-shek's ranks. According to one Western authority on the Chinese navy, most of its junior officers had been trained by the Americans during World War II and had the technological experience that was vital if the new Chinese navy was to have any claim to effectiveness.

At any rate, the new navy was formally established in September 1950 when the various regional forces were put under the command of the PLA's general headquarters. A naval air force was established in 1952. By 1954 the government was ready to reorganize the sea forces, transferring the duties of naval districts to fleets subordinated to naval headquarters in Peking. During this period the navy, like the other arms of the PLA, was receiving assistance from the Soviet Union, which sent surface vessels, submarines (many of which are still operational), and advisors.

The Russians also helped the Chinese develop a shipbuilding industry that emphasized the construction of submarines and small surface craft. In the Soviet Union at that time, the maximum emphasis was being placed on these types; the Russian navy had not yet begun its major development of missile-carrying destroyers and cruisers.

As in the ground and air forces, the navy's principal operational preoccupation is with the Soviet forces—that is, Russia's Pacific fleet. But the navy also has an additional interest that impinges upon the strategic triangle in the Northwest Pacific of Russia–China–America. This interest is Taiwan, whose return to China is one of the People's Republic's national objectives.

China's ambitions in this regard are limited by its naval resources. It is probable that the navy would be adequate to sever the seaborne communications between Taiwan and the offshore islands of Quemoy and Matsu and, with a greater effort, to blockade Taiwan itself. Either action or a combination of both would risk war with the Republic of China on Taiwan, and it is therefore unlikely that the navy would initiate such operations unless Peking was reasonably certain that the United States would remain neutral.

The Mutual Defense Treaty between Taiwan and the United States, State Department officials report, does not cover the offshore islands, but it would obligate the U.S. Navy to break a blockade of Taiwan itself.

The ability of the navy to project China's power is negligible if attacks on the Soviet Maritime Province are under consideration. The navy has only twenty-nine landing craft, all of World War II origin; the supporting forces, destroyers, and frigates would have to operate outside the limits of close air support if the landing were made in an area distant from the mainland. These factors also apply in the case of a landing on Taiwan, whose air force, although aging, probably could punish severely any invasion fleet attacking without air cover.

Quemoy, Matsu, and Taiwan, however, are not the only islands that China claims. Peking also claims all of the Spratly Islands, including Itu Aba, in the South China Sea, which are garrisoned by Taiwan, the Philippines, and Vietnam. China has told the Philippine government that its oil explorations in the Spratly chain infringe upon Chinese sovereignty.

Chinese landing operations on these islands have a much greater chance of success than action against Taiwan and the offshore islands. Here again, even a limited action might promote American intervention, something China at this moment seems anxious to avoid.

Unlike the Soviet and American navies, the Chinese fleet cannot deploy a realistic nuclear missile threat. The only nuclear-missile submarine operational is the old Soviet Golf-class boat built at Dairen in 1964. There is no objective evidence that the Chinese have succeeded in building submarine-launched ballistic missiles with which this boat could be armed. Such boats are expensive, an important consideration to the PLA, and it is unlikely that the missiles, if they are ever produced, could reach Soviet targets that are not already covered by Chinese land-based missiles.

The Chinese also built a nuclear-powered attack submarine early in the 1970s, the first of the Han-class boats. It is still the only vessel built of this class, and its present mission is unknown. One educated guess is that it may be used as an experimental platform for Chinese submarine-launched ballistic missiles.

PLA officers, when discussing the navy, give a strong impression that its technological development has been neglected, which is equally true of the other services, and that a naval expansion program will be part of the general modernization of the PLA. Significantly, the Chinese press early in 1977 accused the Gang of Four of discounting China's need for a powerful navy, a good sign that the new leadership takes a different view.

Yet there are no signs that a larger navy would have any different missions. These remain coastal defense, which includes repelling Soviet naval attacks; the liberation of Taiwan; and the recovery of the Spratly Islands and other "lost" territories. At the moment, the navy has not the means, nor has the government the will, to project Chinese naval power around the world.

This is subject to change. The Chinese rejoice in their self-appointed role as the leaders of the Third World. Aside from extravagant oratory at the United Nations and other international forums, the Chinese have done little to reinforce this position. The deployment of naval forces to ports in Africa and southern Asia is one means, albeit an uncertain one, to announce China's military, as well as political, interest in the welfare of other Third World states. The uncertainty applies to the long-term political reactions to such deployments. Chinese propaganda has consistently criticized the Soviet Union and the United States for "showing the flag" visits by squadrons in the Indian Ocean and elsewhere. Could the Chinese now reverse their propaganda position and carry out the same sort of missions? At the moment, this is out of the question, because of the fleet's weakness. But armed expansion, whether by sea, air, or land, has its own momentum. Chinese naval visits to ports in East Africa and Southeast Asia may be part of the future global military picture.

We have been discussing armed forces of relatively unlimited manpower but limited military sophistication. No one who has seen them can doubt the toughness, high morale, and discipline of the Chinese land, sea, and air forces. They are officered, in the main force at least, by experienced soldiers. But to consider them as effective in an encounter battle against today's Soviet forces is to expect that the American Expeditionary Force of 1917–18 would be able to defeat the Germans of 1944. Morale may be the decisive factor, as Napoleon said, but only when the two sides have equality in weapons.

10

The Last Resort: Tunnels, Militia, and Guerrillas

CHINESE optimism about their prospects of defeating the Soviet Union in war, an optimism that often strikes the visitor as wildly exaggerated, does not rest entirely on the active forces of the PLA. Two other elements of the defense establishment—one passive, the other active—enter into their calculations. The passive element in China's defense is the elaborate system of "tunnels" (in reality, air-raid shelters) that have been dug under cities as large as Peking and under remote farming communes. The active element is the enormous Chinese militia force that would join the regular forces in a fight against invaders.

Whatever their military merits, these two elements have a major psychological importance. The PLA infantryman, shivering in his foxhole along the northern frontier, believes that his wife and children will escape Russian bombs or shells in the shelter near his home. He also counts on the millions of militiamen who will support his efforts.

There is a close connection between the shelters and the militia. In most cases the labyrinthine underground communities would be defended in war by the militia. They would also provide a route by which the militia and party officials could escape from the cities into the countryside. There they would carry on the guerrilla war, which, despite the present drive toward military modernization, remains the ultimate military option for Chinese leaders, especially those whose military education began and ended with the Long March and the subsequent hit-and-run warfare against the Japanese and the Nationalists.

The military rationale for the air-raid shelters is that the civilian and military command would be able to continue to direct a war against the Soviet Union from them. The political impetus came from Chairman Mao Tse-tung, who, a year after the fighting with the Russians on the Ussuri River in 1969, directed the people to dig deep tunnels and store grain everywhere.

The Chinese shelter system thus was started well before the even more elaborate Soviet system, which has been developed since 1972. So extensive is the Russian program that the passive defense efforts of the Soviet Union now are reckoned as important elements in the strategic balance between the United States and the Soviet Union.

The shelter I was shown at Dairen in Manchuria offered striking evidence of the extent of the system and of how, year by year, the Chinese have increased the sophistication of the national system—greater depths, bigger reservoirs for food and water, more elaborate defenses. I was not shown the largest and most important of all shelters, that under Peking, usually termed the new subway, possibly because it is not completed, if such enterprises are ever completed. The Peking shelter will offer refuge to the leaders of the party, the government, and the PLA, and in theory, at least, from it they will direct the war against the Soviet Union.

Dairen deserves an extensive shelter system. It is the largest port in the northeast and, with the neighboring naval base of Port Arthur, now called Liu Shun, forms a conurbation of great strategic importance. The tunnels of Dairen and Port Arthur were built primarily to shelter the workers who would keep the ports working in war.

There are many entrances to the Dairen shelter. The one chosen for me was highly unwarlike. The hotel manager ushered me to a rather dingy room on the first floor, grinned broadly, and pushed a button. The wooden floor slid to one side. Down a flight of steps lay the tunnels of Dairen, twenty thousand meters long, capable of sheltering fifty thousand to sixty thousand people from enemy attack.

Considering China's chronic shortage of modern machinery, the primary tools that created the shelter were pick, shovel, and wheelbarrow. Liu Chen-lin, the foreign ministry's representative, said that half a million workers had been employed at various times on the project. The majority had been volunteers from the city's factories and shops, and the remainder, other volunteers from the agricultural communes on the outskirts of Dairen.

The word *volunteers,* of course, is suspect when employed by officials of an authoritarian regime. But it is probable that in this case the men and women who built the shelters really volunteered. Dairen is within easy range of the Soviet air bases and missile sites in the Maritime Province; an elementary knowledge of geography probably provided all the inducement necessary.

The workers built the shelter between 1970 and 1974. The first section of this underground fortress that I entered had been dug in the first year and a half. The tunnel was about seven meters high and about two meters wide and was lit by naked electric light bulbs backed by tin reflectors. Radio amplifiers supplied an incongruous note—the voice of a soprano. When she flatted, which was often, even the solemn Chinese guides winced. Dimly lit passages led from the main tunnel to reservoirs, ammunition dumps, and first-aid posts.

Dairen's underground fortress contains several large reservoirs, each holding three hundred cubic meters of water, and silos for the storage of grain and rice. There are first-aid posts, clinics, schoolrooms, dormitories, assembly halls, and even a barber shop. One of the guides said that local barbers had pitched in to build their shop. I said they must differ greatly from barbers I had known around the world. His reply was typical. These, he said gently, were *Chinese* barbers inspired by the words of Chairman Mao.

Decontamination centers for use after nuclear, chemical, or bacteriological attacks were scattered through the shelter. Ventilation units had been installed to pump in fresh air, and air-cleaning machines were supposed to keep the air in the shelter reasonably fresh. But the steel doors supposed to seal the tunnel from contamination looked badly built and far from airtight.

Liu said they estimated that the shelter could be filled in ten minutes. Should hostile attacks continue, military production could be carried on by small factories scattered throughout the shelter. Power for these factories would be supplied by mobile power stations such as I later saw being built in Mukden. These were smaller than stations built for surface installation, but the factory chiefs said they had about the same production capacity.

It was obvious that as the work had progressed, tunnel technology had improved. The sections of the shelter built in the first months were only seven to ten meters below ground level and were crudely cut. The newer sections, however, were up to thirty meters down, and large areas had been hewn out of solid rock.

Smaller tunnels have been dug under apartment houses and schools throughout northeastern and eastern China. The Red Guards School's shelter, on the outskirts of Dairen, had been carved into a hillside behind the school. Here again, the shelter was a cooperative effort. Students, teachers, and parents had constructed a shelter sixteen hundred meters long, large enough to accommodate all the students. There were seven underground classrooms, each seating eighty pupils; a clinic; toilets; showers; and a decontamination facility. There was, however, no generator for electricity in the tunnel. One was being procured, I was told hastily. But, the guides pointed out, the earth excavated in building the tunnel had provided the school with a fine new playground.

Some aspects of the shelter program appear rather too elaborate, if, indeed, they are to be used in war. Farther into the hills that tower over Dairen, the Chinese had built what they called the department-store tunnel. A wide, crescent-shaped tunnel had been cut into the rock and stocked with foodstuffs, clothing, bicycles, radios, and even toys; at least that is what it offered a foreign visitor. Despite the salesgirls who stood behind the counters, there was an artificiality about the shelter. The whole scene jarred with the Chinese concept of a People's War. In war, I imagine, the consumer goods would probably be replaced by plain foods, water, ammunition, and weapons.

At the village of Jiao Tang Hwa, about thirty-eight miles southeast of Peking, the shelter is a well-kept relic of the wars against the Japanese and the Nationalists. About eight hundred meters of the shelter area still is maintained for use in an emergency. The village elders, grizzled veterans of the Japanese and national liberation wars, pointed out entrances to the shelter under stoves and in other unlikely places and demonstrated how they would boobytrap the empty houses before going underground. Finally, we clambered up to a fire port, set a few inches above the ground, that commanded the village's principal pig sty. Invading soldiers, they assured me, always headed for the pigsty after they had rushed the village and in two wars they had killed "many, many" Japanese and Nationalists from this fire port.

Military and civilian officials in the cities and the countryside insisted that the shelters would provide effective protection against conventional air attack. But it was evident that they were not aware of the accuracy of modern precision-guided missiles, which can hit relatively small targets, such as the entry to a tunnel or a ventilator. Nuclear attack and the consequent radiation would raise serious problems, they conceded. They recognized that the steel doors installed in the larger shelters as a protection against radiation were not entirely airtight and that the ventilation systems would have to be improved. They thought they could handle a gas attack; masks produced by local industries would be distributed to all civilians.

Serious doubts must remain about the security offered by the shelters in war, especially nuclear war. The U.S. Air Force, hardening the silos for its Minuteman missiles against Soviet attack, aims at a strength that will resist an impact of two thousand pounds per square inch. Obviously, the unhardened surface above Chinese shelters cannot match this resistance. The Chinese will have to allow for major collapse in some sections of their shelters in the event of nuclear attack.

Nor did any of the Chinese with whom I talked in Dairen or elsewhere appear to understand the confusion that follows bombing, even conventional bombing. The Chinese are a disciplined people. But that discipline would be severely tested in an air raid. The death of key personnel, the blocking of streets by debris, and the rupture of water mains and communications lines are the consequences of any bombing attack. It is not simply a question of getting people into shelters, but the Chinese seem to think it is. I put this down to their inexperience. The Chinese were bombed by the Japanese in World War II and before. But they have experienced no raids of the size and severity that might be expected from the Russians, even if conventional weapons are employed. I am sure that the military scientists in Peking are well acquainted with the consequences of nuclear bombing. But local officials and commanders are not.

The defense of the tunnels in the event that invaders overrun a city or village would be left in war to the militia. The militia's ability to provide an effective defense under the conditions I saw seemed questionable.

In the Dairen shelter, machine-gun and rifle ports have been hewn out of the rock or earth at every angle, providing a field of fire down the next stretch of tunnel. Barbed-wire barriers are available to be thrown across the tunnel.

But other, more bizarre defenses were demonstrated proudly. One was a hand-propelled steel fan about four feet in diameter that would be placed across the tunnel, at some hazard to its operator, under the impression that the invaders would throw themselves onto the fan and be sliced to ribbons. I suggested that the invaders would be much more likely, when confronted with the fan, to chuck a grenade at it and its operator. The guides were silent. Another defensive measure was a steel mat about a yard square covered with three-and-a-half-inch steel spikes. Mats such as these were to be strewn throughout the shelter in the path of enemies.

Success in defending the tunnels depends on the armament, training, and leadership of the militia. The Chinese defense ministry's estimates of the numbers, training, and capabilities of the militia are exceedingly high, estimates that appear to derive from the militia's exploits in the Japanese and Nationalist wars.

Wu Hsiu-chen, the deputy chief of staff, reflected this optimism when he told me that "we have more than one hundred million militia" and that "we can say for certain that the equipment for the present militia is better than in the past; at present, for example, the militia is receiving quite enough ammunition. There, in the militia, lies the source of our strength."

An examination of this important part of China's military establishment should begin by saying what the militia is not. It certainly is not 100 million strong if armed and trained forces are counted. It bears only the most remote relationship in training and equipment to the National Guard in the United States or the trained reserves in most Western countries.

The militia—or, to give the full name, the People's Militia—is a part-time, quasi-military organization controlled politically by the Communist party but trained and commanded by the PLA. The militia is subdivided into the basically military service and the Production and Construction Corps. The military service is usually divided into three groupings—ordinary, basic, and armed. Approximately 60 million are in the ordinary category. They receive little training and, aside from certain low-grade duties, would have little significance in war.

The heart of the militia system is the basic organization, probably numbering about 15 million. This consists of former members of the PLA's active forces and politically reliable men in the eighteen-to-thirty-five age group. Retired PLA officers oversee the training of these forces, but once or twice a year, units of the basic militia are exercised under the direction of active-duty PLA officers.

The approximately 5 million men and women of the armed militia are selected from the best of the basic militia. These are the best-trained and best-armed of the whole militia force. They provide armed security patrols and help train basic and ordinary militiamen.

Responsibility for training the militia rests with the provincial military district and is carried out through subordinate commands and various departments of the PLA. Armament usually does not extend beyond rifles, machine guns, and mortars, although some urban militia units have been equipped with antitank and antiaircraft artillery.

The Production and Construction Corps has the primary mission of economic development of some of China's more remote and unproductive areas. The corps's secondary mission is border defense and surveillance in those areas. During the Cultural Revolution the corps came under the control of the Ministry of Defense instead of the Ministry of State Farms and Land Reclamation, which had previously supervised its work. Partly as a result of the ''back to the land'' propaganda of the Cultural Revolution, the Production and Construction Corps was expanded rapidly to a strength of over 3 million. Probably about 15 percent of this number are armed. Again, the weapons are those of the regular armed militia—rifles, light machine guns, and mortars.

In China, as in other authoritarian countries, there is often a startling difference between promise and performance. This is true of the ubiquitous militia. The visitor is shown artillery pieces swaddled in sacking in factories, stacked rifles, and well-oiled machine guns and told that they belong to the militia. The superficial impression is of a force prepared to fight at a moment's notice. The reality is somewhat different.

A textile-machinery factory outside Shanghai boasted a militia three thousand strong—ordinary, basic, and armed. The basic militia, in that factory at any rate, was the best armed and trained, according to a grizzled PLA veteran who directed the training. As so often happened, I was struck not merely by their readiness but by their readiness for a type of war now as dead as the type fought at Gettysburg.

The unit paraded thirty-two strong in neat blue coveralls and bamboo helmets. About one-third were women. All were armed with semiautomatic rifles with fixed bayonets. The unit went through a bayonet drill, that anachronism so beloved by the Chinese military, with cries of "Shah," which means "attack" or "kill," cries so loud that they drowned the iron clamor of the factory.

A whistle blew, and the militia rushed to their antiaircraft guns to demonstrate how they would defend the factory. The covers were torn off the guns, and a hail of fire directed at the balloons hung around the perimeter of the parade ground. The remaining militia knelt and added their rifle fire to the general clamor. The weapons were clean, the alertness exemplary, but it is reasonable to ask whether this demonstration had any relevance to modern war.

The militiamen standing by their weapons were clearly delighted by their demonstration. Evidently, they believed their weapons were the best available. But the quadruple-mount heavy machine guns they fired are primitive compared to the Vulcan multibarrel gun of the U.S. Army or the Soviets' quadruple-mount ZSU 23-millimeter gun. Both of these guns are directed by radar. The officers said that the Chinese machine guns could maintain a rate of fire of 660 rounds a minute in action. This is barely adequate against modern combat aircraft even if there is adequate warning of the attack and radar tracking.

The PLA veteran who commanded the unit admitted there was no radar available. In the event of Soviet attack, he said, warning would come by telephone from a central antiaircraft headquarters in Shanghai. The Russian bombers, he indicated with a sweep of his hand, would come in at low level.

Did he expect machine guns without radar sighting and individually aimed to knock down modern fighters strafing at six hundred miles an hour? He shrugged. Surface-to-air missiles would be more effective, he admitted, but for the present, the factory would have to be defended by the machine guns around us.

Standing there, erect and proud in the cold, clear air, he expressed a combative spirit and admitted the material deficiencies of the militia. If the antiaircraft demonstration had left much to be desired, his forces, he explained, were well trained in marksmanship, grenade throwing, and bayonet drill. The men and women understood and could carry out the precautions necessary in a nuclear attack.

"We drill in antinuclear and antigas warfare, in first aid, and in emergency repairs of equipment," he said defiantly. "We have studied the lessons of Chairman Mao and we are prepared and self-sufficient."

He and other militia commanders in the cities and the countryside left unanswered the question that must strike any visitor: how much of the militia effort is truly relevant to China's defense, and how much is a propaganda effort to tighten the link between the people and the Communist party?

Much of the militia effort displayed was pure show, with little relevance to the realities of modern war—schoolchildren popping away at balloons with their rifles, or marching proudly around a playground; militiamen dueling with bayonets; machine guns preparing to fire at MIG-21s; minute instruction on the achievements of the People's Army, the militia of that day, in the wars against the Japanese and the Nationalists. What connection can this have to the sort of war China will have to fight if the Soviets invade? (I am assuming that the Russian high command keeps its head and restricts the invaders to well-defined objectives rather than mounting a general offensive.)

The propaganda side is clearly important. "The young people must be reminded of the sacrifices of their fathers and mothers; they must not forget what the individual can do in war," a PLA militia instructor said. In Mukden, Nanking, and Peking, other officers and officials said very much the same thing: the young must be reminded of their responsibilities to the country, of what had been done to liberate them. It is a plea not uncommon in other countries, including the Soviet Union.

The central question is the militia's effectiveness in military situations more complex and modern than those foreseen by Chairman Mao. In a long war with the Soviet Union, one in which China is invaded from many points in the north and west, the militia would be important, perhaps decisive. But its effectiveness in an "arena war"—the arena in this case being Manchuria—would be problematical.

The operational plan for the Dairen militia emphasizes the problem. Those militia not required for the defense of the underground shelters would head out of the tunnels into the hills, there to fight a guerrilla war against the invaders. How effective would they be? How effective are any guerrillas under modern conditions?

Quite a few Americans of little experience but extravagant imaginations hold forth at dinner parties about how the ragged guerrillas of the Viet Cong humbled the U.S. Army and Air Force. There were ragged guerrillas there. But anyone who reads the field diaries of units or saw the war at close hand knows that the most effective Vietnamese fighters came from the regulars, the main-force units. Given adequate cover, such as mountains or forests, guerrillas can harry and annoy regular forces. But new weapons and improvements in old ones have increased the odds against them.

In Israel in the summer of 1977 I discussed with Israeli officers the problem posed by the Palestine Liberation Organization guerrillas who had occupied an old fort and some stone houses on a hilltop a mile or so from the Israeli frontier. They scanned the fortifications with their field glasses, and one said, "We'd dust that hill with napalm, and they'd be out of there or dead."

Since 1945, the Russians have made startling claims about the effectiveness of their guerrillas—or as they call them, partisans—in World War II. But the German records show that the partisans were a minor inconvenience. The eastern war was decided not by guerrilla actions but by major battles, such as Stalingrad and Kursk, involving thousands of tanks and aircraft and hundreds of thousands of trained soldiers.

On the basis of high-level statements made in Peking since I left China and on other military information, I believe that the military doctrine of the PLA is being reexamined by the senior military and political authorities, in many cases the same men. In my opinion, one result of this examination will be a gentle, gradual deemphasis of the militia's importance and an intensification of the drive for modernization of the regular armed forces.

Clearly, the government cannot disband the militia; the political and ideological investment has been too great. But it is likely to begin to downgrade the importance of the militia to its operational planning as part of an effort to prepare the PLA to cope with the modern weapons at the disposal of the Soviet forces and, equally important, the modern blitzkrieg tactics that the Russians have evolved to implement their offensive doctrine.

The residual militia mission will be the garrisoning of the air-raid shelters. Even there, militia defense will not be effective unless the men and women are given more modern weapons and static defenses and the shelters themselves are reconstructed to take into account new weapons such as precision-guided bombs or missiles and napalm.

Militiamen and women and the soldiers, sailors, and airmen of the PLA have certain characteristics that should be the envy of other forces. Drawn from the peasant-worker class, which makes up more than 80 percent of the population, the Chinese soldier is a hard and willing worker able to survive and improvise under a wide variety of battlefield conditions. His education is sufficient to enable him to read and understand simple training manuals. He is, however, well below the soldiers in Western armies or the Soviet army in his technical proficiency. But he is well ahead of his Western counterpart in his ability to bear extraordinary physical hardship. The men of the PLA that I saw were all in excellent physical condition.

Motivation is another important plus for the PLA. Every soldier, sailor, and airman has been indoctrinated from a very early age to honor his country and to believe in and support the Communist party. This indoctrination, combined with the high value placed by the Chinese on obedience, is responsible for the firm discipline that was evident in every unit I visited.

In past ages the soldier was held in low repute in China. Two successful wars against the Japanese and the Nationalists and the ever-present and well-advertised threat of Soviet invasion have combined to raise the status of the fighting man in China. A family whose son or daughter is chosen to serve in the PLA is proud.

But to reach full effectiveness, these forces must be given modern weapons. The Russians would not be beaten by peasant marksmen firing from ambush. They can only be held by the PLA if the Chinese high command is ready to recognize that both its doctrine and its weapons are obsolete. War has changed. The individual is still the most important element, but only if he is armed with modern weapons, controlled and commanded by modern means of communication, and carrying out a military doctrine aware of the conditions of modern war.

Rapprochement, Rivalry, or War

THE two antagonists stand face to face in East Asia. In the north are the well-trained, well-disciplined armies and air forces of the Soviet Union, armed with tanks, missiles, and aircraft of a sophistication unmatched in the world, save in the American forces. These are the heirs to the tradition of Suvurov, of Zhukov, of Koniev—true believers in Russian military invincibility, blind followers of the Communist party leadership, possessed of a national xenophobia in which the Chinese are a potential enemy.

To the south are the numberless, faceless legions of the People's Republic of China, deficient in modern weapons, chained to a doctrine evolved by septuagenarians from their memories of battles thirty to forty years ago, obedient, enduring, and enterprising in battle, like their potential enemies imbued with the conviction that their Communist party leadership is all-seeing, all-knowing.

Walter Duranty once remarked that students of the behavior of authoritarian states must always remember that what to the students may appear a government's unlikeliest option may prove in the end to be the likeliest. He was referring to the great switch of 1939, when Hitler's Germany and Stalin's Russia after six years of bitter enmity came to terms and precipitated World War II.

Duranty's words have been much in my mind in the months

since this book was begun. The death of Chairman Mao, the installation of Chairman Hua as his successor, and China's underdeveloped economy and parlous military situation appear to establish conditions under which a new Chinese leader might break with past policies and, taking account of his country's internal and external problems, seek to restore the former relationship with the Soviet Union.

Setting aside the ideological and nationalist arguments against a rapprochement with the Soviet Union, there remain important economic arguments for such a move on China's part. Like Russia in the late 1930s, China desperately needs advanced technology. Much of its industrial structure was designed, and in many cases built, by Russians. The primary weapons of the PLA are Russian or derive from Russian models. Rapid improvement of the republic's economic and military position is more likely to come as a consequence of a new agreement between the two giants than from a gingerly Chinese movement toward the purchase of the military technology of the West.

From the Chinese side these are strong, if not presently acceptable, arguments for rapprochement. But there is a Russian side, too, with equally strong arguments against rapprochement with China.

One basis for these arguments is the present Russian view of the Soviet Union. It is essentially an imperialist view. If all the cant about combating the Western imperialists and the primacy of Marxism is forgotten, the Soviet Union stands today as a great imperialist power whose writ runs from the Baltic to the Pacific, whose authoritarian regime is armored against dissidents by an efficient KGB, and whose power is the central element in the governance of such old and famous states as Poland and Hungary. Occasionally, this new Russian imperium stumbles and fumbles, as did imperial Rome, imperial Spain, and imperial Britain. But its existence is a fact of international life, and that fact has reinforced in the Russian psyche all those characteristics which make drastic changes of basic policy difficult for the governing class, in this case the Communist party.

Undoubtedly, there are theoreticians in the Kremlin who argue that the Soviet Union might be safer and the prospects of political or military victory over the West better if a new accommodation was reached with Peking. But no matter how sensible their arguments (and many sensible ones can be made), the chance that they now will be accepted by the Politburo are remote.

Resume our old association with the Chinese, the theoreticians would advise. The cost in real terms would be no greater than it was in the 1950s when the Russian economy was weaker than it is today. For a few hundred million rubles of economic and military aid each year, the danger of a war on the eastern frontier is eliminated for the time being. Of course, you will be helping to build China's economic and military strength. But China is so far behind in both respects that it will be years before it can really present a threat to Siberia. And, by then, Siberia will be richer and more populous and our own forces will be armed with weapons more advanced than those we would sell to Peking. And, finally, it can be argued, there is always the authoritarian option: break the agreements, withdraw the advisors, and close down trade in products vital to China if it suits the immediate national interest.

American politicians and officials have been so concerned with the Soviet presence in Europe—"NATO is the heart of our foreign policy," President Carter said in May 1977—that they have failed, with a few exceptions, to assess the change that has overtaken the Soviet Union's political and strategic position in Asia.

The Soviet break with China and the beginnings of Sino-American rapprochement have forced the Kremlin to consider its worst possible strategic case: a two-front war against the United States and its allies in Europe, and China and its allies in Asia. Although, it is hoped, such a war is remote, its very possibility imposes heavy burdens on the Soviet Union. As we have seen, Soviet ground forces in Asia have been expanded in numbers and been given more sophisticated weapons—first, after the break with China and, second, after the United States and China began to improve their relations.

Granted a continuation of the Sino-Soviet rift, what can the rulers of the Soviet Union be expected to do in the next decade? Some Russian programs are evident and have been described earlier, such as the continued improvement of the land and air forces in Siberia, the expansion of the Pacific fleet, and the steady economic development of Siberia. But it seems unlikely that the Russians will end there.

The completion of these programs probably will support a major Soviet effort to compete with China for political leadership in Asia, which is one of the fundamental policy aims of the People's Republic. And, although the Chinese will not admit it in conversation, the Russians quite clearly enjoy a favorable position in many Asian countries. This position is the result not of anything the Russians themselves have done or not done but of the residual fear of China in many neighboring capitals, such as Hanoi and New Delhi, to name only two. The Soviet advantage is balanced by equally deep-seated fears of the Russians in Japan and South Korea. Moreover, it is highly unlikely that any Asian country, even the most underdeveloped, would opt for the Soviet Union as a source of technological assistance or as a market for its goods in comparison with the industrialized societies of Japan, Western Europe, and the United States. True, the Russians have concluded economic deals with Japan. But Japan is hardly an underdeveloped country, and it prospers under American security guarantees.

For Moscow the prudent course in the next decade would be a program of mending diplomatic fences and of playing upon Asian fears of China. In this situation arguments for a resumption of the old relationship with China seem unlikely to impress the rulers of the Soviet Union, today or tomorrow.

The Soviet Union is an empire, heir to the empire of the Romanovs. As empires age, they and their rulers become less flexible, less willing to deviate from established principles, less tolerant of competing powers. The aging process often is accompanied by the solidification of national interests (or what are conceived to be those interests), in this case the Soviet position in Asia, which means the provision of adequate military means to repel any attack from outside (meaning China) on that rule.

The second reason why the Russians can be expected at present to reject rapprochement with China is ideological. Chairman Mao and his successors have challenged the Russian leadership in a most sensitive area: Moscow's claim to the leadership of world Communism. The challenge has been made elsewhere, by the Yugoslavs, by the Spanish Communist party, and by sections of the parties in Italy and France. All these developments are important and, indeed, intrinsically dangerous to Moscow's claim to the leadership of international Communism. But no break dealt such a severe blow as China's. This was no minor power defying the northern colossus, but a nation whose population is nearing one billion human beings. China's leaders were not relatively unimportant semibourgeois like Carillo or successful guerrilla leaders like Tito; they were Mao and Chou En-lai, honored and venerated throughout the Marxist world. And, in their ultimate defiance, they challenged the Politburo's policy toward the capitalist world, the ends and means behind its rule of the Soviet Union, and its right to direct the development along Communist lines or, at least, in sympathy with Communism of the states of the Third World.

It is impossible to say precisely which of many causes was the most important in directing a man or a government to take a certain action. Probably, in the case of the Sino-Soviet split, it was Mao's conviction that the Communist world should take a more belligerent attitude toward the capitalists, particularly the United States, that ignited Moscow's hostility to the Chinese party and people.

The immediate consequence of this hostility was to attempt to weaken, by the withdrawal of funds, advisors, and materials, the Chinese economic and military position and thus reduce the impact of China's interference in the Third World. There can be no doubt that, as we have seen, the severance of economic and military aid dealt a grievous blow to China. To a very real degree the Chinese are still struggling to recover from that blow.

The second consequence of the new enmity, or rather the resumption under the red flag of a hostility that has endured since the sixteenth century, was the imposition of a military threat to China. Russians will argue that their enhanced military presence in the Far East represents only an attempt to safeguard Soviet territory there against Chinese expansion, rather than a threat to invade China.

Whatever the Russian objective may be, the reinforcement of the Soviet forces in the Siberian Far East following displays of bellicosity on the Ussuri River has had the effect of forcing the Chinese to take very extensive military measures. What, for example, would be China's economic position today if the millions upon millions of man-hours devoted to digging the shelters had been directed toward the modernization of Chinese industry and agriculture? How much would the economy benefit if a third or a quarter of the PLA divisions now under arms could be disbanded and their men directed into that economy? Is the Chinese balance-of-payments position so good that they can afford to buy Spey engines from Britain or shop around Europe for modern fighters and missiles?

There is little doubt that the confrontation in the Far East has been a far more serious problem for the Chinese than for the Russians. The Chinese military position in Manchuria and farther west is strictly defensive. China has made claims to large areas of the Soviet Maritime Province. But, barring the unlikely event of a complete breakdown of the Soviet government, China's chances of fulfilling those claims by conquering the lost territories are extremely remote. China's problem, in this area, at least, is not the recovery of lost territory but assuring an effective defense of Manchuria and the Peking–Tientsin areas.

China's hope for survival in its present form rests on a rapid modernization of the economy and the military, in that order. If China remains weak in comparison with the Soviet Union, as it is today, Soviet rulers, today and tomorrow, will be tempted by the riches of Manchuria; by the prospect of extirpating, once and for all, the most serious ideological challenge facing the Soviet Communist party; and by the final settlement of the Far Eastern problem, which has plagued Russian governments for centuries.

Does this mean that war between the two giants is imminent? I do not believe so. The potential for war certainly exists. To a Soviet military planner it must be clear that the time to fight China, if Russia has to fight China, is now, before Chinese modernization reduces the chances of victory. Authoritarian states, communist or fascist, have never found it difficult to arrange a cause for war, and uninterrupted propaganda playing upon a patriotic people has done the rest.

The most powerful factor arguing against war in the immediate future is the character of the present Soviet leadership. Leonid Brezhnev and his closest collaborators are elderly men. Elderly men, by and large, are prudent men. In Russia's case, the leaders know what war, even victorious war, can cost a country, including the new danger of nuclear attack. They are aware that any military involvement in Siberia against China would inevitably reduce the Western powers' perception of Soviet strength in Central Europe and, by their calculations, increase the danger of attack there.

The Soviet Union has always considered NATO as an aggressive force directed against the Russians and their allies in Central Europe. Apologists argue that this is only what the Russians say. But do men as experienced as Brezhnev, Suslov, and Gromyko really believe it? They cannot; the whole idea is absurd. The apologists may be assuming too much. The men who rule Russia today are Communists, and to Communists the capitalist West is the enemy, ultimately to be overcome by political or military means. So it is possible that they view the West, with its new aircraft, tanks, missiles, and precision weapons, as an enemy waiting to pounce on the Soviet Union at the first sign that Russian strength in Central Europe has been reduced.

Brezhnev and his colleagues will not be there forever. Will the coming of "the new men" change the Sino-Soviet confrontation? Dozens of Chinese said it would not. By their thinking, the successors to the present Politburo will have been molded by the same heretical views of Marxism as the present rulers; they, too, will be social imperialists hostile to China and its development, presenting a continuing military menace to her northern frontiers and a political rivalry to China's claims to leadership of the Third World. It is impossible to say, of course, whether the dire predictions of the Chinese will be borne out. It is important to realize, however, that this is what the Chinese believe today and that it will take a great deal more than sweet talk from Moscow to convince them that the Soviet attitude toward China has changed. Both peoples will then face that paradox so often found in crises: it is not what is true but what a government or a people believes to be true that counts.

Is war between the Soviet Union and China inevitable? Wars between powers or groups of powers with deep national and ideological differences are not necessarily inevitable. They may become inevitable when one party, by a diplomatic or military coup, establishes a margin of power over the intended victim that makes war inevitable. The Russo-German pact of 1939, and the subsequent German invasion of Poland, is the most recent historical example. In the present situation the conditions that would make war inevitable are remote.

One condition, let us hope sufficiently remote, would be the breakup of NATO and the consequent "Finlandization" of Europe. Relieved then of the prospect of real Western pressure on its western frontier, which for prudence's sake we must believe the Russians now perceive, the Soviet Union might well turn east to deal with the heretics in Peking. Given that European situation, war in Asia would be inevitable. At the moment it is not, although some very knowledgeable people believe it is.

Is war probable? Yes, indeed. In the Chinese and the Russians, Asia accommodates two strongly nationalistic peoples. If Marx had never lived, if Communism had never existed, there would be a probability of war in East Asia. A long frontier guarded on each side by proud and confident fighters and studded by disputed areas lies between the two peoples.

Soldiers, whether they fight under the banner of authoritarianism or democracy, like most of us, are ambitious to make their mark, sometimes heedless of the restrictions placed on their activity by bureaucrats in far-off Moscow or Peking. They also, if well trained, tend to be overconfident, certain that they can engage in, and finish, a minor frontier skirmish with the minimum amount of fuss and the fewest possible political repercussions.

On both sides, the governments and the military high commands are aware of the fruits of victory, which may be more difficult to garner and digest than the two groups of rulers think today. A puzzled British expert asked what on earth the Chinese would do with Vladivostok if they took it. And, in the same vein, what could the Russians do with Manchuria's wealth if they were subjected to continued active and passive resistance? Unhappily, the answer to this second question is that the Russians probably would act with a severity toward the Chinese comparable to that of the Germans toward the Russians in World War II.

The nationalistic and ideological pressures continue in both countries. If war is probable, as I believe it is, it is most likely to start over a border incident—it will take half a century for historians to unravel the truth of the matter—and it will be followed by a full-dress Soviet attack on Manchuria. My estimate now is that such an attack under the present conditions in both forces would be initially successful.

The position of the government of the United States in these circumstances would not be enviable. A very high-ranking Western diplomat asked on my return from China if I thought that in that situation the United States would send military supplies to China. My feeling then and now is that any important arms aid to China in that event would run counter to strong American prejudices.

Here I should perhaps interject that my Chinese hosts did not see the problem in those terms at all. Their view was that the Russians would take on and defeat the NATO powers and then turn on China. This may have been a diplomatic ploy intended to promote advocacy of a strengthening of the Western position vis-à-vis the Warsaw Pact powers. But the argument was put repeatedly and with great vehemence.

American military assistance to a China embroiled in a war with the Soviet Union, assistance short of sending troops or even advisors, would clearly encounter powerful domestic opposition.

To begin, there is the residual, but still powerful, support for the Republic of China on Taiwan, a support not often noticed by pundits of the Boston–Washington axis but still very strong in the Southwest and the northern Middle West. It derives, I believe, from the sentiments of the 1950s, when it was believed, and not always by followers of Joe McCarthy, that the United States had abandoned Chiang Kai-shek and his Nationalists to the Communists and that we owed the new rulers of China nothing. This feeling was exacerbated, understandably, by the Chinese intervention in Korea, the essentially nationalistic reasons for which were never clearly explained to the American people. In consequence, any action by an American administration intended to assist those "dirty Commies" in Peking would be hotly opposed by a considerable section of the American people.

In addition, there would be those, usually few in number, who would take what they considered to be the larger historical view, summed up in the words so often heard during the first phase of the Nazi invasion of Russia—"Let them kill each other off."

Then there is the present, perhaps transient, opposition to any American military involvement overseas. Born of the futility and casualties of Vietnam, this opposition is a very powerful element in the making of American foreign policy. It would certainly figure largely in any national debate over the wisdom of sending arms to China.

A final, mundane argument far removed from global politics that is sure to be raised in the event that the question of arms for an embattled China is raised is simply, What arms? The U.S. armed services, after years in which the army, navy, and air force were limping along on a mixture of past glories and future promises, are now receiving, or about to receive, the modern weapons they have sought. The army, early in the 1980s, will be getting the tanks and surface-to-air missiles it has sought for fifteen years. It is improbable that a service just receiving such weapons would willingly accept their diversion to China. The army and the air force have been bitterly critical since 1973 of new weapons being diverted from them and sent to Israel. It is difficult to believe that they would not strongly resent the shipment of many more new weapons to a country like China, which is not an ally and has for the past twenty years been routinely consigned to the role of one of the "threat" nations in high-level service briefings. We will be told, and rightly, that there are not enough of the new weapons to arm our own forces. Why should they be sent to China?

War between China and Russia would pose complex diplomatic problems for any American government. None of them, however, would be as important or as pressing as that of military aid for the Chinese. If a Sino-Soviet war were to break out today, or any time within the next five years, the Chinese would need extensive outside assistance if they were to continue their resistance.

The American capability to control military events in East Asia is negligible. If war breaks out between the Soviet Union and China, we will face, as we did in 1914 and 1939, the linked questions of whose side we are on and what we ought to do about it. If this duel of the giants begins, its impact on the United States will be tremendous. History will ask the questions. America will have to answer them.

Index